Lecture Notes in Artificial Intelligence   6549

Edited by R. Goebel, J. Siekmann, and W. Wahlster

Subseries of Lecture Notes in Computer Science

Christos Dimitrakakis Aris Gkoulalas-Divanis
Aikaterini Mitrokotsa Vassilios S. Verykios
Yücel Saygin (Eds.)

Privacy and Security Issues in Data Mining and Machine Learning

International ECML/PKDD Workshop, PSDML 2010
Barcelona, Spain, September 24, 2010
Revised Selected Papers

 Springer

Series Editors

Randy Goebel, University of Alberta, Edmonton, Canada
Jörg Siekmann, University of Saarland, Saarbrücken, Germany
Wolfgang Wahlster, DFKI and University of Saarland, Saarbrücken, Germany

Volume Editors

Christos Dimitrakakis
Johann Wolfgang Goethe University, Frankfurt, Germany
E-mail: dimitrakakis@fias.uni-frankfurt.de

Aris Gkoulalas-Divanis
IBM Research – Zurich, Rüschlikon, Switzerland
E-mail: AGD@zurich.ibm.com

Aikaterini Mitrokotsa
Ecole Polytechnice Fédérale de Lausanne, Switzerland
E-mail: katerina.mitrokotsa@epfl.ch

Vassilios S. Verykios
University of Thessaly, Volos, Greece
E-mail: verykios@inf.uth.gr

Yücel Saygin
Sabanci University, Tuzla, Istanbul, Turkey
E-mail: ysaygin@sabanciuniv.edu

ISSN 0302-9743   e-ISSN 1611-3349
ISBN 978-3-642-19895-3   ISBN 978-3-642-19896-0 (eBook)
DOI 10.1007/978-3-642-19896-0
Springer Heidelberg Dordrecht London New York

Library of Congress Control Number: 2011923363

CR Subject Classification (1998): I.2, H.2.8, K.6.5, K.4.1

LNCS Sublibrary: SL 7 – Artificial Intelligence

Typesetting: Camera-ready by author, data conversion by Scientific Publishing Services, Chennai, India

Printed on acid-free paper

Springer is part of Springer Science+Business Media (www.springer.com)

Preface

This volume contains the papers presented at PSDML 2010: ECML/PKDD Workshop on Privacy and Security issues in Data Mining and Machine Learning held on September 24, 2010 in Barcelona, Spain.

The purpose of the workshop was to bring together researchers from different areas of data mining and machine learning, with an interest in privacy and security, to discuss recent results and open problems and to enable future collaborations. We received 21 submissions, each of which received at least 2, and on average 3.6, reviews. We wish to thank the reviewers for their excellent feedback to the authors, which directly contributed to the workshop's success. The committee decided to accept 11 papers for an engaging full-day program touching upon multiple aspects of the workshop's theme.

One theme was data privacy, i.e., how to perform computations on data without revealing the data itself or any sensitive knowledge that can be mined from the data. This was explored for general computations (such as the eigenvector computation paper by Pathak and Raj and the work by Grosskreutz et al. on group discovery), for anonymous data publication (such as the work by Cano and Torra, who studied the suitability of additive noise to protect sensitive microdata while taking data edits into account), and for supervised learning (such as the work by Pathak and Raj on Gaussian classification and the Gavin and Velcin paper on quadratic error minimization).

Security applications, focusing on detecting malicious behavior in computer systems, formed another major part of the workshop schedule. Kruger et al. contribute a method, employing n-grams and matrix factorization, for automatically mapping network payloads onto a low-dimensional space, enabling visualization and anomaly detection. In a similar vein, Mao et al. use generalized n-grams to represent and detect attacks in network traffic, while the problem of filtering in recommender systems is tackled using a soft two-tier classifier employing bag-of-words and other message statistics as features.

Finally, the open problems and position papers session resulted in interesting and fruitful discussions. Charles Elkan presented the idea of using importance weights to preserve privacy in data mining, and Blaine Nelson gave a detailed overview of an adversarial setting where the opponent actively tries to evade detection by the classifier, which raises many interesting theoretical questions.

We would once more like to thank the workshop participants for their interesting contributions, the reviewers for their diligent work and the ECML/PKDD Workshops Chairs for making this workshop possible.

November 2010

Christos Dimitrakakis
Aris Gkoulalas-Divanis
Aikaterini Mitrokotsa
Yücel Saygın
Vassilios Verykios

Conference Organization

Program Chairs

- Christos Dimitrakakis, Goethe University of Frankfurt, Germany
- Aris Gkoulalas-Divanis, IBM Research – Zurich, Switzerland
- Aikaterini Mitrokotsa, EPFL University, Switzerland
- Yücel Saygin, Sabanci University, Turkey
- Vassilios S. Verykios, University of Thessaly, Greece

Program Committee

- Ulf Brefeld, Yahoo Research, Spain
- Michael Bruckner, University of Postdam, Germany
- Mike Burmester, Florida State University, USA
- Kamalika Chaudhuri, University of California at San Diego, USA
- Peter Christen, Australian National University, Australia
- Chris Clifton, Purdue University, USA
- Maria Luisa Damiani, University of Milan, Italy
- Juan M. Estevez-Tapiador, University of York, UK
- Elena Ferrari, University of Insubria, Italy
- Dimitrios Kalles, Hellenic Open University, Greece
- Murat Kantarcioglu, University of Texas at Dallas, USA
- Kun Liu, Yahoo! Labs, California, USA
- Daniel Lowd, University of Oregon, USA
- Grigorios Loukides, Vanderbilt University, USA
- Emmanuel Magkos, Ionian University, Greece
- Bradley Malin, Vanderbilt University, USA
- Mohamed Mokbel, University of Minnesota, USA
- Blaine Nelson, UC Berkeley, USA
- Ercan Nergiz, Sabanci University, Turkey
- Roberto Perdisci, Georgia Institute of Technology, USA
- Pedro Peris-Lopez, TU Delft, The Netherlands
- Aaron Roth, Carnegie Mellon University, USA
- Benjamin I.P. Rubinstein, University of California, USA
- Jianhua Shao, Cardiff University, UK
- Jessica Staddon, PARC, USA
- Angelos Stavrou, George Mason University, USA
- Grigorios Tsoumakas, Aristotle University of Thessaloniki, Greece
- Shobha Venkataraman, AT&T, USA
- Philip S. Yu, University of Illinois at Chicago, USA

External Reviewers

- Acar Tamersoy, Vanderbilt University, USA
- Kamalika Chaudhuri, University of California, USA

Table of Contents

Edit Constraints on Microaggregation and Additive Noise

Isaac Cano and Vicenç Torra

Artificial Intelligence Research Institute (IIIA)
Spanish National Research Council (CSIC)
Campus UAB, Catalonia, Spain
{cano,vtorra}@iiia.csic.es

Abstract. Privacy preserving data mining and statistical disclosure control propose several perturbative methods to protect the privacy of the respondents. Such perturbation can introduce inconsistencies to the sensitive data. Due to this, data editing techniques are used in order to ensure the correctness of the collected data before and after the anonymization.

In this paper we propose a methodology to protect microdata based on noise addition that takes data edits into account. Informally, when adding noise causes a constraint to fail, we apply a process of noise swapping to preserve the edit constraint. We check its suitability against the constrained microaggregation, a method for microaggregation that avoids the introduction of such inconsistencies.

Keywords: Data Editing, Privacy Preserving Data Mining, Constrained Microaggregation, Noise Addition.

1 Introduction

Privacy Preserving Data Mining (PPDM) [1,3,23] aims to develop algorithms for modifying sensitive data in some way, so that the private data and private knowledge remain private even after the mining process. On the other hand, Statistical Disclosure Control (SDC) [30] develops methodologies to ensure that information of the data respondent is not disclosed in any National Statistics publication. SDC involves modifying data so that the risk of identifying individuals is reduced to an acceptable level.

The large volume of data gathered by public agencies and corporations require these methods to protect the privacy of data respondents. In a broad sense, data protection methods can be categorized into data-driven (i.e., general purpose one), and computation-driven (i.e., specific purpose). Computation-driven methods are usually based on cryptographic tools [29] and data-driven ones on the perturbation of the data. That is, the latter methods consist of introducing some noise into the data so that the exact figures of a particular respondent are not disclosed. At present, a large number of perturbative methods exist. In this paper we consider two well-known perturbative methods, the Noise Addition [2,4] and the Microaggregation [12,18,22].

C. Dimitrakakis et al. (Eds.): PSDML 2010, LNAI 6549, pp. 1–14, 2011.

Specifically, when the data to perturb is statistical data, we have to guarantee that it is error-free after the anonymization process due to the inconsistencies that SDC methods can introduce in it. The common approach is to apply Data Editing [17,24,13] techniques in order to guarantee the correctness of both the original and masked microdata. The basic idea is that microdata should satisfy a set of constraints before their release (e.g., non-negative values are not permitted for people's age or when someone is male its number of pregnancies must be zero).

Whilst SDC methods have received ample attention in the literature, the study of perturbation methods in the presence of data edits has not been considered until very recently [28,25]. In this paper we assess the suitability of Additive Noise to ensure consistent data with respect to a subset of edit constraints. Moreover, we compare it to the Constrained Microaggregation in terms of probabilistic information loss and disclosure risk.

The structure of the paper is as follows. Section 2 introduces the basic concepts and the data editing constraints we have considered. In Section 3 we review the constrained microaggregation. In Section 4 we review the correlated and uncorrelated additive noise and we describe how we modified it to deal with the cases where an edit constraint fails. Section 5 presents an evaluation of the results and, finally, Section 6 concludes the paper.

2   Data Editing

Data editing can be broadly defined as the process of detecting errors in statistical data [11]. It is normally accompanied by *error localization*, and *imputation* processes. That is, if there is an error in the data, the erroneous variables have to be identified and the data can be modified in order to fix the error. In general the whole data editing process can be very costly, even requiring human supervision in some stages [13]. For this reason it is very desirable that the statistical disclosure control methods used on edited data do not introduce new errors, so data does not need to be edited again.

The editing process is usually formalized as a set of edit constraints, that the data should satisfy. We present three types of edit constraints from a generic classification [28], and show their applicability in a slightly modified version of the Census data set [10] from the European CASC project [5]. The modification of the dataset, shown in Table 1, is minimal and restricted to the addition of one variable ($V14$) in order to be able to show the applicability of the linear constraints.

- *Constraints on the possible values (EC-PV).* The values of a given variable are restricted to a predefined set. For example, stating that the value of variable *employer contribution for health care* should be in the interval [0, 7500].

EC-PV: *employer contrib. health* $\in [0, 7500]$

Or for example, consider an attribute *age* where a value of 18.5 does not make sense, and only integer positive values are permitted. Similar constraints could involve subsets of variables.

– *One variable governs the possible values of another one (EC-GV)*. The values of a variable v_2 are constrained by the values of the first one. For example, considering the relations between three variables *total person earnings*, *taxable income* and *amount* as:

$$\text{EC-GV: IF } total\ person\ earnings < 1115$$
$$\text{THEN } taxable\ income \leq amount$$

– *Linear constraints (EC-LC)*. Some numerical variables satisfy some linear constraints. That is, a variable can be expressed as a linear combination of a set of other variables. For example, the following relation between *family income*, *person income*, and *other persons income* should hold:

$$\text{EC-LC: } person\ income + other\ person\ income$$
$$= family\ income$$

In general, linear constraints can be expressed as $V = \sum_{i=1}^{K} \alpha_i V_i$, for some values α_i and variables V_i, and the dependent variable V.

In addition to the previous types of constraints, other types of edit constraints can be defined. This is the case of the non-linear constraints and constraints on non-numerical variables.

Table 1. Census dataset description

V1	AFNLWGT	Final weight (2 implied decimal places)
V2	AGI	Adjusted gross income
V3	EMCONTRB	Emplyr. contribution for hlth. insurance
V4	ERNVAL	Business or Farm net earnings in 19..
V5	FEDTAX	Federal income tax liability
V6	FICA	Soc. sec. retirmnt. payroll deduction
V7	INTVAL	Amt. of interest income
V8	PEARNVAL	Total person earnings
V9	POTHVAL	Total other persons income
V10	PTOTVAL	Total person income
V11	STATETAX	State income tax liability
V12	TAXINC	Taxable income amount
V13	WSALVAL	Amount: Total Wage & salary
V14	TOTVAL	Total family income

3   Constrained Microaggregation

Microaggregation is a statistical disclosure control technique, which provides privacy by means of clustering the data into small clusters and then replacing the original data by the centroids of the corresponding clusters.

In this section we will introduce microaggregation and show how it can be used in the presence of edit constraints.

3.1   An Overview of Microaggregation

Microaggregation was originally [12] defined for numerical attributes, but later extended to other domains. E.g., to categorical data in [27] (see also [16]), and in constrained domains in [28].

From the operational point of view, microaggregation is defined in terms of partition and aggregation:

- **Partition.** Records are partitioned into several clusters, each of them consisting of at least k records.
- **Aggregation.** For each of the clusters a representative (the centroid) is computed, and then original records are replaced by the representative of the cluster to which they belong to.

From a formal point of view, microaggregation can be defined as an optimization problem with some constraints. We give a formalization below using u_{ij} to describe the partition of the records in the sensitive data set X. That is, $u_{ij} = 1$ if record j is assigned to the ith cluster. Let v_i be the representative of the ith cluster, then a general formulation of microaggregation with g clusters and a given k is as follows:

$$
\begin{aligned}
\text{Minimize} \quad & SSE = \sum_{i=1}^{g} \sum_{j=1}^{n} u_{ij}(d(x_j, v_i))^2 \\
\text{Subject to} \quad & \sum_{i=1}^{g} u_{ij} = 1 \text{ for all } j = 1, \ldots, n \\
& 2k \geq \sum_{j=1}^{n} u_{ij} \geq k \text{ for all } i = 1, \ldots, g \\
& u_{ij} \in \{0, 1\}
\end{aligned}
$$

For numerical data it is usual to require that $d(x, v)$ is the Euclidean distance. In the general case, when attributes $\mathbf{V} = (V_1, \ldots, V_s)$ are considered, x and v are vectors, and d becomes $d^2(x, v) = \sum_{v \in V}(x_v - v_v)^2$. In addition, it is also common to require for numerical data that v_i is defined as the arithmetic mean of the records in the cluster. I.e., $v_i = \sum_{j=1}^{n} u_{ij} x_i / \sum_{j=1}^{n} u_{ij}$. As the solution of this problem is NP-Hard [22] when we consider more than one variable at a time (multivariate microaggregation), heuristic methods have been developed. MDAV [15] (Maximum Distance to Average Vector) is one of such existing algorithms. A detailed description of the MDAV algorithm is given in Algorithm 1. The implementation of MDAV for categorical data is given in [16].

Privacy is achieved because all clusters have at least a predefined number of elements, and therefore, there are at least k records with the same value.

Algorithm 1. MDAV

Data: X: original data set, k: integer
Result: X': protected data set

1 **begin**
2   **while** $(|X| \geq 3 * k)$ **do**
3   Compute the average record $\bar{x}$ of all records in X;
4   Consider the most distant record x_r to the average record $\bar{x}$;
5   Form a cluster around x_r. The cluster contains x_r together with the $k - 1$ closest records to x_r;
6   Remove these records from data set X;
7   Find the most distant record x_s from record x_r;
8   Form a cluster around x_s. The cluster contains x_s together with the $k - 1$ closest records to x_s;
9   Remove these records from data set X;
10   **if** $(|X| >= 2 * k)$ **then**
11   Compute the average record $\bar{x}$ of all records in X;
12   Consider the most distant record x_r to the average record $\bar{x}$;
13   Form a cluster around x_r. The cluster contains x_r together with the $k - 1$ closest records to x_r;
14   Remove these records from data set X;
15   Form a cluster with the remaining records;
16 **end**

Note that all the records in the cluster replace its own value by the value in the centroid of the cluster. The constant k is a parameter of the method that controls the level of privacy. The larger the k, the more privacy we have in the protected data. Note that when all variables are considered at once, microaggregation is a way to implement k-anonymity.

3.2 Edit Constraints and Microaggregation

In this section we show how the constrained microaggregation copes with the edit constraints listed in Section 2. For a more detailed discussion see [28].

In the rest of this section we will use the following notation. We consider a microdata file with n records $x_1, \ldots, x_n$ that take values over a set of variables $V_1, \ldots, V_m$. We express the value for record x_i in variable V_j by $x_{i,j}$.

Constraints on the possible values (EC-PV). In order to enforce constrains on the possible values, we can require the cluster representatives of $x_1, \ldots, x_N$ denoted by $\mathbb{C}(x_1, \ldots, x_N)$ to be in the interval defined between the minimum and the maximum of the elements in the cluster. That is, the function $\mathbb{C}$ has to satisfy *internality*. Formally,

$$\min_i x_i \leq \mathbb{C}(x_1, \ldots, x_N) \leq \max_i x_i$$

Note that if the constraint is that $x_i \in [a, b]$ for some a and b, it is clear that for edited data, we have $x_i \in [a, b]$, and thus, this constraint implies that $\mathbb{C}(x_1, \dots, x_N) \in [a, b]$.

It can be proved that both the *arithmetic mean* and the *geometric mean* do satisfy internality [28]. So, $\mathbb{C}$ can be any of these two functions.

One variable governs the possible values of another one (EC-GV). Although this case normally requires a case by case approach, in general any monotonic function $\mathbb{C}$, permits us to generate a protected file with $V_1 < V_2$ for variables V_1 and V_2 if in the original file it also holds $V_1 < V_2$. In fact, the condition $x_{i,j} \leq x_{i,k}$ for all i and $j \neq k$ implies $\mathbb{C}(x_{1,j}, \dots, x_{N,j}) \leq \mathbb{C}(x_{1,k}, \dots, x_{N,k})$, corresponds to the monotonicity of $\mathbb{C}$.

EC-GV constraints, such as the one presented in Section 2, can be summarized as:

$$\text{IF } V8 < 1115 \text{ THEN } V13 \leq V12.$$

These constraints can be satisfied by partitioning the dataset in subsets according to the antecedent of the rule, and then applying microaggregation separately to each subset using a monotonic function $\mathbb{C}$. In this case the data is partitioned in two sets, one with records satisfying $V8 < 1115$, and the other with records with $V8 \geq 1115$.

Linear constraints (EC-LC). A linear constraint can be expressed as follows: if we assume that V is the dependent variable (cf. Table 2), we have that $V = \sum_{i=1}^{K} \alpha_i V_i$, for some values α_i and variables V_i.

Assuming that the original data (already edited) satisfies the linear constraint, i.e., $x_j = \sum_{i=1}^{K} \alpha_i x_{j,i}$, we need to consider which function is suitable for computing the cluster representative.

Table 2 shows the representation of a single cluster of size N. The function $\mathbb{C}$ is the cluster representative or centroid, which we assume to be a function of the data in the cluster. More specifically, we presume that the representative of the variable V is a function of the values of the records for V, that is, $\mathbb{C}(x_1, \dots, x_N)$. Similarly, the representative for variable V_i is $\mathbb{C}(x_{1,i}, \dots, x_{N,i})$. The representatives are shown in the last row of Table 2. The arithmetic mean is the most general solution for $\mathbb{C}$.

Table 2. Representation of a single cluster in microaggregation

V	V_1	$\dots$	V_K
x_1	$x_{1,1}$	$\dots$	$x_{1,K}$
$\vdots$	$\vdots$		$\vdots$
x_N	$x_{N,1}$	$\dots$	$x_{N,K}$
$\mathbb{C}(x_1, \dots, x_N)$	$\mathbb{C}(x_{1,1}, \dots, x_{N,1})$	$\dots$	$\mathbb{C}(x_{1,K}, \dots, x_{N,K})$

4   Additive Noise

Masking by adding noise [2,4] was first tested extensively by Spruill [26] and basically consists of adding random noise to the original data. Generally, the noise distribution is Gaussian with mean zero, to preserve means, and the variance of the noise distribution commonly reflects either complete independence or the correlation structure of the original, unmasked data. In this section we first review a perturbation scheme that minimizes the number of failed edits and later we propose a perturbation procedure to deal with those cases where the edit constraints fail.

4.1   Edit Constraints and Additive Noise

If we want to anonymize original microdata by means of additive noise, it may cause edit constraints to start failing. In order to minimize the number of failed edits, Shlomo and De Waal [25] proposed an alternative method for generating univariate and multivariate random noise for continuous variables:

- *Univariate Random Noise:* Select the amount of uncorrelated random noise to add to the variable z by defining the parameter δ with a value larger than 0 and less than or equal to 1. When $\delta = 0$ no noise is added whilst when $\delta = 1$ we obtain the case of fully modelled synthetic data. After setting δ to the desired value, calculate the contribution d_1 of the variable z as $d_1 = \sqrt{(1 - \delta^2)}$. Then, generate Gaussian random noise ϵ independently for each record with a mean of $\mu' = ((1 - d_1)/\delta)\mu$ and the original variance σ^2 of the variable z, where μ is the original mean of the variable. Finally, calculate the masked variable z' for each record i $(i = 1, \cdots, n)$ as the linear combination $z' = d_1 \times z_i + \delta \times \epsilon_i$. Note that, since the random noise is generated independently of the original variable z both the mean E and variance Var of the masked z' and the original variable z are equal, this is $E(z) = E(z')$ and $Var(z) = Var(z')$.
- *Multivariate Random Noise:* When several variables are connected through a linear edit constraint (EC-LC), we have to add correlated random noise to the variables simultaneously in order to preserve as much as possible the means and covariance structures. Considering that three variables x, y, z have to satisfy the linear constraint $x + y = z$, generate multivariate Gaussian random noise $(\epsilon_x, \epsilon_y, \epsilon_z)^T \sim N(\mu', \Sigma)$, where the vector μ' contains the corrected means of each of the three variables based on the noise parameter $\delta : \mu'^T = (\mu'_x, \mu'_y, \mu'_z) = (((1 - d_1)/\delta)\mu_x, ((1 - d_1)/\delta)\mu_y, ((1 - d_1)/\delta)\mu_z)$ and the matrix Σ is the original covariance matrix. Then, for each separate variable, calculate its corresponding masked variable by means of the linear combination described above (i.e., for record $i : z'_i = d_1 \times z_i + \delta \times \epsilon_{zi}$).

4.2   Noise Swapping

Generally, the perturbation scheme of Shlomo and De Waal preserve constraints on the possible values (EC-PV) and linear constraints (EC-LC) but it can also be the case that some individuals fail the edit constraints. Nevertheless, the perturbation scheme of Shlomo and De Waal can not directly deal with constraints where one variable governs the possible values of another one (EC-GV) so in this section we propose a new perturbation schema that combines both the univariate and multivariate random noise in order to deal with EC-GV constraints.

In case of the edit constraint on the possible values, the addition of uncorrelated random noise following the proposal of Shlomo and De Waal can lead to masked values outside of the attribute's possible values. This can be because either the attribute barely follows a Gaussian distribution or the noise generated for a particular individual makes it to happen to be outside its possible values. In order to minimize the number of failed edits, Shlomo and De Waal proposed to generate the random noise within percentiles of the attribute. However, still can be a great number of failed edits. To fix these inconsistencies, one possible solution is to force the inconsistent individuals to be within its range of possible values by establishing boundaries for the minimum and maximum values but this can lead to a greater information loss.

Nevertheless, we propose to fix these inconsistencies by swapping the noise of the different individuals. That is, when a perturbed individual falls out of the possible values, its associated noise is swapped with a randomly-selected candidate individual if and only if both the perturbed and the candidate individuals stay within their possible values after adding their swapped noise. This process is repeated until the inconsistence is fixed or a maximum number or attempts.

In case of linear constraints, the addition of correlated random noise with the previous perturbation scheme barely produces the linear relationship between the attributes to fail. If some inconsistencies appear, swapping the correlated noise of the individuals seemed to be enough in our experiments to preserve the linear constraints. However, whilst the addition of correlated random noise preserve the linear constraint between attributes, it do not guarantee the single attributes to stay within their possible values as the constrained microaggregation does. Because of that, in case of linear constraints, the noise swapping will be considered successful if and only if both the linear constraints between the attributes and the constraint on the possible values of the single attributes are preserved.

Finally, in order to deal with the EC-GV type of edit constraints, we propose the perturbation schema illustrated in Figure 1. We consider the following notation for the three different variables involved in the EC-GV constraint:

$$\text{EC-GV: IF } Antecedent=\text{True THEN } V1 \leq V2$$

The proposed perturbation schema satisfies the EC-GV constraints by partitioning first the dataset in two subsets according to the antecedent in the rule (i.e., one subset A_1 with all the records that make the Antecedent come true and another subset A_2 with the remaining records). Then, the subset A_2 is protected by means of univariate random noise with noise swapping. Each variable is considered separately. Subset A_1 is protected by applying univariate random noise with noise swapping to the records that corresponds to the Antecedent and

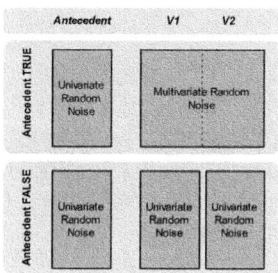

Fig. 1. Graphical representation of the proposed schema to deal with EC-GV constraints that combines both the univariate and multivariate random noise

multivariate random noise with noise swapping together to the variables $V1$ and $V2$. In order to keep the relation $V1 \leq V2$ when the multivariate random noise is added, we need to introduce an additional variable $V_{aux} = V2 - V1$ so that we can create a multivariate random noise from V_{aux}, $V1$ and $V2$ that holds the linear relation $\epsilon_{aux} = \epsilon1 - \epsilon2$. Finally, the values of $V1$ and $V2$ that fall in A_1 are perturbed using the $\epsilon1$ and $\epsilon2$ respectively.

Worth to mention that we have tried different variations of the proposed perturbation schema to satisfy EC-GV constraints (e.g., generating univariate random noise to perturb the whole Antecedent or generating multivariate random noise to perturb $V1$ and $V2$ in the subset A_2) but they obtained worse results in terms of probabilistic information loss and disclosure risk. Because the space limitations, we do not include in this paper the explicit numerical evaluations of the different perturbation schemes tested.

5   Experiments

In our experiments, we used as a test dataset one of the reference datasets [5] used in the European project CASC. We refer to the "Census" dataset which contains 1080 records with 13 numerical attributes labeled from $v1$ to $v13$. This dataset was used in CASC and by several authors as in e.g. [6,7,9,14]. As described in Section 2, we have added one new variable to the "Census" dataset to be able to assess the linear constraint $v9 + v10 = v14$.

In case of additive noise, we have considered an amount of noise $0.01 \leq \delta \leq 0.4$ with increments of 0.01 whilst in case of the constrained microaggregation we have considered k-anonimity $2 \leq k \leq 98$ with increments of 2. Moreover, for each δ and k we have evaluated both perturbative approaches with respect to risk and information loss using record-linkage algorithms (i.e., Distance-Based Record Linkage, Probabilistic Record Linkage and Interval Disclosure), Probabilistic Information Loss (PIL) measures [19] and the standard score (SCORE) [31,8] (computed as $score = 0.5 * PIL + 0.5 * DR$).

On the one hand, to assess the noise swapping we have considered two scenarios regarding noise addition and linear constraints. In the first scenario ($S1$),

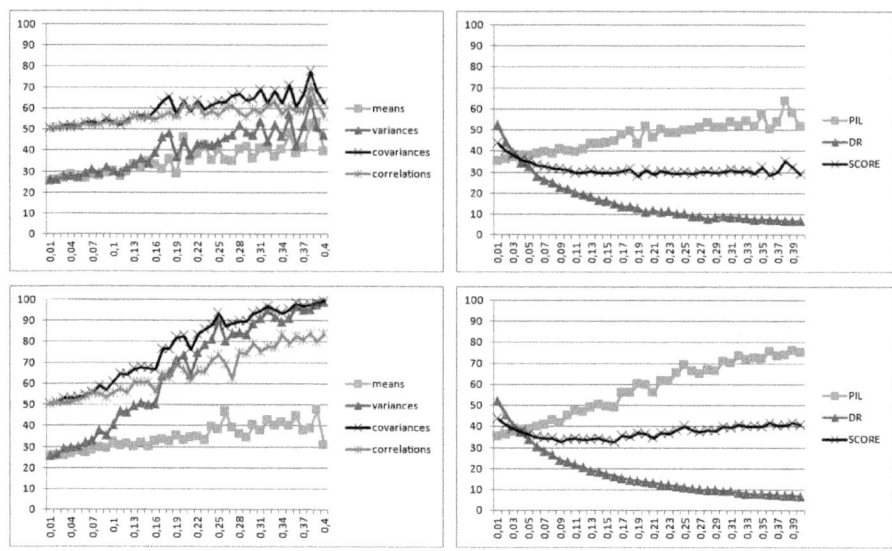

Fig. 2. Detailed probabilistic information loss (left) and SCORE (right) when protecting the dataset by adding noise and preserving the edit constraints. Results obtained when applying the procedure proposed by Shlomo and De Waal with noise swapping (up) and when also preserving the constraints on the possible value of the attributes within the linear constraint (down).

we have protected the dataset in order to preserve the linear constraints without forcing the masked values of the attributes $v9, v10$ and $v14$ to be within their possible values while in the second scenario $(S2)$ we do force the masked values to be within their possible values. Figure 2 shows the results obtained in both scenarios. The main difference between both scenarios is that in $S2$ the probabilistic information loss regarding variances, covariances and correlations is much greater than in $S1$ when incrementing the amount of noise. This is also reflected in the $SCORE$ of both scenarios, whilst in $S1$ the average $SCORE$ is around 30, in $S2$ it is around 40.

On the other hand, to assess the suitability of the procedure proposed by Shlomo and De Waal to preserve edit constraints, we have compared it with the constrained microaggregation. We have considered in this case the additive noise scenario $S2$ because the constrained microaggregation do preserve the values of the attributes involved in a linear constraint to remain inside their possible values. Figure 3 shows that the results obtained with constrained microaggregation and the scenario $S2$ of the additive noise are very similar. The main difference is that with constrained microaggregation the probabilistic information loss increases in a more exponential fashion when incrementing k but the average $SCORE$ of both approaches are around 40. It is worth mentioning that constrained microaggregation offers k-anonymity so even though they got similar SCORE the constrained microaggregation offers better disclosure risk.

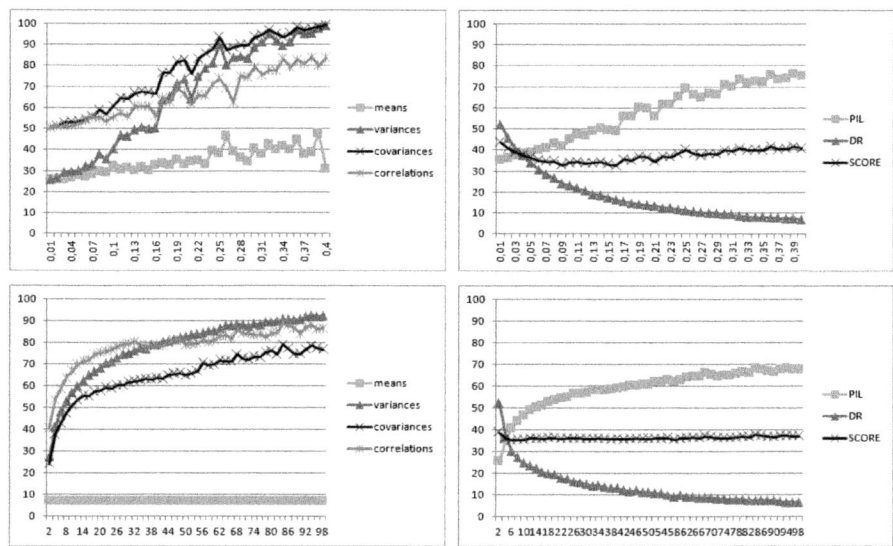

Fig. 3. Detailed probabilistic information loss (left) and SCORE (right) when protecting the dataset by the procedure proposed by Shlomo and De Waal with noise swapping (up) and constrained microaggregation (down)

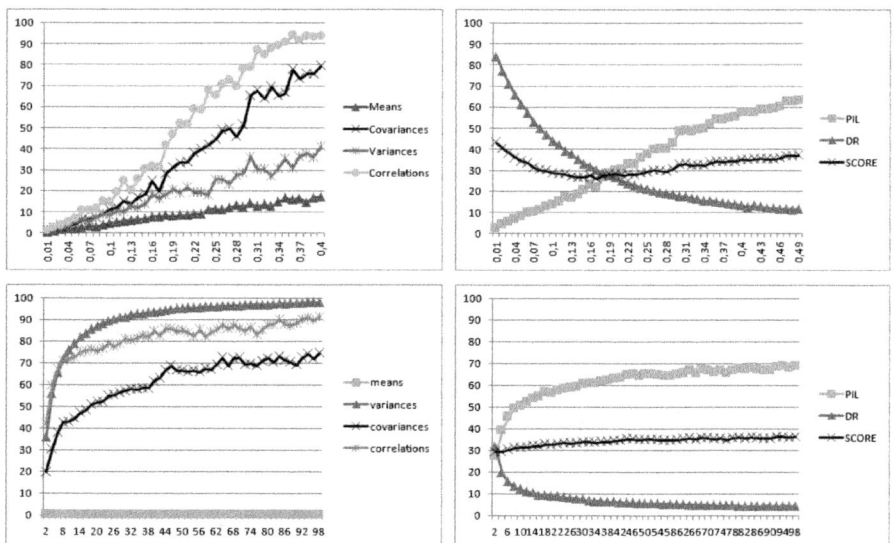

Fig. 4. Detailed probabilistic information loss (left) and SCORE (right) when dealing with the EC-GV constraint by means of the proposed perturbation schema (up) and the constrained microaggregation (down)

Finally, we have compared our proposed perturbation schema to satisfy EC-GV constraints with the constrained microaggregation. Specifically, the EC-GV constraint considered is *IF V7 < 1115 THEN V13 ≤ V12*. Figure 4 shows that the proposed schema obtains better SCORE (i.e., for an amount of noise in between 0.1 and 0.25 the proposed schema obtains a SCORE below 30 whilst the constrained microaggregation obtains values above it) because variances, covariances and correlations are better preserved.

6   Conclusions

In this paper we have proposed a methodology to protect microdata based on noise addition that take data edits into account and we have assessed its suitability to ensure consistent data with respect to a subset of edit constraints.

In addition, we have shown that constrained microaggregation obtains similar results regarding disclosure risk and probabilistic information loss compared to the noise addition with noise swapping in case of edit constraints on the possible values, linear constraints and constraints where one variable governs the possible values of another one.

As future work we consider the extension of the proposed methodology to support more edit constraints.

Acknowledgments

Partial support by the Spanish MICINN (projects eAEGIS TSI2007-65406-C03-02, ARES - CONSOLIDER INGENIO 2010 CSD2007-00004) is acknowledged.

References

1. Aggarwal, C.C., Yu, P.S.: Privacy Preserving Data Mining: Models and Algorithms. Springer, Heidelberg (2008)
2. Brand, R.: Microdata protection through noise. In: Domingo-Ferrer, J. (ed.) Inference Control in Statistical Databases. LNCS, vol. 2316, pp. 97–116. Springer, Heidelberg (2002)
3. Clifton, C., Marks, D.: Security and privacy implications of data mining. In: Proceedings of the ACM SIGMOD Workshop on Research Issues on Data Mining and Knowledge Discovery, pp. 15–19 (1996)
4. Kim, J.J.: A method for limiting disclosure in microdata based on random noise and transformation. In: Proceedings of the ASA Section on Survey Research Methodology, pp. 303–308. American Statistical Association, Alexandria (1986)
5. Brand, R., Domingo-Ferrer, J., Mateo-Sanz, J.M.: Reference datasets to test and compare SDC methods for protection of numerical microdata. Technical report, European Project IST-2000-25069 CASC (2002)
6. Domingo-Ferrer, J., Mateo-Sanz, J.M., Torra, V.: Comparing SDC methods methods for microdata on the basis of information loss and disclosure risk. In: Pre-proceedings of ETK-NTTS 2001, Luxemburg, Eurostat, vol. 2, pp. 807–826 (2001)

7. Domingo-Ferrer, J., Sebé, F., Solanas, A.: A polynomial-time approximation to optimal multivariate microaggregatio. Computers and Mathematics with Applications 55(4), 714–732 (2005)
8. Domingo-Ferrer, J., Torra, V.: A quantitative comparison of disclosure control methods for microdata. In: Doyle, P., Lane, J.I., Theeuwes, J.J.M., Zayatz, L.V. (eds.) Confidentiality, Disclosure, and Data Access: Theory and Practical Applications for Statistical Agencies, pp. 111–133. Elsevier, Amsterdam (2001)
9. Domingo-Ferrer, J., Torra, V.: Ordinal, continuous and heterogeneous k-anonymity through microaggregation. Data Mining and Knowledge Discovery 11(2), 195–212 (2005)
10. U.S. Census Bureau. Data Extraction System, http://www.census.gov/
11. Chambers, R.: Evaluation criteria for statistical editing and imputation. National Statistics Methodological series No.28 (January 2001)
12. Defays, D., Nanopoulos, P.: Panels of enterprises and confidentiality: the small aggregates method. In: Proc. of 92 Symposium on Design and Analysis of Longitudinal Surveys, Statistics Canada, pp. 195–204 (1993)
13. De Waal, T.: An overview of statistical data editing. Statistics Netherlands (2008)
14. Domingo-Ferrer, J., Torra, V., Mateo-Sanz, J.M., Sebé, F.: Empirical Disclosure risk assessment of the ipso synthetic data generators. In: Monographs in Official Statistics-Work Session On Statistical Data Confidenciality, Luxemburg, Eurostat, pp. 227–238 (2006)
15. Domingo-Ferrer, J., Mateo-Sanz, J.: Practical data-oriented microaggregation for statistical disclosure control. IEEE Transactions on Knowledge and Data Engineering 14(1), 189–201 (2002)
16. Domingo-Ferrer, J., Torra, V.: Ordinal, continuous and heterogeneous k-anonymity through microaggregation. Data Mining and Knowledge Discovery, 195–212 (January 2005)
17. Granquist, L.: The new view on editing. Int. Statistical Review 65(3), 381–387 (1997)
18. Hansen, S., Mukherjee, S.: A Polynomial Algorithm for Optimal Univariate Microaggregation. IEEE Trans. on Knowledge and Data Engineering 15(4), 1043–1044 (2003)
19. Mateo-Sanz, J.M., Domingo-Ferrer, J., Sebé, F.: Probabilistic information loss measures in confidentiality protection of continuous microdata. Data Mining and Knowledge Discovery 11, 181–193 (2005) ISSN: 1384-5810
20. Moore, R.: Controlled data swapping techniques for masking public use microdata sets, U. S. Bureau of the Census (1996) (unpublished manuscript)
21. Nin, J., Herranz, J., Torra, V.: Rethinking Rank Swapping to Decrease Disclosure Risk. Data and Knowledge Engineering 64(1), 346–364 (2008)
22. Oganian, A., Domingo-Ferrer, J.: On the complexity of optimal microaggregation for statistical disclosure control. Statistical Journal of the United Nations Economic Commision for Europe 18(4), 345–353 (2001)
23. O'Leary, D.E.: Knowledge Discovery as a Threat to Database Security. In: Proceedings of the 1st International Conference on Knowledge Discovery and Databases, pp. 107–516 (1991)
24. Pierzchala, M.: A review of the state of the art in automated data editing and imputation. In: Statistical Data Editing, Vol. 1, Conference of European Statisticians Statistical Standards and Studies N. 44, UN Statistical Commission and Economic Commission for Europe, pp. 10–40 (1995)
25. Shlomo, N., De Waal, T.: Protection of Micro-data Subjecto to Edit Constraints Against Statistical Disclousure. Journal of Official Statistics 24(2), 229–253 (2008)

26. Spruill, N.L.: The Confidentiality and Analytic Usefulness of Masked Business Microdata. In: Proceedings of the Section on Survey Research Methods, pp. 602–610. American Statistical Association (1983)
27. Torra, V.: Microaggregation for categorical variables: A median based approach. In: Domingo-Ferrer, J., Torra, V. (eds.) PSD 2004. LNCS, vol. 3050, pp. 162–174. Springer, Heidelberg (2004)
28. Torra, V.: Constrained microaggregation: Adding constraints for data editing. Transactions on Data Privacy 1(2), 86–104 (2008)
29. Vaidya, J., Clifton, C., Zhu, M.: Privacy Preserving Data Mining. Springer, Heidelberg (2006)
30. Willenborg, L., De Waal, T.: Elements of Statistical Disclosure Control. Springer, New York (2001)
31. Disclosure risk and probabilistic information loss measures for continuous microdata web site, http://ppdm.iiia.csic.es/

Preserving Privacy in Data Mining
via Importance Weighting

Charles Elkan

Department of Computer Science and Engineering
University of California, San Diego,
La Jolla, CA 92093-0404
elkan@cs.ucsd.edu

Abstract. This paper presents a fundamentally new approach to allowing learning algorithms to be applied to a dataset, while still keeping the records in the dataset confidential. Let D be the set of records to be kept private, and let E be a fixed set of records from a similar domain that is already public. The idea is to compute and publish a weight $w(x)$ for each record x in E that measures how representative it is of the records in D. Data mining on E using these importance weights is then approximately equivalent to data mining directly on D. The dataset D is used by its owner to compute the weights, but not revealed in any other way.

1 Introduction and Framework

Suppose that a hospital possesses data concerning patients, their diseases, their treatments, and their outcomes. The hospital faces a fundamental conflict. On the one hand, to protect the privacy of the patients, the hospital wants to keep the dataset secret. On the other hand, to allow science to progress, the hospital wants to make the dataset public. This conflict is the issue addressed by research on privacy-preserving data mining. How can a data owner simultaneously both publish a dataset and conceal it?

In this paper, we propose a new approach to resolving this fundamental tension between publishing and concealing data. The new approach is based on a mathematical technique called importance weighting that has proved to be valuable in several other areas of research [Hastings, 1970]. The essential idea is as follows. Let D be the set of records that the owner must keep confidential. Let E be a different set of records from a similar domain, and suppose that E is already public. The owner should compute and publish a weight $w(x)$ for each record x in E. Given x in E, its weight is large if x is similar to the records in D, while its weight is small otherwise. Data mining on E using the weights will then be approximately equivalent to data mining on D. The owner uses D privately to compute the weights, but never reveals D in any way.

Note that the proposed approach is non-interactive. The owner chooses E, and normally there will only be one dataset E and one set of weights. Data users, and adversaries, know the contents of E, but do not get to select E in any way.

C. Dimitrakakis et al. (Eds.): PSDML 2010, LNAI 6549, pp. 15–21, 2011.

A learning algorithm can be any statistical analysis method, including any supervised or unsupervised data mining method. The class of learning algorithms that we consider consists of methods that use the dataset D indirectly, by computing averages over it. Suppose that D contains records of type X, meaning that each record in D is an element of the space X. For example, if each record in D is a real-valued vector of length k, then $X = \mathbb{R}^k$. Let b be any real-valued function of X, i.e. $b : X \rightarrow \mathbb{R}$. The empirical average over D of b is

$$\bar{b} = \frac{1}{|D|} \sum_{x_i \in D} b(x_i).$$

Assume that the samples x_i are drawn independently and identically distributed (iid) from a fixed probability distribution f over the space X. The empirical average is then an estimate of the expectation of b over X given f.

The point of a learning algorithm, or of any statistical analysis, is to induce some property of the distribution f, rather than merely to obtain a measurement of the dataset D. The goal of an insider (that is, a data owner), is to allow outsiders to estimate properties of f without revealing D. In general, properties of f are expectations. An insider can estimate the expectation of the function $b(x)$ using the empirical distribution:

$$E[b(x)|x \sim f(x)] \hat{=} \frac{1}{|D|} \sum_{x_i \in D} b(x_i).$$

Different learning algorithms require estimates of different expectations relative to the distribution $f(x)$. The question is, how can the data owner allow outsiders to estimate all these expectations without revealing the specific x_i records in D to them?

Note that the framework adopted here for learning is the statistical queries model of [Kearns, 1998]. The operation of a learning algorithm is divided into two parts. One part is an algorithm that takes as given the availability of measurements of population averages. The other part is a procedure for obtaining estimates of these measurements. The importance sampling method proposed here is a privacy-preserving procedure for obtaining these estimates.

2   Preserving Privacy via Importance Weighting

Let f be any probability distribution over X and let b be any real-valued function over X. The definition of the expectation of b with respect to f is

$$E[b(x)|x \sim f(x)] = \int_{x \in X} b(x)f(x)dx.$$

Now let g be a different probability distribution over X, and consider the following equations:

$$\int b(x)f(x)dx = \int b(x)f(x)\frac{g(x)}{g(x)}dx = E[b(x)\frac{f(x)}{g(x)}|x \sim g(x)].$$

In words, the expectation of b with respect to the distribution f is equal to the expectation of $b(x)f(x)/g(x)$ with respect to the distribution g. This result is sometimes called the importance sampling identity [Hastings, 1970, Press, 2004] and has been used in recent research on sample-selection bias and covariate shift [Shimodaira, 2000, Smith and Elkan, 2007, Cortes et al., 2010]. The ratio $w(x) = f(x)/g(x)$ is called the importance of x.

For the importance sampling identity to be true, $g(x)$ must be positive for all x such that $f(x)$ is positive, i.e. the support of g must be a superset of the support of f. This condition is required to avoid division by zero. If $f(x) = g(x) = 0$ for any x, one can define $f(x)/g(x) = 0$ for that x.

In order to apply importance weighting to achieve privacy-preserving data mining, let the confidential dataset D be a random sample from the distribution f over X. A statistical query concerning D is an expectation

$$E[b(x)|x \sim f(x)] = \int b(x)f(x)dx$$

that would be estimated by the owner of D as

$$\frac{1}{|D|} \sum_{x_i \in D} b(x_i).$$

Now, let E be a random sample from a different distribution g over X that is known to an outsider. The fact that D and E are samples over the same space X means that, in database terminology, they have the same schema. The outsider can then estimate $E[b(x)|x \sim f(x)]$ as

$$\frac{1}{|E|} \sum_{x_i \in E} b(x_i)w(x_i).$$

In order to compute this estimate, for any b, the outsider does not need any access to D. The outsider does need to know the weights $w(x_i)$. However, these weights are the same for all b. The weights can be computed by the data owner based on its knowledge of D and E, and then published, once and for all.

The importance-weighting approach to privacy-preserving data mining is based on the assumption that an appropriate dataset E exists and is public. There are several possibilities for how E might exist. First, E might be a dataset that was revealed previously, perhaps inadvertently. At the time E was revealed, there was a breach of privacy, but now, one might as well use E for future research that does not breach privacy any further. Second, E might consist of information about individuals who have given consent for data concerning them to be published. For example, a hospital can gather consent for data release from some patients, and then compute weights that allow the consenting patients to be representative of all patients. Third, E might even consist of artificially generated synthetic data.

The method proposed above is different from two previous approaches that may appear similar at first sight. Some recent research has considered how to publish a version D' of D that preserves privacy yet is such that functions in a certain class have similar values on D' and D [Blum et al., 2008]. In the proposal above, no new dataset D' is created or published; instead an existing dataset E is reused, and only scalar weights are published. Other research has considered how to answer subset-sum queries interactively in a differentially private way [Blum et al., 2005]. A subset-sum query asks the data owner to evaluate a function on a subset of D. The proposal above is non-interactive: the data owner does not answer queries at all. The data owner merely designates a dataset E and publishes one set of weights, once and for all.

3   How to Compute Importance Weights

For each data point x_i in E, its importance weight $w(x_i)$ is the ratio of the probability density of x_i according to two different distributions. Both distributions are over the space X, which in general has high dimensionality; the dimensionality is the length of the x_i vectors. Estimating high-dimensional densities is difficult at best, and often infeasible [Scott, 1992]. Fortunately, we can estimate the ratio $w(x)$ without estimating $f(x)$ and $g(x)$, as follows.

Let F be the combined dataset $D \cup E$ where samples from D are extended with the label $s = 1$ and samples from E are extended with the label $s = 0$. Suppose that we use F to learn a model of $p(s = 1|x)$. Then,

$$p(s = 1|x) = \frac{p(x|s = 1)p(s = 1)}{p(x)}$$

by Bayes' rule. Therefore,

$$p(s = 1|x) = \frac{f(x)p(s = 1)}{f(x)p(s = 1) + g(x)p(s = 0)} = \frac{1}{1 + \frac{g(x)p(s=0)}{f(x)p(s=1)}}.$$

As above, let $w(x) = f(x)/g(x)$ and let $r = p(s = 0)/p(s = 1)$. We can derive

$$w(x) = \frac{r}{1/p(s = 1|x) - 1}. \tag{1}$$

The equation above lets us write each weight $w(x)$ as a deterministic transformation of $p(s = 1|x)$. The equation is correct as a statement of probability theory. Its practical usefulness depends on being able to estimate the probability $p(s = 1|x)$ for each x in the dataset E. Fortunately, in general we can learn to estimate these probabilities accurately. To do so, we apply a supervised learning method that yields well-calibrated conditional probability predictions to the union of the D and E datasets. The simplest method with this property is logistic regression, but many other appropriate methods exist also [Zadrozny and Elkan, 2001].

To clarify, only the data owner knows both datasets D and E. Using these, the owner trains the model $p(s = 1|x)$, and applies this model to each example x_i in E. The owner then computes and publishes $w(x_i)$ for each of these examples, non-interactively, using Equation (1). Outsiders know the dataset E and the published numerical weights. They are not given access to anything else.

Each dataset D and E is treated as a random sample from a corresponding population. The two populations may be more similar or less similar. If the populations happen to be identical, then it will be the case that $w(x_i)$ equals the same constant for all x_i in E. In separate research, we have developed a variant of regularized logistic regression that allows for lower and upper bounds L and U for predicted probabilities:

$$0 < L \leq \min_x p(s = 1|x) < \max_x p(s = 1|x) \leq U < 1.$$

If D and E come from indistinguishable populations, then the new variant of logistic regression will in principle learn that $L = U$.

The data owner does not need to publish the model used to compute weights (only the numerical weights themselves). However, if an adversary happened to know this model, it could compute $p(s = 1|x)$ for any data record x. If this value is high, then x is more typical of records in D than of records in E. But that simply means x is representative of the population from which D is drawn. The adversary cannot conclude that x actually appears in D.

The approach just explained to estimate the ratio of two probability densities, without needing to estimate the two densities individually, is something of a folk result. Variations of it have been discovered and used independently several times [Zadrozny, 2004, Smith and Elkan, 2007, Tsuboi et al., 2009]. To be useful in practice, the approach requires careful regularization.

4   Research Questions

The importance-weighting approach has two major drawbacks. The first obvious issue is that an appropriate dataset E must already exist and be public. A less obvious issue is that the dataset E may be too good, that is too similar to D. Suppose for the sake of argument that E is a superset of D. Then the ideal weights will be $w(x) > 0$ for each x in D, and $w(x) = 0$ for each x that is in E but not in D. In general, weights will be high for examples in E that are representative of D. An adversary will know this, but cannot conclude that a record in E with a high weight appears "as is" in D.

The following research questions need answers. They are related to each other, so the order in which they are stated here is somewhat arbitrary and does not reflect their relative importance. The first questions concern importance weighting in general, while later ones are specifically related to privacy.

1. Is logistic regression the best supervised learning method for the data owner to use to estimate $p(s = 1|x)$, or does a better alternative exist? What variety of smoothing or regularization is best?
2. How should D and E be divided into training, validation, and test sets for the purpose of computing weights?

3. For some x_i in E, the estimated value of $w(x_i)$ will be large. These x_i will have disproportionate influence in estimates of $E[b(x)]$ for all functions b. How can large values of $w(x_i)$ be avoided, while still maintaining correctness?

The variant of logistic regression with lower and upper bounds mentioned above should help answer the last question above, because Equation (1) implies that bounds on $p(s = 1|x)$ correspond to bounds on the importance weights.

The following research questions ask what theoretical guarantees concerning information disclosure can be proved for the importance-weighting approach. We conjecture that under some conditions, the approach can be proved to satisfy the definition of differential privacy [Dwork, 2008]. Intuitively, the more general a statistical query is, the higher the accuracy with which it can be answered using E and the published weights. Queries that in fact ask about a single potential record in D will only be answered with very low precision.

The specific research questions are the following:

1. Characterize the uncertainty in estimates

$$E[b(x)|x \sim f(x)] \triangleq \frac{1}{|E|} \sum_{x_i \in E} b(x_i)w(x_i)$$

   by computing confidence intervals. What are the quantities on which these intervals depend?
2. Intuitively, knowing the expectation of an indicator function such as

$$b(x) = I(lastname(x) = \text{Obama})$$

   destroys privacy, whereas a function such as

$$b(x) = I(age(x) \geq 40)$$

   is irrelevant to privacy. Provide a formal definition of privacy-destroying and privacy-irrelevant functions.
3. Show that if $b(x)$ is privacy-destroying then the uncertainty in its estimated expectation is high, while if $b(x)$ is privacy-irrelevant then the uncertainty is small.
4. Show that publishing the dataset E with the weights $w(x_i)$ for x_i in E satisfies the definition of differential privacy for D.
5. Under interactive models of differential privacy, the number of queries allowed must be sublinear in the size of D. When learning importance weights, is this "privacy budget" relevant? If so, how can one avoid exceeding it?

There is a simple intuitive argument why differential privacy is guaranteed for the importance-weighting approach. The only information that is computed and revealed from the confidential dataset D is a single logistic regression function. And regularized logistic regression can be trained while respecting differential privacy [Chaudhuri and Monteleoni, 2008, Chaudhuri and Sarwate, 2009]. Intuitively, if the published weights $w(x)$ are approximately unchanged whether or not any particular record is included in D or excluded from D, then the importance-weighting approach satisfies differential privacy. And because the weights are based on logistic regression, they do satisfy differential privacy. Making this argument precise is a priority for continued research.

Acknowledgments. The author is grateful to anonymous referees for comments that helped in clarifying the ideas of this position paper.

References

[Blum et al., 2005] Blum, A., Dwork, C., McSherry, F., Nissim, K.: Practical privacy: the SuLQ framework. In: Proceedings of the 24th ACM Symposium on Principles of Database Systems, pp. 128–138. ACM Press, New York (2005)

[Blum et al., 2008] Blum, A., Ligett, K., Roth, A.: A learning theory approach to non-interactive database privacy. In: Proceedings of the 40th Annual ACM Symposium on Theory of Computing, pp. 609–618. ACM Press, New York (2008)

[Chaudhuri and Monteleoni, 2008] Chaudhuri, K., Monteleoni, C.: Privacy-preserving logistic regression. In: Proceedings of the 22nd Annual Conference on Neural Information Processing Systems (NIPS), pp. 289–296 (2008)

[Chaudhuri and Sarwate, 2009] Chaudhuri, K., Sarwate, A.D.: Privacy constraints in regularized convex optimization. Arxiv preprint arXiv:0907.1413 (2009)

[Cortes et al., 2010] Cortes, C., Mohri, M., Riley, M., Rostamizadeh, A.: Sample selection bias correction theory. In: Algorithmic Learning Theory, pp. 38–53. Springer, Heidelberg (2010)

[Dwork, 2008] Dwork, C.: Differential privacy: A survey of results. In: Agrawal, M., Du, D.-Z., Duan, Z., Li, A. (eds.) TAMC 2008. LNCS, vol. 4978, pp. 1–19. Springer, Heidelberg (2008)

[Hastings, 1970] Hastings, W.K.: Monte Carlo sampling methods using Markov chains and their applications. Biometrika 57(1), 97–109 (1970)

[Kearns, 1998] Kearns, M.: Efficient noise-tolerant learning from statistical queries. Journal of the ACM 45(6), 983–1006 (1998)

[Press, 2004] Press, W.H.: How to use Markov chain Monte Carlo to do difficult integrals (including those for normalizing constants) (2004), Draft working paper available at http://www.nr.com/whp/workingpapers.html

[Scott, 1992] Scott, D.W.: Multivariate density estimation: Theory, practice, and visualization. Wiley-Interscience, Hoboken (1992)

[Shimodaira, 2000] Shimodaira, H.: Improving predictive inference under covariate shift by weighting the log-likelihood function. Journal of Statistical Planning and Inference 90(2), 227–244 (2000)

[Smith and Elkan, 2007] Smith, A., Elkan, C.: Making generative classifiers robust to selection bias. In: Proceedings of the SIGKDD International Conference on Knowledge Discovery and Data Mining (KDD), pp. 657–666. ACM Press, New York (2007)

[Tsuboi et al., 2009] Tsuboi, Y., Kashima, H., Bickel, S., Sugiyama, M.: Direct Density Ratio Estimation for Large-scale Covariate Shift Adaptation. Journal of Information Processing 17, 138–155 (2009)

[Zadrozny, 2004] Zadrozny, B.: Learning and evaluating classifiers under sample selection bias. In: Proceedings of the 21st International Conference on Machine Learning, pp. 903–910. ACM Press, New York (2004)

[Zadrozny and Elkan, 2001] Zadrozny, B., Elkan, C.: Obtaining calibrated probability estimates from decision trees and naive Bayesian classifiers. In: Proceedings of the 18th International Conference on Machine Learning, pp. 609–616. Morgan Kaufmann, San Francisco (2001)

Quadratic Error Minimization in a Distributed Environment with Privacy Preserving

Gérald Gavin and Julien Velcin

Laboratory ERIC
University of Lyon

Abstract. In this paper, we address the issue of privacy preserving data-mining. Specifically, we consider a scenario where each member j of T parties has its own private database. The party j builds a private classifier h_j for predicting a binary class variable y. The aim of this paper consists in aggregating these classifiers h_j in order to improve the individual predictions. Precisely, the parties wish to compute an efficient linear combinations over their classifier in a secure manner.

1 Introduction

We consider a scenario where T parties with private databases wish to cooperate by computing a data-mining algorithm for the union of these databases. Since the databases are all confidential, no party wishes to divulge any content to any other. Let us suppose that each party j has inferred a prediction function (classifier) h_j to predict a binary class variable y. Parties could be interested in collaborating to improve each individual prediction performance. A solution would consist in aggregating the different classifiers h_j to build an overall better one $\hat{h}$. The simplest way to combine these classifiers consists in predicting the majority class. This approach is naive when, for instance, most of the parties have almost the same low quality classifier. The aim of this paper is to propose a more appropriate approach. The natural evolution of the previous approaches consists of using linear combinations, i.e. weighted votes. Many ways are proposed in literature to build such combinations. The most famous algorithm is certainly Adaboost. This algorithm builds convex combinations maximizing margins (see [19]). In [20], the authors propose upper-bounds on the generalization error independent on the combination size.

A key problem that arises in any collection of data is confidentiality. The need for privacy is sometimes due to law (e.g., medical databases) or can be motivated by business interests. In this paper, the parties do not wish to share any information about their private data or their classifier h_j. These privacy constraints restrict the choice of the aggregating algorithm: it should be essentially "arithmetic", meaning that the only allowed operations are additions and multiplications. This excludes, for instance, the algorithm Adaboost which requires logarithms and exponential computations. In order to satisfy both machine learning and privacy constraints, we choose to minimize the quadratic error on a convex

C. Dimitrakakis et al. (Eds.): PSDML 2010, LNAI 6549, pp. 22–35, 2011.

C. This quadratic error is close to the exponential error minimized by Adaboost. In addition, this optimization can be done with a simple descent gradient algorithm. However, the projection operator is not "arithmetic" if C is the set of the convex combinations. To overcome this issue, the convexity constraint is partially removed, i.e. the positivity constraint on the coefficients α_i is released. In other words, the parties will build a linear combination $h = \alpha_1 h_1 + ... + \alpha_T h_T$ minimizing the quadratic error under the constraint $\sum_{j=1}^{T} \alpha_j = 1$.

In Section 3, we propose an algorithm, called QEM, that achieves this optimization process. This algorithm is experimented in Section 4: it is shown that this weighting scheme can be dramatically better than the naive one (equivalent to a simple vote). In Section 6, we present the protocol PDEM that allows the parties to securely implement this scheme. The cryptographic tools used in this paper are the threshold homomorphic encryption schemes [9], [8] allowing to securely compute any arithmetical circuit [6]. These tools are presented in Section 5. PDEM is shown to be both correct and private against any adversary.

2   Related Work

In [22], [24],[5] the authors propose two-party protocols to build a decision tree, an SVM or a neural network. In these papers it is assumed that a database is horizontally or vertically partitioned. Parties then jointly build a classifier on the whole database. However, intermediate computations are made public, leaking information about private data. For instance, in [22], the entropy computations are public. In [24], the authors assume that parties do not collude, i.e. an adversary controls at most one party. Pinkas and Lindell [15] focus on the problem of decision tree learning with the popular ID3 algorithm. Their protocol is shown secure against passive (semi-honest) adversaries. In [10], authors propose protocols that allow two or more participants to construct a boosting classifier without explicitly sharing their data sets. However, these protocols are not private, even against passive adversaries. In [13], the authors extend the notion of privacy preservation or secure multi- party computation to gradient-descent-based techniques. However, the proposed two party protocols are costly and they are not shown secure against active adversaries. The main protocol of this paper is shown to be correct and private against any passive or active adversaries.

3   Quadratic Error Minimization

Let us suppose that the parties agree on a sample z_n of n instances. Let $y_i \in \{-1, 1\}$ be the class of the instance i and x_{ij} the information (e.g. a predictive variables vector) known by party j about instances i. We also suppose that parties have inferred a classifier h_j in order to predict the class variable y. We will denote by h_{ij} the class predicted by the classifier h_j on the instance i, i.e. $h_{ij} = h_j(x_{ij})$. In this section, we propose to build a linear combination over the classifiers h_j minimizing the quadratic error, noting that this error is close to the one minimized by Adaboost, i.e. the exponential error. Minimizing quadratic error under convexity constraints can be done in polynomial time with gradient descent algorithms. However the convexity constraint implies a projection phase which is not "arithmetic". Thus, the classical cryptographic tools are not adapted for this algorithm. The solution that we propose consists of relaxing this convexity constraint. For concreteness, the positivity constraint is removed and we propose to find a linear combination $h = \alpha_1 h_1 + ... + \alpha_T h_T$ minimizing the quadrating error under the constraint $\sum_{j=1}^{T} \alpha_j = 1$. By removing the positivity constraint, $\sum_{i=1}^{T} |\alpha_i|$ can be larger than 1. The performance could be degraded if this sum is too large [1]. To overcome this, we penalize large weight combinations by adding a regularization term $\gamma \sum_{i=1}^{T} \alpha_i^2$ to the quadratic error where γ is a parameter.

3.1 Quadratic Error

In this section, I will denote the identity matrix of size T. We denote by C the (convex) set of the linear combinations over the classifiers h_j such that the sum of the coefficients is equal to 1,

$$C = \left\{ \sum_{j=1}^{T} \alpha_j h_j \mid \forall j \in \{1, ..., T\} \; \alpha_j \in \mathbb{R} \; ; \; \sum_{j=1}^{T} \alpha_j = 1 \right\}$$

An element $h \in C$ is a real function: on an instance $i = 1, ..., n$, $h(x_{i1}, ..., x_{iT}) = \sum_{j=1}^{T} \alpha_j h_{ij}$. For sake of simplicity, $h(x_{i1}, ..., x_{iT})$ will be denoted by $h(i)$. It is classically transformed into a binary classifier $\bar{h}$ by applying the function Sign, i.e. $\bar{h} = \text{Sign}(h)$. As discussed previously, this section proposes an algorithm to minimize, over C, the error $er(h)$[1] being defined by,

$$er(h) = \frac{1}{n} \sum_{i=1}^{n} (h(i) - y_i)^2 + \gamma \sum_{j=1}^{T} \alpha_j^2$$

In the next lemma, it is shown that for any $h \in C$, the error $er(h)$ only depends on the values $(m_{jk})_{(j,k) \in \{1,...,T\}^2}$ defined by

$$m_{jk} = \frac{1}{n} \sum_{i=1}^{n} (h_{ij} - y_i)(h_{ik} - y_i)$$

This coefficient represents the common error between the party j and the party k. Let us observe that m_{jk} is smaller than the error of the classifiers h_j and h_k and that m_{jj} is equal to the classification error of h_j computed on z_n. In the following, M will denote the $T \times T$ matrix of the coefficients m_{jk}, i.e. $M = [m_{jk}]$.

---

[1] It is straightforward to see that $er(h)$ upper-bounds the classification error of $\bar{h}$. The exponential error is equal to $\frac{1}{n} \sum_{i=1}^{n} e^{-h(i)y_i}$.

Lemma 1. *Let $\gamma \in \mathbb{R}$ be a regularization parameter. M is symmetric, defined positive and for any $h \in C$,*

$$er(h) = \alpha^T(M + \gamma I_T)\alpha$$

Proof. Let h be a convex combination $h = \sum_{j=1}^{T} \alpha_j h_j$ such that $\sum_{j=1}^{T} \alpha_j = 1$.

First, let us consider the quantity $Q(h) = \frac{1}{n}\sum_{i=1}^{n}(h(i) - y_i)^2$.

$$Q(h) = \frac{1}{n}\sum_{i=1}^{n}\left(\sum_{j=1}^{T}\alpha_j h_{ij} - y_i\right)^2$$

By using the fact that $\sum_{j=1}^{T} \alpha_j = 1$ we can state

$$Q(h) = \frac{1}{n}\sum_{i=1}^{n}\left(\sum_{j=1}^{T}\alpha_j(h_{ij} - y_i)\right)^2.$$ By developing and by inverting sums, we get the following result

$$Q(h) = \sum_{j=1}^{T}\sum_{k=1}^{T}\alpha_j\alpha_k\left(\frac{1}{n}\sum_{i=1}^{n}(h_{ij} - y_i)(h_{ik} - y_i)\right)$$

Thus $Q(h) = \alpha^T M \alpha$. The result is obtained by noticing that

$$er(h) = Q(h) + \alpha^T(\gamma I)\alpha$$

$\square$

In the next section, we propose a gradient descent algorithm to minimize $er(h)$.

3.2 Gradient Descent Algorithm

In this section, we are looking for an algorithm which minimizes $er(h)$. In next sections, this algorithm will be transformed for observing a secure multi-party protocol. In order to use classical cryptographic primitives, the only allowed computations are arithmetic operators ($+$ and $\times$). It excludes, for example, algorithms requiring normalization steps. The following algorithm satisfies these constraints.

Algorithm QEM

Inputs: $K \in \mathbb{N}$, $\gamma \in \mathbb{Q}$ and $\rho \in \mathbb{Q}$

1. $\alpha = (1/T)_{j=1,...,T}$
2. For $k = 1$ to K
   (a) $P = (M + \gamma I)\alpha$
   (b) $\alpha_j = \alpha_j + \frac{\rho}{T}\left(\sum_{i=1}^{T}(P_j - P_i)\right)$ for all $j = 1...T$

Proposition 1. *For "small" values of ρ, QEM converges to the combination which minimizes the quadratic error over the convex C.*

Proof. (Sketch.) As $M + \gamma I$ is positive definite, the associated bilinear form is elliptic. Thus, the projected gradient algorithm converges if ρ is small enough. It suffices to see that the projection over C in step 2.b is correct. $\qquad\square$

Remark 1. By convention, $\alpha = (1/T)_{j=1,\dots,T}$ at the 0th iteration.

4 Experiments

In this section, we experimentally compare our weighting scheme to the uniform scheme consisting of weighting each classifier by $1/T$. In all of our experiments, we choose $\gamma = 0$ and $\rho = 2T^{-2}\sum_{j=1}^{T} m_{jj}^{-1}$. The tests are made on classical benchmarks used in machine learning (they can be found on the UC Irvine Machine Learning Repository)

Name	Variables number	Instances Number
Waveform	21	5000
BreastW	31	569
Clean	167	476
CreditG	25	1000

In our problem, each party has a partial view of the database. In the following, n designates the instances number and p designates the number of explicative variables. In our experiments, each party j only knows a subset of p_j explicative variables, randomly chosen, such that p_j is a random number belonging to $\{1, \dots, p/5\}$. Each party j knows the value of these p_j variables for all the instances. However, each party j knows the class value of a subset z_j of instances: the cardinality of z_j is n_j where n_j is a random number belonging to $\{n/20, \dots, n/3\}$.

Then each party j builds a decision tree h_j with the classical method C4.5 (see [18]). The coefficients m_{jk} (let us recall that m_{jk} is the common error between the classifiers h_j and h_k) are computed over $\bigcup_{j=1}^{T} z_j$ ($\approx z_n$ the whole training set when T sufficiently large).

The parameters of these experiments will be the number of parties T and the iterations numbers K in QEM. The generalization error are estimated with 10-folds cross-validation.

Results. In all of our experiments, the generalization error significantly and sometimes drastically decreases with the iteration number (see **fig. 1**). Let us recall that classifiers h_i are uniformly weighted at the first iteration. At convergence, the error rate is sometimes half of the error rate during the first iteration. Secondly, the convergence is reached quickly. After 10 iterations, approximatively 50% of the improvements are already done. In our opinion, this completely validates our approach.

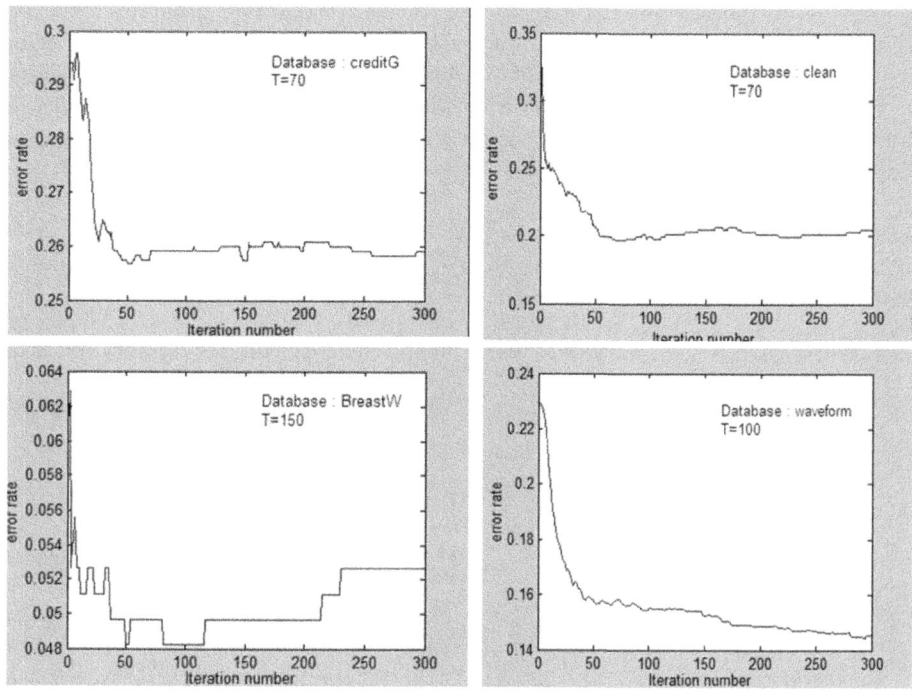

Fig. 1. Cross-validation error of the linear combinations obtained at each iteration of QEM

5   Cryptographic Tools

Homomorphic encryption schemes (El Gamal [8], Paillier [17], Boneh [2]...) have been shown relevant for secure multi-party computation. The most famous one of them is attributed to Paillier. This encryption scheme is probabilist, the public key is a k-bit RSA modulus μ chosen at random and an element $g \in Z_{\mu^2}^*$ of order divisible by μ. The plaintext space for this system is Z_μ. In [7], the cryptosystem is generalized to have plaintext space Z_{μ^s} for any s smaller than the factor of μ and g has order divisible by μ^s. To encrypt $a \in Z_{\mu^s}$, one chooses $r \in Z_{\mu^s}$ at random and computes the ciphertext as $E_{pk}(a) = g^a r^{\mu^s} \mod \mu^{s+1}$. The private key sk is the factorization of n, i.e. $\lambda(\mu)$ or equivalent information. This encryption scheme is shown semantically secure[2] under the well-known DCRA assumption (see [17]). This encryption scheme is additively homomorphic. Indeed the product of two encryptions is an encryption of the sum of the encrypted value, i.e. $E_{pk}(a)E_{pk}(b) \mod \mu^2$ is an encryption of $a + b$. Several threshold versions have been proposed in the literature [9]. In these versions, the public key pk is

---

[2] Encryptions cannot be distinguish from random values.

known by all parties but the private key sk is shared between parties such that the decryption can be done only if at least t parties agree on it. In the following, we say that S is a $(t, T)-$threshold encryption scheme if the secret key is shared between T parties such that the decryption requires at least t honest parties. To build the main protocols of this paper, the additional protocols Mult, Sign and EncryptBit are needed.

Definition 1. *Let S be a $(t, T)-$threshold homomorphic encryption scheme semantically secure. The encryption function is denoted by E_{pk} and we assume the existence of the protocols Mult, Sign and EncryptBit defined by:*

1. **Mult.** *Given an encryption of a and b, parties can securely compute an encryption of ab*
2. **Sign.** *Let ξ a security parameter. Given an encryption of a value x such that $|x| < \mu/2^{\xi-1}$, parties can securely compute an encryption of the sign of x.*

$$\text{Sign}(x) = \begin{cases} 0, & \text{if } x = 0 \\ 1, & \text{if } x > 0 \\ -1, & \text{otherwise} \end{cases}$$

3. **EncryptBit.** *A party j builds an encryption B of a bit $b \in \{0, 1\}$. EncryptBit is a $\Sigma-$protocol [12] allowing the party j to prove that B encrypts a bit without revealing it.*

These protocols are assumed secure under composition [3] against any adversary controlling less than t parties.

A version of protocol Mult can be found in [6]. The protocol Sign can be found in [11] and [21]. Concretely, let X be an encryption of $|x| < 2^{\xi-1}$. Parties compute encryptions of each bit of the binary decomposition of $v = x + 2^{\xi-1} \in \{0, ..., 2^{\xi}\}$ with the protocol BITREP found in [21]. Then, parties compare v with $2^{\xi-1}$ with a comparison protocol found in [11]. A version of EncryptBit can be found in [7]. The communication cost and the time complexity of these protocols are linear with respect to the parties numbers, i.e. $O(T)$.

Notations. *Let X, Y be encryptions of x, y, i.e. $X = E_{pk}(x)$ and $Y = E_{pk}(y)$. $X \oplus Y$ and $X \ominus Y$ will denote an encryption of $x + y$ and $x - y$. These encryptions can be obtained by using the homomorphic properties of the encryption scheme S. In the same way, $X \otimes Y$ will denote an encryption of xy. This encryption is obtained by invoking Mult.*

6   The Protocols

In this section, we assume that parties have jointly generated a pairwise (pk, sk) by invoking the function Generation of a $(t, T)-$threshold homomorphic encryption scheme S satisfying the definition 1. The domain of E_{pk} is assumed to be the ring $\mathbb{Z}_\mu$. Let us assume the existence of an adversary A controlling several parties. A knows private data of all controlled parties and it can replace any controlled party in the protocol. Here, adversaries can be active, meaning that they can deviate from the protocol in any way [16]. In this section, the protocols are shown correct and private against any adversaries. A rigorous definition of correctness and privacy, when inputs are committed, is given in appendix A. Intuitively, a protocol is said to be correct if an honest party outputs the correct value (or does not output anything if the protocols fails). A protocol is said to be private against an adversary A if A cannot learn anything about the private data of an honest party (except what it can learn with the output and its own private data). In our case, A will not learn anything about the coefficients m_{jk}, the class values y_{ij}, the coefficients α_j and the values h_{ij}.

6.1   Protocol PQEM

In order to use classical and efficient cryptographic primitives, QEM should be defined over a finite ring $\mathbb{Z}_\mu$. Contrarily to the computation over floats, truncations are forbidden. It implies that the domain size is linked to the computations number. This will be discussed in section 6.4.

At each iteration k in PQEM, an encryption of a coefficients vector α' is computed. This vector is proportional to the coefficients vector α computed at the kth iteration in QEM, i.e. $\alpha' = C\alpha$ (here, $C = T(auv)^k$). Thus, the classifiers $\mathsf{Sign}(\alpha'_1 h_1 + ... + \alpha'_1 h_T)$ and $\mathsf{Sign}(\alpha_1 h_1 + ... + \alpha_1 h_T)$ are equal. In this sense, PQEM is correct.

Protocol PQEM

Let $\gamma, \rho \in \mathbb{Q}$ be parameters and M be a symmetric, defined positive, rational matrix. Let a, u, v be integers such that $\widetilde{\rho} = v\rho/T$, $\widetilde{\gamma} = a\gamma$ are integers and $\widetilde{M} = uM$ is an integer matrix.

Public inputs: *Let $K \in \mathbb{N}$. let $\widetilde{M}_{jk}$ be encryptions of $\widetilde{m}_{jk}$. It is also known $\widetilde{\rho}$, $\widetilde{\gamma}$, a, v and U, an encryption of u, i.e. $U = E_{pk}(u)$*

1. $\Delta_j = E_{pk}(1)$ for all $j = 1, ..., T$

2. For $k = 1$ To K
   (a) $P_j = a \otimes \left(\bigoplus_{j'=1}^{T} \widetilde{M}_{jj'} \otimes \Delta_{j'} \right) \oplus \left(\widetilde{M}_{jj} \otimes \widetilde{\gamma} \right)$ for all $j = 1...T$
   (b) $\Delta_j = (v \otimes a \otimes U \otimes \Delta_j) \oplus \left(\bigoplus_{k=1}^{T} (P_j \ominus P_k) \right) \otimes \widetilde{\rho}$ for all $j = 1...T$

Lemma 2. *Assume the encryption scheme S semantically secure. Let N_k the Manhattan norm $(\|.\|_1)$ of the vector α outputted at the kth iteration of QEM and $w = auv$. Assuming $\mu > Tw^K N_K$, PQEM is correct and private against any adversary controlling less than t parties.*

Proof. Assuming correctness of the protocol Mult (operator $\otimes$), it is easy to establish, for instance by recurrence, that Δ_j encrypts $Tw^K \alpha_j \mod \mu$ where α is the coefficients vector computed at the Kth iteration in QEM. Thus if $\mu > Tw^K N_K$, Δ_j encrypts $Tw^K \alpha_j$.

Assuming Mult secure under composition, Mult can be replaced by a trusted party (see [3]). As Mult output a random encryption, by replacing Mult by a trusted party, an adversary A only receives encryptions. Assuming the encryption scheme S semantically secure, encryptions are computationally indistinguishable from random values. It proves privacy.   □

Remark 2. In all our experiments, $N_K \approx 1$ meaning that the absolute values of the negative coefficients are small.

6.2   Protocol **PDEM**

Let us suppose that each party j has a private database D_j containing a binary variable y. Each party j has built a private classifier h_j to predict a class variable y. Here, it is assumed that parties agree on an instances list[3]. We denote the predicted values of h_j in instance i by h_{ij}, and the class value of instance i in the private database D_j of party j by y_{ij}. By convention $y_{ij} = 0$ if this value is missing in D_j. Note that y_{ij} can differ from the true class value y_i of instance i, i.e. $y_{ij} \neq y_i$. At the beginning of the protocol PDEM, each party j broadcasts encryptions of h_{ij} and y_{ij} for each instance $i = 1, ..., n$.

First, the parties must agree on the class value of each instance i, i.e. y_i. We propose to define y_i as the class the most represented among the values $(y_{ij})_{j=1,...,T}$, i.e. $y_i = \text{sign}\left(\sum_{j=1}^{T} y_{ij}\right)$. Note that y_i is correct only if a majority of parties knows this value and $y_i = 0$ if the class 1 and -1 are equally represented or if this value is unknown by all the parties, i.e. $y_{ij} = 0$ for all $j = 1, ..., T$. So the first step of PDEM consists of computing an encryption of y_i, computed as described previously. It is done by using homomorphic properties and the protocol Sign.

Let E be the set of instances for which the class y_i is defined, i.e. $E = \{i \mid y_i \neq 0\}$. The instances $i \notin E$ are discarded. Then parties have to securely compute encryptions of the common errors m_{jk}. These errors are computed over E. Precisely, parties compute encryptions of the integers $|E|m_{jk}$ defined by

$$|E|m_{jk} = \sum_{i \in E}(h_{ij} - y_i)(h_{ik} - y_i)$$

Finally parties execute PQEM.

---

[3] The method for this is not explained here.

Protocol PDEM

Let $K \in \mathbb{N}$, $\gamma \in \mathbb{Q}$, $\rho \in \mathbb{Q}$ be parameters chosen a priori. Let $a, v \in \mathbb{N}$ be integers such that $\widetilde{\gamma} = \gamma a \in \mathbb{N}$ and $\widetilde{\rho} = v\rho/T \in \mathbb{N}$. Each party has computed a classifier h_j. For each $i = 1, ..., n$, each party $j = 1, ..., T$ computes and broadcasts encryptions Y_{ij}, H_{ij} of y_{ij}, h_{ij}.

Public inputs: *K, $\widetilde{\gamma}$, $\widetilde{\rho}$, a, v, Y_{ij}, H_{ij}, $(i, j) \in \{1, ..., n\} \times \{1, ..., T\}$.*

1. each party j prove that $Y_{ij} \otimes Y_{ij}$ and $H_{ij} \otimes H_{ij}$ encrypt a bit by invoking EncryptBit for all $i = 1...n$

2. $U = E_{pk}(0)$

3. For $i = 1$ to n

   (a) compute $Y_i = \mathsf{Sign}\left(\bigoplus_{j=1}^{T} Y_{ij} \right)$

   (b) $U = U \oplus Y_i \otimes Y_i$

4. compute encryption $\widetilde{M}_{jk}$ of um_{jk} where U is the encrypted value of u for $(j, k) \in \{1, ..., T\}^2$,

$$\widetilde{M}_{jk} = \bigoplus_{i=1}^{n} Y_i \otimes Y_i \otimes (H_{ij} \ominus Y_i) \otimes (H_{ik} \ominus Y_i)$$

5. invoke the weighting scheme $\mathsf{PQEM}(K, [\widetilde{M}_{jk}], U, \widetilde{\gamma}, \widetilde{\rho}, v, a)$: the parties output the encryptions Δ_j computed.

Remark 3. U encrypts a value $u \leq n$ equal to the cardinal of $E = \{i \mid y_i = 0\}$. As, a, v and n are public, parties can bound auv with anv.

Lemma 3. *Assume the encryption scheme S semantically secure. Assume the protocols Mult, Sign and EncryptBit secure under composition. Let us state $w = avn$. Assume $\mu > Tw^K N_K$, PDEM is correct and private against any adversary controlling less than $t - 1$ parties.*

Proof. Assuming correctness of the protocol EncryptBit, Y_{ij} encrypts a bit. Thus, $\bigoplus Y_{ij}$ encrypts a value smaller than $T < \mu/2^\xi$. Thus, assuming Sign is correct, Y_j encrypts a bit. Assuming Mult is correct, at each step k, the computed encryptions of $u = |E|$, um_{jk} and $Tw^k \alpha_j$ are correct modulo μ. Assuming $Tw^K N_K < \mu$ implies that $Tw^K \alpha_j \mod \mu = Tw^K \alpha_j$ for all $j = 1, ..., T$.

Assuming Mult, EncryptBit, Sign are secure under composition, these protocols can be replaced by a trusted party. These protocols output encryptions. By replacing them by trusted parties, an adversary A only receives encryptions. Assuming the encryption scheme S semantically secure, encryptions are computationally indistinguishable from random values. It proves privacy. $\square$

6.3   Protocol Prediction

In this section, it is assumed that parties have already executed PDEM and they get encryptions Δ_j of $Tw^K\alpha_j$ for all $j = 1, ..., T$ (see previous section). Let x be a new instance. To securely compute the sign of $\alpha_1 h_1(x) + ... + \alpha_T h_T(x)$, each party j computes $h_j(x)$ and broadcasts its encryption Y_j. Then parties jointly compute an encryption of $Tw^K(\alpha_1 h_1(x) + ... + \alpha_T h_T(x))$ by applying Mult. Then, by invoking protocol Sign, parties get the predicted class.

Protocol Prediction

$PDEM(K, \widetilde{\gamma}, \widetilde{\rho}, a, v, (Y_{ij}, H_{ij})_{(i,j) \in \{1,...,n\} \times \{1,...,T\}})$ *should have been invoked: parties have outputted an encryption Δ_j of $Tw^K\alpha_j$. Let x be a new instance. Each party j computes $y_j = h_j(x)$.*

Public inputs: *encryptions $Y_j = E_{pk}(y_j)$ and Δ_j for $j = 1, ..., T$,*

1. each party j proves that $Y_j \otimes Y_j$ encrypts a bit by invoking EncryptBit.

2. compute $C = \bigoplus_{j=1}^{T} \Delta_j \otimes Y_j$

3. output $y =$Sign(C)

Lemma 4. *Assuming the encryption scheme semantically secure and assuming that $\mu > 2^\xi Tw^K N_K$, Prediction is correct and private against any adversary controlling less than t parties.*

Proof. As EncryptBit and Mult are correct steps 1 and 2 are correct. To prove correctness of step 3, it suffices to see that the encrypted value by C is smaller than $Tw^K N_K$. As $\mu > 2^\xi Tw^K N_K$, the protocol Sign is secure (see definition 1). Thus, the output is correct. Privacy is shown by the same way than for lemma 1 and 2.   □

Thus, in order to ensure correctness and privacy of PDEM+Prediction, $\mu > 2^\xi Tw^K N_K$. By assuming $N_K \approx 1$ (according to remark 2) and by recalling (according to remark 3) that w can be upper-bounded by a public value $w' = anv$, μ should be chosen such that

$$\mu = O\left(2^\xi Tw'^K\right)$$

6.4   Complexity

The number of encryptions/decryptions/modular exponentiations computations is linear with respect to T in the protocols Sign, EncryptBit and Mult. The number of invocations of Sign, EncryptBit and Mult is equal to $O(nT^2 + KT)$. Thus, the number of encryptions/decryptions/modular exponentiations computations is equal to

$$O(nT^3 + KT^2)$$

Furthermore, we noted in the previous section that the domain size $\lceil \log_2 \mu \rceil$ is linear (neglecting logarithm factors) in K ($\log \mu = O(\log T + \xi + K \log w')$). As the encryptions/decryptions/modular exponentiations complexities are in $O(\log^3 \mu)$ for classical homomorphic encryption schemes (Paillier, El Gamal), the complexity of PDEM is

$$O\left(K^3 T^2 (nT + K)\right)$$

The protocol Mult is invoked T times by Prediction. Thus, the number of encryptions/decryptions/modular exponentiations computations is quadratic with respect to T in Prediction. By taking into account the domain size, the complexity is

$$O\left(K^3 T^2\right)$$

These computational costs are not relevant for many real applications. Truncations would be interesting in order to reduce the domain size expansion ($\lceil \log \mu \rceil$). In [14], the authors propose a secure multi-party protocol to compute $x \mod a$ and x/a (integer division) given a public divisor a and an encryption of x. This protocol could be used to compute truncations.

7 Discussion and Future Work

PDEM and Prediction were shown both correct and private against any adversary. However a "malicious" adversary A can always alter its inputs. It could choose "malicious" inputs in order to get relatively large weights α_j for the parties it controls. To get relatively large weights, A is interested in choosing a classifier h_j with a low empirical error (even if h_j has a very bad generalization error). In other words, if it knows the class value of a majority of instances, it could input a classifier with a low empirical error: for instance, it could choose the classifier which predicts the correct class when it is known and random ones (or better than random) for the others. Thus our scheme is not robust against an adversary which knows a large number of class values.

Furthermore, to predict the class of a new instance x, each party j should input an encryption of $h_j(x)$ in Prediction. An adversary could input an encryption of the other class in order to change the prediction of the aggregated classifier.

To overcome this issue, the classifiers h_j should belong to a restricted class whose VC-dimension [23] should be adapted to the number of instances. For instance, parties could only propose decision trees or neural networks of size lower than a given size. To ensure this, the classifiers h_j should be committed such that any party can compute an encryption of the predicted class. However, in this case, information about individual classifiers would be leaked. An other way to proceed would consist in making statistical controls on inputs. It should be also interesting to consider the regret minimization setting of online learning where several experts can be combined to make an aggregate prediction in spite of adversaries [4].

Acknowledgements. The authors thank the reviewers for their helpful comments.

References

1. Bartlett, P.L.: For valid generalization the size of the weights is more important than the size of the network. In: NIPS, pp. 134–140 (1996)
2. Boneh, D., Goh, E.-J., Nissim, K.: Evaluating 2-dnf formulas on ciphertexts. In: Kilian, J. (ed.) TCC 2005. LNCS, vol. 3378, pp. 325–341. Springer, Heidelberg (2005)
3. Canetti, R.: Universally composable security: A new paradigm for cryptographic protocols. In: FOCS, pp. 136–145 (2001)
4. Cesa-Bianchi, N., Lugosi, G., Stoltz, G.: Minimizing regret with label efficient prediction. IEEE Transactions on Information Theory 51(6), 2152–2162 (2005)
5. Chen, T., Zhong, S.: Privacy-preserving backpropagation neural network learning. Trans. Neur. Netw. 20(10), 1554–1564 (2009)
6. Cramer, R., Damgård, I., Nielsen, J.B.: Multiparty computation from threshold homomorphic encryption. In: Pfitzmann, B. (ed.) EUROCRYPT 2001. LNCS, vol. 2045, pp. 280–299. Springer, Heidelberg (2001)
7. Damgård, I., Jurik, M.: A generalisation, a simplification and some applications of paillier's probabilistic public-key system. In: Kim, K.-c. (ed.) PKC 2001. LNCS, vol. 1992, pp. 119–136. Springer, Heidelberg (2001)
8. Elgamal, T.: A public key cryptosystem and a signature sheme based on discrete logarithms. IEEE Transactions on Information Theory 31, 469–472 (1985)
9. Fouque, P., Stern, J.: Fully distributed threshold rsa under standard assumptions. In: IACR Cryptology ePrint Archive: Report 2001/2008 (February 2001)
10. Gambs, S., Kégl, B., Aïmeur, E.: Privacy-preserving boosting. Data Min. Knowl. Discov. 14(1), 131–170 (2007)
11. Garay, J.A., Schoenmakers, B., Villegas, J.: Practical and secure solutions for integer comparison. In: Okamoto, T., Wang, X. (eds.) PKC 2007. LNCS, vol. 4450, pp. 330–342. Springer, Heidelberg (2007)
12. Goldwasser, S., Micali, S., Rackoff, C.: The knowledge complexity of interactive proof-systems (extended abstract). In: STOC, pp. 291–304 (1985)
13. Han, S., Ng, W.K., Wan, L., Lee, V.C.S.: Privacy-preserving gradient-descent methods. IEEE Trans. Knowl. Data Eng. 22(6), 884–899 (2010)
14. Guajardo, J., Mennink, B., Schoenmakers, B.: Modulo reduction for paillier encryptions and application to secure statistical analysis. In: Sion, R. (ed.) FC 2010. LNCS, vol. 6052, pp. 375–382. Springer, Heidelberg (2010)
15. Lindell, Y., Pinkas, B.: Privacy preserving data mining. In: Bellare, M. (ed.) CRYPTO 2000. LNCS, vol. 1880, pp. 36–54. Springer, Heidelberg (2000)
16. Goldreich, O., Michali, S., Wigderson, A.: How to play any mental game or a completeness theorem for protocols with honest majority. In: STOC, pp. 218–229 (1987)
17. Paillier, P.: Public-key cryptosystems based on composite degree residuosity classes. In: Stern, J. (ed.) EUROCRYPT 1999. LNCS, vol. 1592, pp. 223–238. Springer, Heidelberg (1999)
18. Ross Quinlan, J.: C4.5: Programs for Machine Learning. Morgan Kaufmann, San Francisco (1993)

19. Schapire, R.E.: Theoretical views of boosting. In: Fischer, P., Simon, H.U. (eds.) EuroCOLT 1999. LNCS (LNAI), vol. 1572, pp. 1–10. Springer, Heidelberg (1999)
20. Schapire, R.E., Freund, Y., Barlett, P., Lee, W.S.: Boosting the margin: A new explanation for the effectiveness of voting methods. In: ICML, pp. 322–330 (1997)
21. Schoenmakers, B., Tuyls, P.: Efficient binary conversion for paillier encrypted values. In: Vaudenay, S. (ed.) EUROCRYPT 2006. LNCS, vol. 4004, pp. 522–537. Springer, Heidelberg (2006)
22. Vaidya, J., Clifton, C., Kantarcioglu, M., Scott Patterson, A.: Privacy-preserving decision trees over vertically partitioned data. TKDD 2(3) (2008)
23. Vapnik, V.: Principles of risk minimization for learning theory. In: NIPS, pp. 831–838 (1991)
24. Yu, H., Vaidya, J., Jiang, X.: Privacy-preserving svm classification on vertically partitioned data. In: Ng, W.-K., Kitsuregawa, M., Li, J., Chang, K. (eds.) PAKDD 2006. LNCS (LNAI), vol. 3918, pp. 647–656. Springer, Heidelberg (2006)

A   Correctness and Privacy Definition

Let us start to define the distance between 2 distributions.

Definition 2. *Let D and D' 2 probability distribution defined over X. For a subset $A \subseteq X$, let's denote $D_A(D, D') = |D(A) - D'(A)|$ the distance between D and D' defined by*

$$d(D, D') = \max_{A \subseteq S} d_A(D, D') \tag{1}$$

This allows us to define the notion computational indistinguishability

Definition 3. *Let D and D' 2 probability distributions over X. These distributions are computationally indistinguishable, $D \equiv^c D'$, if for all polynomial size boolean circuit C,*

$$|P(C(x) = 1 | x \leftarrow D) - P(C(x) = 1 | x \leftarrow D')|$$

is negligible.

The classical security notions are linked to this notion of indistinguishability.

Definition 4. *Let π be a two party-protocol which computes the functionality (f_1, f_2). Inputs (x, y) are assumed committed. Party 1 is honest and party 2 is controlled by a polynomial adversary A. The adversary A may commit $C_A(y)$ instead of y where C_A is a non-uniform p.p.t. Let $\text{OUTPUT}_{\pi,A}(x, y)$ be the outputted value by the honest party and $\text{VIEW}_{\pi,A}(x, y)$ the sequence of all received values of the adversary A.*

1. *A protocol is correct if*

$$\text{OUTPUT}_{\pi,A}(x, y) = \begin{cases} \bot & \text{if the protocol fails;} \\ f_1(x, C_A(y)) & \text{otherwise.} \end{cases}$$

2. *It is private if there exists a non-uniform p.p.t S such that*

$$\text{VIEW}_{\pi,A}(x, y) \equiv^c S(y, f_2(x, C_A(y)))$$

Secure Top-k Subgroup Discovery

Henrik Grosskreutz, Benedikt Lemmen, and Stefan Rüping

Fraunhofer IAIS, Schloss Birlinghoven, Sankt Augustin, Germany
firstname.lastname@iais.fraunhofer.de

Abstract. Supervised descriptive rule discovery techniques like subgroup discovery are quite popular in applications like fraud detection or clinical studies. Compared with other descriptive techniques, like classical support/confidence association rules, subgroup discovery has the advantage that it comes up with only the top-k patterns, and that it makes use of a quality function that avoids patterns uncorrelated with the target. If these techniques are to be applied in privacy-sensitive scenarios involving distributed data, precise guarantees are needed regarding the amount of information leaked during the execution of the data mining. Unfortunately, the adaptation of secure multi-party protocols for classical support/confidence association rule mining to the task of subgroup discovery is impossible for fundamental reasons. The source is the different quality function and the restriction to a fixed number of patterns – i.e. exactly the desired features of subgroup discovery. In this paper, we present a new protocol which allows distributed subgroup discovery while avoiding the disclosure of the individual databases. We analyze the properties of the protocol, describe a prototypical implementation and present experiments that demonstrate the feasibility of the approach.

1 Introduction

The question of the privacy of data can be an important aspect in the real-world application of data mining. In privacy-sensitive scenarios, in particular those with distributed data, a failure to guarantee certain privacy-preserving constraints means that data mining can not be applied at all. As an example, consider the case of competing mail order companies. To a large part, these companies make money by knowing their customers better than their competitors do. On the other hand, they lose money due to fraud. Typically, the risk of disclosing sensitive customer information by far outweighs the chances of reducing expenses by a joint fraud detection effort. Only privacy-preserving data mining techniques will allow an analysis of fraud patterns over all companies.

In applications like the above, descriptive techniques like rule mining are very popular, as they have the potential to provide more insight than numerical methods like SVMs or neural networks. Actually, protocols have been proposed that allow secure association rule mining over distributed databases [10]. These, however, rely on the classical support/confidence framework, which has been observed to have effects undesired in some settings [22,3,9]: In particular, there is a danger to come up with huge amounts of rules which are not significant or do not express a correlation.

C. Dimitrakakis et al. (Eds.): PSDML 2010, LNAI 6549, pp. 36–49, 2011.

For this reason, several alternative (non-secure) rule mining approaches have been proposed, that deviate from the classical support/confidence framework. These include subgroup discovery [11], contrast set mining [2] and correlated itemset mining [16]. These approaches share many similarities, and are sometimes subsumed under the name *supervised descriptive rule discovery* [17]. The key differences compared to classical support/confidence association rule mining is (i) the different quality function used to assess the patterns, and (ii) the intention to collect only a small set of k patterns (instead of collecting all patterns satisfying some minimal threshold constraint).

Unfortunately, it is *impossible* to adapt existing secure association rule mining protocols like [10] to a supervised descriptive rule discovery task like subgroup discovery. The reason lies in the different quality functions. The existing protocols rely on the property that in the support/confidence framework *every globally large itemset must be locally large at least at one of the sites*. However, an analogous property does not hold for the new quality functions: the globally best rules are not guaranteed to also be among the locally best rules of any site, neither exactly nor approximately [19,24].

In this paper, we present a secure protocol for the task of top-k subgroup discovery. To the best of our knowledge, this is the first approach that tackles any of the above-mentioned supervised descriptive rule discovery tasks. Our approach assumes horizontally partitioned data, that is, all sites use the same set of attributes and the quality of every subgroup depends on all databases. The approach finds patterns in the union of the databases, without disclosing the local databases.

The remainder of this paper is structured as follows: After a brief review of some basic definitions in Section 2, we present our new protocol in Section 3 and prove that it is secure. Next, we describe a prototypical implementation in Section 4, before we conclude in Section 5.

2 Preliminaries

In this section, we will briefly go over the most important notions from secure multi-party computation and subgroup discovery.

2.1 Privacy-Preserving Data-Mining and Secure Multi-party Computation

Privacy-preserving data mining has emerged to address the situation when the use of data mining techniques is desired, but the data to be mined may not be disclosed or brought together due to privacy considerations. One of the most important lines of research in privacy-preserving data mining is the family of approaches based on *secure multi-party computation* [18,7]. Here, the premise is that the data is distributed over different parties, and the goal is to obtain some result without revealing the (private) data of one party to another. A classical example is Yao' famous millionaires problem [25]: two millionaires want to learn who is richer without revealing the precise amount of their wealth. In the context of data mining, the input would be databases and the result a bunch of patterns. We will now review the most important definitions of secure multi-party computation. The following presentation is based on Goldreich [7] (with some simplifications, as we consider a less general scenario).

Multi-Party Computation. A multi-party problem, or *task*, is casted by specifying a mapping from sequences of inputs (one input per party) to sequences of outputs (one output per party). We refer to this mapping as the desired *functionality*, denoted $f : (\{0,1\}^*)^S \rightarrow (\{0,1\}^*)^S$, where S denotes the number of parties. That is, f is a mapping of the combined input $\bar{x} = (x_1, \ldots, x_S)$ to the combined output $(f_1(\bar{x}), \ldots, f_S(\bar{x}))$: the first party with input x_1 wishes to obtain $f_1(\bar{x})$, the second party with input x_2 wishes to obtain $f_2(\bar{x})$, etc. Clearly, the output of every party can depend on all inputs, $x_1, \ldots, x_S$.

In this paper, we consider multi-party computation in the *semi-honest model*, arguably the most commonly used model in privacy-preserving data-mining (e.g. [13,20,10]). The semi-honest model assumes that every party follows the protocol properly with the exception that it keeps a record of all intermediate computations and messages. One motivation for the semi-honest model is that parties who want to mine data for their mutual benefit will follow the protocol to get correct results. Another argument is that in a complex software implementation, it might not be easy to deviate from the specified protocol, definitely more difficult than merely recording the registers and messages. Finally, such records may be available anyway through some standard activities of the operating systems, which makes "totally honest" behavior hard to enforce.

A Definition of Secure Computation. Intuitively, a protocol π securely computes a functionality f if whatever a semi-honest party can obtain after participating in the protocol could be obtained from the input and output available to that party. This is formalized according to the simulation paradigm, which requires that every party's view in a protocol execution can be simulated given only its input and output. As the actual execution may involve messages based on random numbers, the simulator does not need to generate *exactly* what is seen during the actual execution. The following definition makes this precise:

Definition 1. *Let $f = (f_1, \ldots, f_S)$ be a deterministic S-ary functionality and π be a multi-party protocol for computing f. For a party i, let $\mathsf{view}_i^\pi(\bar{x})$ denote its view, i.e. its input x_i and the sequence of messages it has received. We say that π securely computes f in the presence of semi-honest adversaries without collusion if there exist probabilistic polynomial-time algorithms $S_i, 1 \leq i \leq S$, also called* simulators, *such that for every party the view is computationally indistinguishable from the simulation:*

$$\{(S_i(x_i, f_i(\bar{x})))\}_{\bar{x} \in (\{0,1\}^*)^S} \equiv^C \{\mathsf{view}_i^\pi(\bar{x})\}_{\bar{x} \in (\{0,1\}^*)^S} \tag{1}$$

Here, $\equiv^C$ denotes computational indistinguishability. Loosely speaking, the simulations are computationally indistinguishable from the views if for every polynomial-time distinguisher D the probability that D distinguishes a view and the simulation decreases super-polynomially in the length of the input. The details can be found in [7]. For our purpose, it is sufficient to note that any random number in a view is computationally indistinguishable from another random number drawn from the same probability distribution.

Yao's Generic Circuit Solution. Yao has presented a generic solution that allows the secure evaluation of *any* two-party functionality [26,14]. The solution is based on the encryption and secure evaluation of circuits. While in principle this implies that it is possible to securely compute any kind of (two-party) data mining task simply by using a circuit calculating the outcome of the data mining task, this naive approach would result in huge circuits whose inputs would be entire databases – an approach which is not feasible in practice [18]. However, the use of Yao's circuit encryption scheme can be very useful to securely compute some sub-functionality.

2.2   Subgroup Discovery

Subgroup discovery is a supervised descriptive rule learning task. In this paper, we only consider binary labeled data, thus a *subgroup description* can be seen as the antecedent of a rule whose consequence is the positive class.

Formally, let $\mathcal{A} = A_1, \ldots, A_m$ be a sequence of m sets we refer to as *attributes*. Beside these attributes, there is a special binary set $\{+, -\}$ called the *label*. A *data record* over $\mathcal{A}$ is an $m+1$-tuple $D = (a_1, \ldots, a_m, l) \in A_1 \times \cdots \times A_m \times \{+, -\}$. A *database* $\mathcal{D}$ over $\mathcal{A}$ is a multiset of data records over $\mathcal{A}$. We use the expression $\mathcal{D}^+$ to denote the sub-multiset of all $+$-labeled data records in $\mathcal{D}$. Formally, thus $\mathcal{D}^+ = \{(a_1, \ldots, a_m, l) \in \mathcal{D} \mid l = +\}$. Similarly, $\mathcal{D}^-$ denotes the sub-multiset of all $-$-labeled data records in $\mathcal{D}$.

The subgroup description language considered here is the language of conjunctions of attribute/value equality constraints. We formalize this as follows: a *constraint* over $\mathcal{A}$ is an expression $(A_i = v)$ with $i \in \{1, \ldots, m\}$ and $v \in A_i$. The language of *subgroup descriptions* over $\mathcal{A}$, denoted by $\mathcal{L}_\mathcal{A}$, is then the power set of constraints over $\mathcal{A}$. In the following, we drop the index $\mathcal{A}$ because it is always clear from the context. Given a subgroup description $s \in \mathcal{L}$, we call the number of constraints it is built of its *length*, denoted by $length(s)$.

We will now turn to the semantics of subgroup descriptions: a data-record $(a_1, \ldots, a_m, l) \in \mathcal{D}$ satisfies a subgroup description $s \in \mathcal{L}$, if for all $(A_i = v) \in s$ it holds that $a_i = v$. Then the *extension* of s in $\mathcal{D}$, denoted by $\mathcal{D}[s]$, is the sub-multiset of $\mathcal{D}$ containing the data records that satisfy s.

The "interestingness" of a subgroup description is measured by a *quality function*, which is a mapping from a database and a subgroup description to the reals. The idea is that high function values indicate interesting patterns. In this paper, we consider the *Piatetsky-Shapiro* quality function, which is (factor) equivalent to the *weighted relative accuracy* [12]. This function, which is arguably one of the most common subgroup quality functions, is defined as follows:

$$q(\mathcal{D}, s) = n(\mathcal{D}, s) \left(p(\mathcal{D}, s) - p_0(\mathcal{D}) \right). \tag{2}$$

Here, $n(\mathcal{D}, s) = |\mathcal{D}[s]|$ denotes the size of the subgroup, $p(\mathcal{D}, s) = |\mathcal{D}^+[s]| / |\mathcal{D}[s]|$ the fraction of records with positive label in the subgroup and $p_0(\mathcal{D}) = |\mathcal{D}^+| / |\mathcal{D}|$

the fraction of positive records in the overall population. Subgroup discovery is concerned with finding high-quality subgroups, as precised in the next section.

3   Distributed Secure Subgroup Discovery

We assume that there are $S \geq 2$ sites (or parties) participating in the computation, each holding a private database $\mathcal{D}_i$ ($1 \leq i \leq S$) built over the same set of attributes. Instead of directly considering the task of top-k subgroup discovery, we first consider a specialization of this problem, namely finding a *single* subgroup of maximum quality. This task can be seen as the special case where $k = 1$. We will describe later (in Section 3.4), how given a solution to this task, we can iteratively collect a set of k subgroups. Beside the subgroup description, we want to learn its quality, because this tells us whether the subgroup describes a significant phenomenon or merely a manifestation of noise in the data. The task we consider is thus the following:

Task 1. *Top-1 Subgroup Discovery Given private databases* $\mathcal{D}_1, \ldots, \mathcal{D}_S$ *at Sites 1 to S (each built over the same set of attributes) together with a length limit L, calculate and distribute a maximum quality subgroup description* s_{max} *of length* $\leq L$ *together with its quality. That is, compute a pair* $\langle s_{max}, q_{max} \rangle \in \mathcal{L} \times \mathcal{R}$ *such that*

$$q_{max} = \max_{\{s \in \mathcal{L} \mid length(s) \leq L\}} q(\mathcal{D}, s),$$

$$length(s_{max}) \leq L \text{ and } q(\mathcal{D}, s_{max}) = q_{max}$$

where the quality function q (defined in Equation 2) is evaluated wrt. the disjoint union of the local databases, $\mathcal{D} = \bigoplus_{i=1}^{S} \mathcal{D}_i$.

It turns out that Task 1 is unexpectedly hard: First, as shown by Scholz [19], the globally best rules may perform poor at all local sites, and moreover the local quality of a subgroup can arbitrarily deviate from its global quality (no matter whether a relative or an absolute definition of support is applied). The consequence is that separately analyzing one (or all) local databases is of no help in finding the best global subgroup. This is unlike the situation in the classical support/confidence framework, where every globally large itemset must be locally large at least at one of the sites, a property exploited in protocols like [4,10]. The reason for this difference is the different quality function used in subgroup discovery. As a consequence, the distributed association rule mining protocols cannot be adapted to the task of subgroup discovery, and instead a distributed global subgroup mining protocol has been proposed [24] which computes the global quality of every subgroup essentially by polling the local support counts from all participating sites.

   In the context of secure computation, we face an additional difficulty: the standard approach of non-secure subgroup discovery algorithms – keeping track of the best subgroups observed so far together with their quality during the traversal of the search space [23,8,24] – results in a security leak. The reason is, loosely speaking, that the sequence of increments of the best quality cannot be simulated from the outcome. This sequence, however, reveals a lot of information about the data, as it induces a partial order over the quality of *all* subgroups visited during the exploration of the search space. For this reason, we compute the maximum-quality subgroup in two steps, by subsequently solving the following two sub-tasks:

- first, we compute the maximum of all subgroup qualities, that is, the value q_{max}. This is done in a way that only the maximum becomes known, but no ordering between subgroup qualities;
- second, we use this quality to securely find a maximum-quality subgroup.

We will discuss these two steps in Sections 3.1 and 3.2, respectively, before we present the overall protocol in Section 3.3 and turn to the task of *top-k* subgroup discovery in Section 3.4.

3.1 Computing the Maximum Quality

Our solution to the first sub-task works as follows: In a first phase, the sites collectively traverse the space of subgroup descriptions. For every subgroup description, the protocol ensures that Site 1 obtains a random value r_i, and Site S a second value $\tilde{q}_i + r_i$, where $\tilde{q}_i$ represents the quality of the subgroup (actually, $\tilde{q}_i$ is an integer-valued multiple of the subgroup quality, as explained below). The motivation for the distributed storage of r_i and $\tilde{q}_i + r_i$ is that none of the parties must learn the value $\tilde{q}_i$. In a second phase, Site 1 and Site S use the garbled qualities $\tilde{q}_i + r_i$ and the offsets r_i to securely calculate the maximum quality. We remark that the first phase is inspired by the garbled quality calculation in [5], while the second phase shares some similarity with the maximum computation in [13].

Computing the Garbled Qualities $\tilde{q}_i + r_i$. We will now describe these two phases in more detail. We first observe that the Piatetsky-Shapiro quality (Equation 2) can be rewritten as follows [6]: $q(\mathcal{D}, s) = |\mathcal{D}^+[s]| (1 - p_0(\mathcal{D})) - |\mathcal{D}^-[s]| p_0(\mathcal{D})$. Given that $\mathcal{D} = \bigoplus_{i=1}^{S} \mathcal{D}_i$, this means that the quality can be expressed as a sum of local values:

$$q(\mathcal{D}, s) = \sum_{i=1}^{S} \left(|\mathcal{D}_i^+[s]| (1 - p_0(\mathcal{D})) - |\mathcal{D}_i^-[s]| p_0(\mathcal{D}) \right). \tag{3}$$

All that is required to compute the local summands is the value $p_0(\mathcal{D})$. Moreover, all summands are multiples of $1/|\mathcal{D}|$, because p_0 is a multiple of $1/|\mathcal{D}|$. Thus, assuming that every site has knowledge of $|\mathcal{D}|$, we can reduce the computation to arithmetics on integers. In fact, the $\tilde{q}_i$ mentioned earlier are simply the integers obtained by multiplying the quality of the i-th subgroup and $|\mathcal{D}|$. As final observation, we note that the values of the integers $\tilde{q}_i$ do not exceed $|\mathcal{D}|^2$.

Based on these observations, we realize the computation of the values r_i and $\tilde{q}_i + r_i$ at Sites 1 resp. S as follows: Site 1 generates a random number r_i uniformly distributed in $[0, \dots, M]$, where M is a some power of 2 constant such that $M > |\mathcal{D}|^2$. Site 1 adds it local support, $(|\mathcal{D}_1^+[s_i]|(1 - p_0) - |\mathcal{D}_1^-[s_i]|p_0) \cdot |\mathcal{D}|$ to r_i, and sends the sum (modulo M) to Site 2. Sites 2 to (S-1) add their local support and send the result to the next site. Finally, Site S obtains the result, which according to Equation 3 corresponds to $\tilde{q}_i + r_i$.

Obtaining the Maximum. Once the first phase of the computation is completed, Site 1 has a list of values $r_1, \dots, r_R$, and Site S another list $\tilde{q}_1 + r_1, \dots, \tilde{q}_R + r_R$, where R denotes the number of subgroup descriptions visited during the traversal. In the second phase, only *two* sites are involved. This is an important difference to the first phase, as it means that now we could apply a generic two-party solution like Yao's encrypted circuit scheme [26].

However, due to the potentially very large number of inputs this may result in an in-feasibly large circuit, so we reduce the problem to smaller subproblems: We successively shorten the two lists by iteratively replacing *two* values by *one* at *both* Sites 1 and S. Thereby, we take care that while the length of the two lists decrease, together they still allow the reconstruction of q_{max}. This is done by replacing two values r_α, r_β at Site 1 by a *new* random value r', and the two corresponding values $r_\alpha + \tilde{q}_\alpha$, $r_\beta + \tilde{q}_\beta$ at Site S by $r' + \max(\tilde{q}_\alpha, \tilde{q}_\beta)$. The use of a new random number r' is important, as it will allow us to prove that the parties learn nothing new during the replacements[1]. The replacements take place until only one pair of values remains, whose difference reveals the quality q_{max}. Figure 1 illustrates the overall idea.

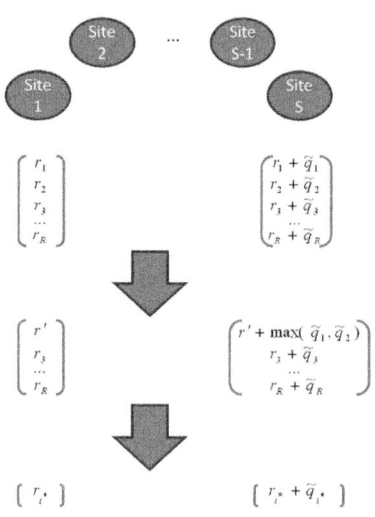

Fig. 1. Maximum Quality Calculation

To put the above into action, all we need is a secure solution for the following functionality: Provided Site 1's input (r_α, r_β, r') and Site S's input $(r_\alpha + \tilde{q}_\alpha, r_\beta + \tilde{q}_\beta)$, calculate the combined output $(\perp, (\max(\tilde{q}_\alpha, \tilde{q}_\beta) + r') \mod M)$, i.e. Site 1 learns nothing and Site S learns the garbled maximum. Here, all inputs and outputs are integers in $[0, \dots, M]$.

We realize this functionality using an encrypted circuit [26]. A detailed description of the circuit encryption scheme is beyond the scope of this paper (see the excellent presentation in [14] for details). The bottom line is that given some boolean circuit, this scheme allows to generate an encrypted representation of that circuit, together with an encoding table for the boolean input gates.

---

[1] Simply dropping one of the pairs would not be secure, as it would reveal which subgroup has the higher quality; this also explains why we cannot store an encrypted representation of the subgroup description together with its garbled quality.

Given this representation, plus cryptographic keys representing a particular set of boolean inputs, it is possible to calculate the (plain) value of the boolean outputs - but no additional information beyond that.

Using this encryption scheme, Site 1 proceeds as follows: First, it generates a boolean circuit that computes the above functionality. The circuit has input wires for the boolean representation of r_α, r_β, $\tilde{q}_\alpha + r_\alpha$, $\tilde{q}_\beta + r_\beta$ and r', and the output wires represent $(\max(\tilde{q}_\alpha, \tilde{q}_\beta) + r') \mod M$. The circuit calculates the output using some inverters and ripple-carry adders, a well-known type of digital circuit. Site 1 generates the encrypted representation of the circuit and sends the circuit (without the encoding table) to Site S, together with the keys representing its own input bits. Now all that Site S needs to calculate the output are the keys representing its own input. For this purpose, we make use of an additional ("third") party, T: Site 1 sends the encoding table for the inputs of Site S to Site T. Site S sends its (plain) input bits to Site T and obtains the corresponding cryptographic keys. Given this information, Site S can evaluate the encrypted circuit and thus obtain $(r' + \max(\tilde{q}_\alpha, \tilde{q}_\beta)) \mod M$. None of the parties learn anything else than the result. We remark that if $S > 2$, the role of Site T can be implemented by one of the sites $2, ..., (S - 1)$, e.g. Site 2, after some minor preprocessing.[2]

3.2   Computing a Maximum Quality Subgroup

Once the maximum quality q_{max} is computed, it is straightforward to solve Task 1 and compute a maximum quality subgroup. Basically, all that has to be done is to check, for every subgroup s_i, whether $q_i \geq q_{max}$, which is equivalent to $\tilde{q}_i + r_i \geq r_i + q_{max} \cdot |\mathcal{D}|$. The first subgroup satisfying this inequality is returned as outcome. The values $\tilde{q}_i + r_i$ are known at Site S after execution of Protocol 1, and moreover the values r_i, q_{max} and $|\mathcal{D}|$ are known at Site 1, so all that is needed is to securely compute the greater-or-equal test. This test, however, is equivalent to Yao' famous millionaires problem [25], and many solutions exist for this task (e.g. [21]).

3.3   The Protocol

We now have all ingredients for a secure solution for Task 1. Protocol 1 assumes the length limit L as input, together with local database $\mathcal{D}_i$, $i, 1 \leq i \leq S$.

First, the sites securely calculate $|\mathcal{D}|$ and $|\mathcal{D}^+|$. As $|\mathcal{D}|$ is the sum of the local $|\mathcal{D}_i|$, this reduces to the secure calculation of a sum of local values – a standard task in multi-party computation, for which efficient protocols exist (see e.g. [5]). Same for $|\mathcal{D}^+|$. The values $|\mathcal{D}|$ and $|\mathcal{D}^+|$ are distributed to all sites, which will enable them to calculate p_0 and hence the local values in Equation 3. Next, Site 1 and Site S initialize a local queue, $\mathcal{Q}_1$ resp. $\mathcal{Q}_S$. These will be used to store the values $r_1, ..., r_R$ (at Site 1) resp. $\tilde{q}_1 + r_1, ..., \tilde{q}_1 + r_R$ (at Site S).

---

[2]   All that is required is that before the circuits are generated, Site 1 and Site S replace every r_i by $r_i + r'_i$, where r'_i is a newly generated random value. This prevents the third party from drawing conclusions by relating the observed inputs from Site S with the intermediate sums observed earlier.

Protocol 1. Maximum Subgroup Quality Computation
INPUT: length limit L and local databases $\mathcal{D}_1, \ldots, \mathcal{D}_S$

1: Site 1 initiates the secure calculation of $|\mathcal{D}|$ and $|\mathcal{D}^+|$ and broadcasts the result
2: Site 1 creates a local iterator *iter* and a queue $\mathcal{Q}_1$, Site S creates a local queue $\mathcal{Q}_S$

3: **while** hasNext(*iter*) **do**
4:   Site 1 calculates and broadcasts $s_i = $ next(*iter*)
5:   Site 1 generates a random number r_i uniformly in $[0, \ldots, M]$, enqueues r_i in $\mathcal{Q}_1$, adds its local support $(|\mathcal{D}_1^+[s_i]| (1 - p_0) - |\mathcal{D}_1^-[s_i]| p_0) \cdot |\mathcal{D}|$ to r_i and sends the result (mod M) to Site 2
6:   Sites $2, ..., S - 1$ add their local support to the intermediate sum and send the result (mod M) to the next site
7:   Site S adds its local support to the sum and enqueues the result, $\tilde{q}_i + r_i$ (mod M), in $\mathcal{Q}_S$
8: **end while**

9: **while** $\mathcal{Q}_1$ contains more than 1 value **do**
10:   Site 1 dequeues r_α and r_β from $\mathcal{Q}_1$, generates a random number r' uniformly in $[0, \ldots, M]$ and enqueues r' in $\mathcal{Q}_1$
11:   Site 1 generates and encrypts a circuit that computes $(\max(\tilde{q}_\alpha, \tilde{q}_\beta) + r') \mod M)$ from $r_\alpha, r_\beta, \tilde{q}_\alpha + r_\alpha, \tilde{q}_\beta + r_\beta$ and r'. It sends the circuit to Site S together with the cryptographic keys corresponding to the input bits for r_α, r_β and r'.
12:   Site 1 sends the encoding table for the remaining inputs to Site T
13:   Site S dequeues $(r_\alpha + \tilde{q}_\alpha)$ and $(r_\beta + \tilde{q}_\beta)$ from $\mathcal{Q}_S$, asks Site T for the corresponding cryptographic keys, evaluates the encrypted circuit and enqueues the result, $(r' + \max(\tilde{q}_\alpha, \tilde{q}_\beta) \mod M)$, in $\mathcal{Q}_S$
14: **end while**

15: Sites 1 and S calculate q_{max} by exchanging the two remaining values
16: **for** every subgroup descriptions s_i **do**
17:   **if** $\tilde{q}_i + r_i \geq r_i + q_{max} \cdot |\mathcal{D}|$ **then return** $\langle s_i, q_{max} \rangle$
18: **end for**

OUTPUT: s_{max} and q'_{max} (same output at all sites)

Thereafter, the protocol iterates over all subgroup descriptions (Line 3 to 8). This is orchestrated by Site 1, which makes use of an iterator *iter* to generate all subgroup descriptions satisfying the length limit. The iterator traverses the space of subgroup descriptions in a canonically depth-first, left-to-right order, according to the lexicographic order of the constraints. Using this iterator, Site 1 generates the next subgroup description s_i and informs all sites that s_i is the next subgroup description to be considered. Next, the parties collectively calculate r_i and $\tilde{q}_i + r_i$. As discussed earlier, the latter value is computed by iteratively adding the local support and sending the intermediate result to the next site. The values r_i resp. $r_i + \tilde{q}_i$ are separately stored in the queues $\mathcal{Q}_1$ and $\mathcal{Q}_S$ at Sites 1 and S, respectively.

When the second loop starts at Line 9, all candidate subgroups have been considered. The protocol will now determine a pair of values $r_{i^*}, (r_{i^*} + \tilde{q}_{i^*})$

such that $\tilde{q}_{i^*}$ is maximal. This is done by iteratively replacing (a pair of) *pairs* at Sites 1 and S simultaneously by (a pair of) *single values*. To this end, in every iteration of Line 11 a new encrypted circuit is generated at Site 1, which is evaluated afterwards by Site S, resorting to a third party T (which can optionally be implemented by Site 2 as discussed earlier). The loop ends when only one pair of values remains, which allows the calculation of the quality q_{max}.

Once the figure q_{max} is calculated, the protocol re-iterates over all subgroups (in Line 16) until a subgroup with maximum quality is met. This subgroup is returned as result together with its quality, and the execution ends.

Protocol 1 is secure, as precised by the following theorem:

Theorem 1. *Protocol 1 privately solves Task 1, revealing only $|\mathcal{D}|$ and $|\mathcal{D}^+|$ (in the semi-honest model, assuming no collusion).*

Proof. We have to specify how every site can simulate its *view* given the result, the leaked information and its own input. Recall that the simulation does not need to generate the *exact* same sequence of messages – it suffices that its output is computationally indistinguishable from the view (which involves messages based on random numbers).

The simulator generates execution traces following the algorithmic skeleton of Protocol 1, i.e. by iterating over the subgroup descriptions. This ensures that the simulations have the same overall structure as the views. We will now go over every line of the protocol involving communication and describe how the simulator can generate data computationally indistinguishable from the observed messages. To this end, we will describe how the simulator generates such data in a first paragraph "(S)", before we prove that this data is computationally indistinguishable from the actual messages in a second paragraph "(I)".

Line 1: (S) The protocol computes $|\mathcal{D}|$ and $|\mathcal{D}^+|$ using an existing secure-sum sub-protocol, e.g. [5]. Goldreich's *Composition Theorem* [7] says that given secure protocols for sub-tasks, they can be dealt with in a transparent way: all we need to show is that the simulator can predict the outcome of the sub-protocol. Given that $|\mathcal{D}|$ and $|\mathcal{D}^+|$ is part of the simulator's input, it can output these very values. (I) The values in the view and in the simulation are computationally indistinguishable because they are identical.

Line 4: (S) The simulator generates the next subgroup using the iterator *iter*. (I) The subgroup in the view and in the simulation coincide, because the traversal is performed in a canonical way.

Lines 5 to 7: (S) Sites 2 to S generate a random number uniformly in $[0, \ldots, M]$. (I) Given that r_i was randomly generated uniformly in $[0, \ldots, M]$, the local sum in the view is also uniformly distributed in $[0, \ldots, M]$. Hence, it is computationally indistinguishable from the random number in the simulation, because two random numbers generated from the same distribution are computationally indistinguishable [7].

Lines 11 to 13: The execution of these lines result in the following messages: (i) Site S receives an encrypted circuit representation together with a set of cryptographic keys that allow the evaluation of the circuit; (ii) Site T receives an encoding table, plus the values $(r_\alpha + \tilde{q}_\alpha)$ and $(r_\beta + \tilde{q}_\beta)$.

(S) For *Site S*, the simulator generates a new encrypted circuit, and uses its representation to simulate the circuit in the view. As simulation of the input r', it uses the encryption table to encode the bits of a newly generated random number generated uniformly in $[0, \ldots, M]$. To simulate the other inputs, it uses the encryption table to encode some arbitrary boolean values. For *Site T*, the simulator generates an encrypted circuit and uses the encoding table as simulation of the table in the view. Moreover, it generates two random numbers as simulation of the two inputs from Site S.

(I) For *Site S*, recall that all can be extracted from an encrypted circuit, given a particular set of input keys, is the outcome [14]. The outcome of the circuit in the view is a random number uniformly distributed in the domain $[0, \ldots, M]$, which is independent from all values observed so far (recall that Site 1 generates a *new* random offset in every iteration). The same is true for the circuit in the simulation, thus the view and the simulation are computationally indistinguishable. For *Site T*, the encoding table in the view is computationally indistinguishable from that in the simulation because both essentially consist of a set of cryptographic keys generates by the same cryptographic key generation mechanism. The inputs from Site S in the view are computationally indistinguishable from the random numbers in the simulation because both are uniformly distributed in $[0, \ldots, M]$, and are independent from all values observed so far.

Line 15: (S) The simulator generates q_{max}, which it is part of its input. (I) obvious.

Line: 17: (S) Again, due to the composition theorem the simulator only has to generate the result of the test (plus, optionally, s_{max}). This is straightforward, given that s_{max} is part of the input. (I) obvious.   □

3.4   Top-k Subgroup Discovery and the Weighted Covering Scheme

It is straightforward to extend our solution to collect a set of subgroups. The simplest way is to iteratively collect the k highest-quality subgroups one after another, thereby solving the top-k subgroup discovery task. This only requires a minor modification of the iterator, ensuring that all subgroups collected so far will be ignored during subsequent search space traversals.

A more sophisticated approach would be to use the weighted covering scheme [12]. Here again, the idea is to iteratively search for the maximum subgroup, however using a definition of quality that accounts for *record weights*. After every iteration, the weights of the records covered by the subgroup collected so far is decreased by multiplication with some rational number. This results in a definition of quality which is equivalent to the following:

$$q^w(\mathcal{D}, s) = \sum_{i=1}^{S} \left(\left| \mathcal{D}_i^+[s] \right|^w (1 - p_0(\mathcal{D})^w) - \left| \mathcal{D}_i^-[s] \right|^w p_0(\mathcal{D})^w \right). \tag{4}$$

Here, $|\mathcal{D}|^w$ denotes the sum of the weights of the records in $\mathcal{D}$, and similarly $p_0(\mathcal{D})^w = |\mathcal{D}^+|^w / |\mathcal{D}|^w$. All that needs to be done to implement the weighted covering scheme is thus to make use of this quality definition instead of that in

Equation 3. Given that Equation 4 is a sum of local values, and that these values are rational numbers which can be computed locally given the set of subgroups collected in the previous iterations, the adaptation is thus straightforward.

4 Prototypical Implementation

Our prototype was implemented in Java. For the encryption of the circuits, we used the AES cipher with 128 bit keys implemented in the lightweight API of the crypto-library Bouncycastle (http://www.bouncycastle.org). To compute secure sums, we used the secure sum protocol described in [5]. For secure comparisons, we used the efficient solution for Yao' millionaires problem described in [21]. The quality calculation is realized without sophisticated data structures like FpTrees, as the prototype is merely intended as a proof-of-concept.

We have evaluated the performance of our implementation on different datasets from the well-known UCI repository [1]. All datasets where randomly split into three parts, which were used as local datasets. The experiments were performed on three Core 2 Duo E8400 PCs with 2GB RAM, connected by an Ethernet LAN. The length limit, L, was set to 3. Figure 2 visualizes the result. Beside the overall runtime ("total"), it shows the proportions of the runtime spent (i) for the distributed calculation of the garbled subgroup qualities ("qual."), and (ii) for the evaluation

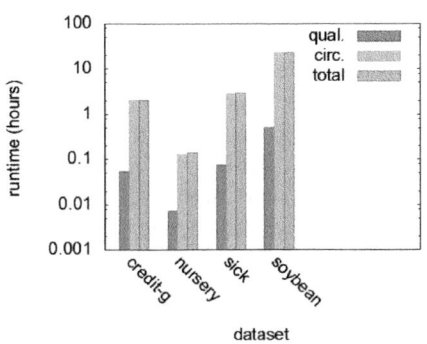

Fig. 2. Runtime of the prototype

of the encrypted circuits ("circ."). These two components correspond to the first resp. second `while` loop of Protocol 1. The figure shows that the most costly part is the encryption and evaluation of the circuits.

Compared with state-of-the-art non-secure subgroup discovery algorithms [12,8], the computation is (extremely) slow. Nevertheless, the experiments show that our approach is applicable in practice. The runtime is sufficient to process data sets of realistic size in a few hours, which is quite often sufficiently fast for practical use. In scenarios where a failure to guarantee privacy means that data mining can not be applied at all, the users may very well be willing to invest this time if that allows to find valuable patterns which could not be obtained otherwise.

5 Conclusions

In many pattern mining settings, the data to be analyzed is sensitive, which makes the use of privacy-preserving techniques mandatory. Although approaches exist to securely find association rules in distributed data, these cannot be adapted to supervised descriptive mining tasks like subgroup discovery. The source for the difficulties are precisely the features that distinguish subgroup discovery from classical association rule mining: (i) the different quality function, and (ii) the aim to collect only k patterns.

In this paper, we have presented a new secure protocol that allows secure subgroups discovery on horizontally partitioned data. While the basic protocol only solves the top-1 subgroup discovery task, it can be iterated to collect a set of k subgroups. We have analyzed the properties of our protocol and have shown that it leaks only little information, namely the size of the database and the share of positive records. Finally, we have reported on a prototypical implementation and experiments which demonstrate the feasibility of the approach.

In the experiments it has become clear that the improvements in security and privacy come at the price of a high runtime. While the worst-case complexity of our algorithm is the same as for a non-secure solution, i.e. exponential in the number of attributes, in practice it is much slower than the latter. One reason is of course the slowdown caused by communication and encryption overhead. Another reason is that approaches of speeding up subgroup discovery, such as optimistic estimate pruning [8] or local counting pruning [24] were not considered here. The reason is that they need to exchange additional information between local parties, which make them problematic in a secure computation setting. It would be worthwhile to investigate the effective severity of such information leaks. Clearly, knowledge about optimistic estimates tells something about the private data, but it is not really clear how much. In particular, does it allow to reconstruct (part of) the data? This question is closely related to the so-called task of *inverse frequent set mining* [15]. We leave the investigation of these issues to future work.

Another interesting question is whether the protocols presented in this paper can be adapted to other quality functions used in supervised descriptive rule discovery. Finally, it would be desirable to extend the security guarantees to colluding parties. One standard approach in the cryptographic community to deal with collusion issues is to divide the information into different parts, and to use different routes for the different calculations (e.g. [10]). Whether such an approach is applicable is left to future work.

References

1. Asuncion, A., Newman, D.: UCI machine learning repository (2007)
2. Bay, S.D., Pazzani, M.J.: Detecting group differences: Mining contrast sets. Data Min. Knowl. Discov. 5(3), 213–246 (2001)
3. Brin, S., Motwani, R., Silverstein, C.: Beyond market baskets: Generalizing association rules to correlations. In: Peckham, J. (ed.) SIGMOD Conference, pp. 265–276. ACM Press, New York (1997)
4. Cheung, D., Han, J., Ng, V., Fu, A., Fu, Y.: A fast distributed algorithm for mining association rules. In: International Conference on Parallel and Distributed Information Systems, p. 0031 (1996)

5. Clifton, C., Kantarcioglu, M., Vaidya, J., Lin, X., Zhu, M.Y.: Tools for privacy preserving distributed data mining. SIGKDD Explor. Newsl. 4(2) (2002)
6. Fürnkranz, J., Flach, P.A.: Roc 'n' rule learning-towards a better understanding of covering algorithms. Machine Learning 58(1), 39–77 (2005)
7. Goldreich, O.: General Cryptographic Protocols. In: The Foundations of Cryptography, vol. 2. Cambridge University Press, Cambridge (2004)
8. Grosskreutz, H., Rüping, S., Wrobel, S.: Tight optimistic estimates for fast subgroup discovery. In: ECML/PKDD (1). Springer, Heidelberg (2008)
9. Hämäläinen, W., Nykänen, M.: Efficient discovery of statistically significant association rules. In: ICDM, pp. 203–212. IEEE Computer Society, Los Alamitos (2008)
10. Kantarcioglu, M., Clifton, C.: Privacy-preserving distributed mining of association rules on horizontally partitioned data. IEEE Transactions on Knowledge and Data Engineering 16(9), 1026–1037 (2004)
11. Klösgen, W.: Explora: A multipattern and multistrategy discovery assistant. In: Advances in Knowledge Discovery and Data Mining (1996)
12. Lavrac, N., Kavsek, B., Flach, P., Todorovski, L.: Subgroup discovery with cn2-sd. Journal of Machine Learning Research 5, 153–188 (2004)
13. Lindell, Y., Pinkas, B.: Privacy preserving data mining. In: Bellare, M. (ed.) CRYPTO 2000. LNCS, vol. 1880, p. 36. Springer, Heidelberg (2000)
14. Lindell, Y., Pinkas, B.: A proof of yao's protocol for secure two-party computation. Technical report (2004)
15. Mielikäinen, T.: On inverse frequent set mining. In: Workshop on Privacy Preserving Data Mining (2003)
16. Nijssen, S., Guns, T., Raedt, L.D.: Correlated itemset mining in roc space: a constraint programming approach. In: KDD, pp. 647–656 (2009)
17. Novak, P.K., Lavrač, N., Webb, G.I.: Supervised descriptive rule discovery: A unifying survey of contrast set, emerging pattern and subgroup mining. Journal of Machine Learning Research 10 (2009)
18. Pinkas, B.: Cryptographic techniques for privacy-preserving data mining. SIGKDD Explor. Newsl. 4(2), 12–19 (2002)
19. Scholz, M.: On the tractability of rule discovery from distributed data. In: ICDM, pp. 761–764. IEEE Computer Society, Los Alamitos (2005)
20. Shaneck, M., Kim, Y., Kumar, V.: Privacy preserving nearest neighbor search. In: ICDM Workshops, pp. 541–545 (2006)
21. Shundong, L., Yiqi, D., Daoshun, W., Ping, L.: Symmetric encryption solutions to millionaire's problem and its extension. In: 1st International Conference on Digital Information Management (2006)
22. Webb, G.I.: Discovering significant rules. In: KDD 2006: Proceedings of the 12th ACM SIGKDD International Conference on Knowledge Discovery and Data Mining, pp. 434–443. ACM, New York (2006)
23. Wrobel, S.: An algorithm for multi-relational discovery of subgroups. In: Komorowski, J., Zytkow, J. (eds.) PKDD 1997. LNCS, vol. 1263, pp. 78–87. Springer, Heidelberg (1997)
24. Wurst, M., Scholz, M.: Distributed subgroup mining. In: Fürnkranz, J., Scheffer, T., Spiliopoulou, M. (eds.) PKDD 2006. LNCS (LNAI), vol. 4213, pp. 421–433. Springer, Heidelberg (2006)
25. Yao, A.C.-C.: Protocols for secure computations (extended abstract). In: FOCS. IEEE, Los Alamitos (1982)
26. Yao, A.C.-C.: How to generate and exchange secrets. In: 27th Annual Symposium on Foundations of Computer Science, 1985, pp. 162–167 (October 1986)

ASAP: Automatic Semantics-Aware Analysis of Network Payloads

Tammo Krueger[1,3], Nicole Krämer[2,3], and Konrad Rieck[3]

[1] Fraunhofer Institute FIRST, Germany
[2] Weierstrass Institute for Applied Analysis and Stochastics, Germany
[3] Berlin Institute of Technology, Germany

Abstract. Automatic inspection of network payloads is a prerequisite for effective analysis of network communication. Security research has largely focused on network analysis using protocol specifications, for example for intrusion detection, fuzz testing and forensic analysis. The specification of a protocol alone, however, is often not sufficient for accurate analysis of communication, as it fails to reflect individual semantics of network applications. We propose a framework for semantics-aware analysis of network payloads which automatically extracts semantics-aware components from recorded network traffic. Our method proceeds by mapping network payloads to a vector space and identifying communication templates corresponding to base directions in the vector space. We demonstrate the efficacy of semantics-aware analysis in different security applications: automatic discovery of patterns in honeypot data, analysis of malware communication and network intrusion detection.

1 Introduction

Automatic analysis of network data is a crucial task in many applications of computer security. For example, intrusion detection systems often require parsing of network payloads for identification of attacks [1, 2, 3], fuzz testing tools build on automatically crafting network messages from protocol specifications [4, 5, 6], and forensic analysis depends on inspecting network data involved in security incidents [7, 8, 9]. In these and several other security applications, the analysis of communication—whether from live traffic or recorded traces—critically depends on automatic extraction of meaningful patterns from network payloads, such as application parameters, cookie values and user credentials.

A large body of security research has thus focused on analysis of network data using protocol specifications [10, 11, 12]. The specification of a protocol defines the basic structure of its communication as well as the syntax of its network messages. While these analysis techniques are successful in parsing network data, they are by design confined to the examination of protocol syntax. However, attacks and security threats are rarely reflected in syntax alone but in semantics, functionality realized on top of protocol specifications. As an example, malicious software often employs standard network protocols for communication. However, parsing of corresponding network traffic is not sufficient for accurate analysis,

C. Dimitrakakis et al. (Eds.): PSDML 2010, LNAI 6549, pp. 50–63, 2011.

and significant manual effort is necessary for deducing relevant information from parsed content. What is needed are techniques capable of automatically identifying and extracting semantics-aware components from communication, thereby reducing the gap between protocol syntax and semantics.

In this paper, we propose a framework for automatic, semantics-aware analysis of network payloads (ASAP). This framework is orthogonal in design to specification-based approaches and automatically extracts semantics-aware components from recorded traffic—even if the underlying protocols are unknown. To this end, ASAP ignores any protocol specification and exploits occurrences and combinations of strings for inferring communication templates which are more focused on the semantics instead of the syntax of communication. The main contributions of this framework are:

1. *Alphabet extraction for network payloads.* For automatic analysis, we devise a technique for extracting an alphabet of strings from network payloads. The alphabet concisely characterizes the network traffic by filtering out unnecessary protocol or volatile information via a multiple testing procedure and embeds the payloads into a vector space.

2. *Analysis using matrix factorization.* The method proceeds by identifying base directions in this vector space using concepts of matrix factorization, which combines these letters to meaningful building blocks.

3. *Construction of communication templates.* Discovered base directions are transformed to communication templates—conjunctions of strings—which give insights into semantics of communication and provide a basis for interpretation of traffic beyond syntax-based analysis.

Empirically, we demonstrate the capabilities of semantics-aware analysis in different security applications. First, we conduct experiments on network traffic captured using honeypots where we pinpoint exploited vulnerabilities as well as attack sources using the ASAP framework. Second, we apply semantics-aware analysis for investigation of network traces recorded from malware executed in sandbox environments. We exemplarily extract typical communication patterns for the malware *Vanbot*. Finally, we employ our framework in the domain of network anomaly detection by mapping payloads into a low-dimensional space without accuracy loss yet significantly increased runtime performance.

2   The ASAP Framework

The ASAP framework proceeds in three analysis stages, which are outlined in Figure 1. First, an alphabet of relevant strings is extracted from raw network payloads and used to map these payloads into a vector space for analysis. Second, concepts of matrix factorization are applied for identification of base directions in the vector space, characterizing usage patterns of mapped payloads. Third, each of these base directions is traced back to a conjunction of strings from the underlying alphabet and results in a template of typical communication content.

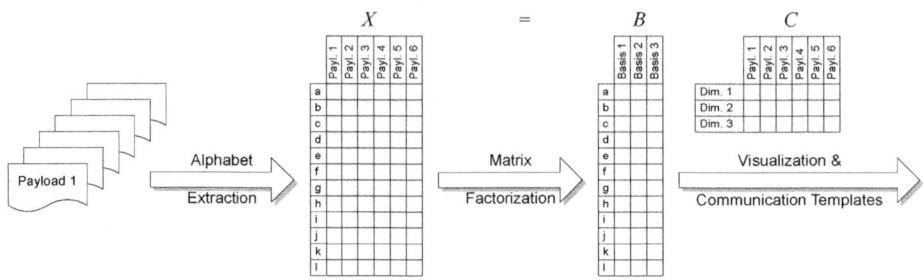

Fig. 1. Overview of the ASAP framework

2.1   Alphabet Extraction for Network Payloads

A payload p is a string of bytes contained in network communication. For describing and characterizing the content of a payload, we automatically extract an *alphabet S* of relevant strings from a set of payloads which provides the ground for inferring communication templates. The alphabet S is initially constructed from a set of basic strings and then refined using filtering and correlation techniques.

Basic strings. Depending on the network data to be analyzed, we build the alphabet from a different set of basic strings. If we consider a protocol with distinct delimiter bytes, such as HTTP, SMTP or FTP, we base the alphabet on *tokens*—the set of all strings separated by delimiters. For a set of delimiter bytes D, such as space or carriage return, tokens can be defined as

$$S = \{\{0, \ldots, 255\} \setminus D\}^{*}.$$

However, for binary network protocols such as DNS, SMB and NFS, we need to define the basic strings differently, as no delimiter symbols are available. In these cases we apply the concept of *n-grams* which denotes the set of all strings with fixed length n. Formally, this set of basic strings can be defined as

$$S = \{0, \ldots, 255\}^{n}.$$

Alphabet filtering and correlation. Strings within network payloads naturally appear with different frequency, ranging from volatile to constant occurrences. For instance, every HTTP request is required to contain the string HTTP in its header, whereas other parts such as timestamps or session numbers are highly variable. Both, constant and highly volatile components, do not augment semantics and thus are filtered from the alphabet S. More precisely, we employ a statistical *t-test* for identifying non-constant and non-volatile strings by testing whether their frequency is significantly different from 0 and 1. We apply the correction proposed by Holm [13] to avoid problems with multiple testing.

   With the remaining alphabet, we apply a correlation analysis to combine co-occurring strings. That is, for each string $s \in S$ we compute the Pearson correlation coefficient to all other strings and group strings which are highly correlated, i.e. have a correlation coefficient of roughly one. Hence, we combine elements of S which co-occur in the analyzed data and thereby further refine our alphabet. Together, filtering and correlation compact the alphabet and lead to a focused representation of S ignoring both static and volatile information.

Map to vector space. Using the alphabet S, we map a network payload p to an $|S|$-dimensional vector space, such that each dimension is associated with a string $s \in S$. In particular, we define a mapping function ϕ as

$$\phi : P \to \{0,1\}^{|S|}, \quad \phi : p \mapsto (I(s,p))_{s \in S},$$

where P is the domain of all considered payloads and $I(s,p)$ an indicator function returning 1 if the string s is contained in p and 0 otherwise. Note, that the mapping ϕ is *sparse*, that is, the vast majority of dimensions is zero, allowing for linear-time algorithms for extraction and comparison of vectors [14].

2.2 Matrix Factorization

The mapping of network payloads to a vector space induces a geometry, reflecting characteristics captured by the alphabet S. For instance, payloads sharing several substrings appear close to each other, whereas network payloads with different content exhibit larger geometric distances. The focused alphabet of the ASAP framework enables us now to identify semantics-aware components *geometrically.* In particular, we apply the concept of matrix factorization for identifying base directions in the vector space. Given a set of payloads $P = \{p_1, \ldots p_N\}$ we first define a data matrix X containing the vectors of P as columns by

$$X := [\phi(p_1), \ldots, \phi(p_N)] \in \mathbb{R}^{|S| \times N}.$$

For determining semantics-aware components, we seek a representation of X that retains most information but describes X in terms of few base directions. This can be achieved in terms of a matrix factorization of X into two matrices $B \in \mathbb{R}^{|S| \times L}$ and $C \in \mathbb{R}^{L \times N}$ such that $L \ll |S|$ and

$$X \approx BC = \overbrace{\begin{bmatrix} b_1 \ldots b_L \end{bmatrix}}^{\text{basis}} \underbrace{\begin{bmatrix} c_1 \ldots c_N \end{bmatrix}}_{\text{coordinates}}. \tag{1}$$

The columns $b_1, \ldots, b_L \in \mathbb{R}^{|S|}$ of B form a new basis for the N payloads, where the dimensions of each base direction b_i are associated with the alphabet S. As we show in later experiments, this relation of base directions and the alphabet can be exploited to construct communication templates from a matrix factorization. The columns $c_1, \ldots, c_N \in \mathbb{R}^L$ of C form a new set of coordinates for the payloads in a low-dimensional space, which can be used for visualization.

In general, matrix factorization methods differ in the constraints imposed on the matrices B and C. In this paper, we study two standard techniques widely used in the field of statistics and data analysis: Principal Components Analysis (PCA) [15, 16] and Non-negative Matrix Factorization (NMF) [17].

In PCA, we seek base directions, which are orthogonal and capture as much of the variance inside the data as possible. Formally, the ith direction b_i consecutively maximizes the variance of $X^\top b_i$ under the constraint that all base directions are mutually orthonormal:

$$b_i = \underset{\|b\|=1}{\arg\max} \operatorname{var}\left(X^\top b\right) \quad \text{s.t. } b \perp b_j, \, j < i.$$

In NMF, the orthogonality constraints are replaced by the requirement that the matrix B and C only contain non-negative entries. Non-negative entries in the basis vectors are a more natural representation for sequential data, as each string contributes positively to the basis representation. For a fixed dimensionality L, the factorization (1) is defined in terms of the minimization criterion

$$(B,C) = \underset{B,C}{\arg\min} \|X - BC\| \quad \text{s.t. } b_{ij} \geq 0, \, c_{jn} \geq 0.$$

2.3   Construction of Communication Templates

After identification of base directions B in the vector space, every payload can be expressed as a tuple of coordinates. For the interpretation, it is now crucial to find a re-mapping of these coordinates to a meaningful representation, that can be used to judge semantical content of network communication.

In case of tokens as basic strings of the alphabet we can simply select all tokens exceeding a specific threshold inside the base directions for constructing a template. For alphabets of n-grams we can try to concatenate occurring n-grams and regain parts of the original ordering. For example, if we have a basis containing the 3-grams Hos ∧ ost ∧ st: we can easily infer, that these tokens overlap and can be concatenated to Host:.

Obviously, there is no guarantee against false concatenation. Therefore we propose a greedy algorithm, which takes the calculated values for each token of the alphabet into account: By sorting the n-grams according to their assigned weights and using this inherent ordering for the matching process, we ensure a data-driven reassembly of n-grams. We first pick the token with the highest weight and look for overlaps to the other tokens, which are also ordered by their respective weights. If we find an overlap, we merge the n-grams and remove the corresponding token from the list of pending tokens. With this merged token we restart the procedure until no more overlaps are found. This token is then added to the representation list and the procedure is repeated for the next token with the highest value left, until no more tokens are in the pending list.

3   Experiments and Applications

After presenting the ASAP framework, we turn to an empirical evaluation of its capabilities in different security applications. First, we study the framework on

```
GET static/3lpAN6C2.html HTTP/1.1
Host: www.foobar.com
Accept: */*
```
———————— *Request for static content* ————————

```
GET cgi/search.php?s=EhOYKj3r3wD2I HTTP/1.1
Host: www.foobar.com
Accept: */*
```
———————— *Search query* ————————

```
GET cgi/admin.php?action=rename&par=dBJh7hSOr5 HTTP/1.1
Host: www.foobar.com
Accept: */*
```
———————— *Administrative request* ————————

Fig. 2. Example payloads of the artificial dataset

a toy dataset, which allows us to establish an understanding of how communication templates are inferred from communication (Section 3.1). We then proceed to real-world applications, where network traces containing malicious communication are analyzed for interesting components, such as exploited vulnerabilities and attack sources (Section 3.2 and 3.3). Finally, we apply our framework in the field of network anomaly detection by reducing the processing of network data using communication templates (Section 3.4).

3.1   A Showcase Analysis

For our first experiment, we consider an artificial dataset of HTTP communication where we have total control over protocol syntax and semantics. We simulate a web application supporting three different types of requests, whose network payloads are depicted in Figure 2. The first payload reflects a request for static content, the second payload resembles a search query and the last payload corresponds to an administrative request, in which the action parameter is one of the following `rename`, `move`, `delete` or `show`. All requests are equipped with random parts (the name of the static web page, the search string and the administration parameter) to simulate usual fluctuation of web traffic.

Using this web application, we generate a dataset of 1,000 network payloads with a uniform distribution of the three request types. We then apply the ASAP framework to this dataset as detailed in Section 2.1–2.3 using tokens as basic strings with delimiters selected according to the specification of HTTP. Based on the extracted alphabet, we then apply matrix factorization algorithms, namely Principal Component Analysis (PCA) and Non-negative Matrix Factorization (NMF) for determining base directions in the vector space of payloads. Finally, we construct communication templates for these base directions.

The extracted alphabet S consists of 8 "letters" (tokens combined by the co-occurrence analysis are grouped by brackets and the $\wedge$ operator):

$S = \{$`static`, `cgi`, (`search.php` $\wedge$ `s`), (`action` $\wedge$ `admin.php` $\wedge$ `par`), `rename`, `move`, `delete`, `show`$\}$.

Table 1. Templates extracted for the artificial dataset. The templates have been constructed using tokens as basic strings and NMF as factorization.

Communication Templates

1) `static`
2) `cgi ∧ (search.php ∧ s)`
3) `cgi ∧ (action ∧ admin.php ∧ par)`
4) `cgi ∧ (action ∧ admin.php ∧ par) ∧ move`
5) `cgi ∧ (action ∧ admin.php ∧ par) ∧ rename`
6) `cgi ∧ (action ∧ admin.php ∧ par) ∧ delete`
7) `cgi ∧ (action ∧ admin.php ∧ par) ∧ show`

Note that the alphabet does not contain tokens related to HTTP syntax or highly volatile parts of the data and thereby concentrates the following analysis on parts, which are more likely to capture the semantics of the application.

Results for the application of matrix factorization algorithms to the artificial dataset are visualized in Figure 3. For the algorithms PCA and NMF, base directions (matrix B) are shown, where the x-axis details the different directions and the y-axis the contribution of individual alphabet symbols.

While both techniques perform a matrix factorization of the payload data, the matrices differ significantly. PCA yields positive and negative contributions in the matrix B indicated by different colors. Although a certain structure and relation of alphabet symbols may be deduced from the matrix, a clear separation of different elements is not possible. By contrast, the NMF matrix shows a crisp representation of the base directions. Static and search requests are clearly reflected in individual base directions. The remaining base directions correspond to administrative requests, where different combinations of action types and other alphabet symbols have been correctly identified.

Due to this superior performance, we restrict our analysis to base directions determined using the NMF algorithm in the following. Communication templates resulting from the NMF matrix in Figure 3 are presented in Table 1. The templates accurately capture the semantics implemented in the example application.

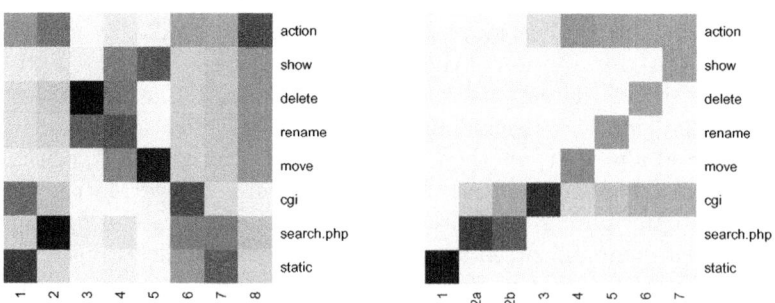

Fig. 3. Visualization of bases for PCA (left) and NMF (right) on the artificial dataset. Colors signify the intensity of the entry ranging from -1 (red) to 1 (blue).

A set of 7 templates is constructed which covers static access of web content, search queries and different administrative tasks. Note that two base directions in Figure 3 are identical, resulting in a total of 7 templates. The templates even exhibit hierarchical structure: template 3 resembles a basic administrative request with all following templates being special cases for particular administrative actions,which renders NMF as prominent candidate for the construction of easily comprehensible communication templates.

3.2   Analysis of Honeypot Data

Network honeypots have proven to be useful instruments for identification and analysis of novel threats. Often however, the amount of data collected by honeypots is huge, such that manual inspection of network payloads becomes tedious and futile. The proposed ASAP framework allows for analyzing such large datasets of unknown traffic and extracts semantically interesting network features automatically.

We illustrate the utility of our framework on network data collected using the web-based honeypot *Glastopf* (http://glastopf.org). The honeypot captures attacks against web applications, such as remote file inclusions (RFI) and SQL injection attacks, by exposing typical patterns of vulnerable applications to search engines. The honeypot has been deployed over a period of 2 months and collected on average 3,400 requests per day. For our experiments, we randomly pick 1,000 requests from the collected data and apply our framework using tokens as underlying alphabet. In particular, we extract 40 communication templates using the base direction identified by NMF from the embedded HTTP payloads. The templates are shown in Table 2. Note that 12 templates have been omitted as they contain redundant or unspecific information.

The extracted communication templates can be classified into three categories: *semantics of malware*, *vulnerabilities* and *attack sources*. For example, the first templates reflect different options supplied to a web-based malware. Malicious functionality such as preparing a remote shell (`shellz`), setting up an IRC bouncer (`psybnc`) or scanning for vulnerable hosts (`scannerz`) are clearly manifested in strings of the templates. The following templates characterize vulnerabilities of web applications including corresponding file and parameter names. Finally, the last set of templates corresponds to domain and host names used as sources of remote file inclusions. Often not only the originating host but also parts of the complete URL have been discovered.

Note that although the communication templates have been generated from raw HTTP traffic, no syntactic and protocol-specific strings have been extracted, demonstrating the ability of ASAP to focus on semantics of communication.

3.3   Analysis of Malware Communication

A second application domain for the proposed framework is the automatic analysis of malware communication. While there exist several methods for automatic collection and monitoring of malware [18, 19, 20, 21], analysis of monitored

Table 2. Templates for honeypot dataset. The templates have been constructed using tokens as basic strings and NMF as factorization.

Communication Templates	Description
1) modez ∧ shellz ∧ csp.txt	Semantics of RFI malware
2) modez ∧ psybnc ∧ csp.txt	—
3) modez ∧ botz ∧ bot.txt	—
4) modez ∧ scannerz ∧ bot.txt	—
5) mosConfig.absolute.path ∧ option ∧ http	Vulnerability (VirtueMart)
6) mosConfig_absolute_path ∧ option ∧ Itemid	—
7) com_virtuemart ∧ show_image_in_imgtag.php ...	—
8) com_virtuemart ∧ export.php ∧ php.txt	—
9) shop_this_skin_path ∧ skin_shop ∧ standard ...	Vulnerability (Technote)
10) board_skin_path ∧ Smileys ∧ http	Vulnerability (GNUBoard)
11) board ∧ skin ∧ http	—
12) write_update.php ∧ files ∧ 1	—
13) write_comment_update.php ∧ files ∧ http	—
14) delete_all.php ∧ admin ∧ zefa.txt	—
15) delete_comment.php ∧ http ∧ fx29id1.txt	—
16) appserv ∧ appserv_root ∧ main.php	Vulnerability (Appserv)
17) _SERVER ∧ DOCUMENT_ROOT ∧ media	Vulnerability (PHP)
18) error.php ∧ dir ∧ 1	Misc. RFI vulnerabilities
19) errors.php ∧ error ∧ php.txt ∧ bot.txt	—
20) administrator ∧ index.php ∧ raw.txt	—
21) admin ∧ include ∧ http	—
22) med.buu.ac.th ∧ com_mylink ∧ stealth ...	Sources of attacks
23) http ∧ med.buu.ac.th ∧ com_mylink ∧ components	—
24) http ∧ www.hfsb.org ∧ sites ∧ 10225 ∧ img	—
25) zerozon.co.kr ∧ eeng ∧ zefa.txt	—
26) http ∧ zerozon.co.kr ∧ photos ∧ count	—
27) http ∧ musicadelibreria.net ∧ footer	—
28) qqe.ru ∧ forum ∧ Smileys	—

malware communication still requires significant manual effort. As a remedy, we apply the ASAP framework for discovery of typical components in malware communication. In particular, we analyze the communication of 20 malware binaries that has been recorded during repetitive executions of each binary in a sandbox environment [see 22]. Since we do not know, which kind of protocols are contained in the traffic, we apply the ASAP framework using 4-grams as basic strings and extract base directions via the NMF algorithm. From the 20 binaries, we pick *Vanbot* as an example and present the respective communication templates in Table 3 as they particularly emphasize the capabilities of our framework.

First, we observe that the extracted components clearly separate protocol semantics: three components contain IRC related strings (1, 2, 4), while one component contains HTTP data (3). A closer look reveals, that the first two components contain IRC communication typical for *Vanbot*: the malware joins two IRC channels, namely #las6 and #ns, and signifies the start of a TFTP service. The

Table 3. Templates for communication of a malware binary. The templates have been constructed using 4-grams as basic strings and NMF as factorization.

Communication Templates

1) MODE #las6←→USER b ∧ JOIN #las6 ∧ 041- Running TFTP wormride...
2) c←→MODE #ns←→USER ∧ c +xi←→JOIN #ns ∧ ub.28465.com←→PONG :hub.2
3) GET /1al222.exe HTTP/1.0←→Host: zonetech.info ∧ /lb3.ex ∧ /las1.ex...
4) x←→USER e020501 . . . ∧ JOIN &virtu3 ∧ NICK bb ∧ CK gv ∧ R h020

HTTP component in turn comprises update requests, where the malware tries to download updates of itself from different hosts. Interestingly, our analysis also extracts an IRC component (4), which contains typical communication of the *Virut* malware, for example, as indicated by the channel name #virtu3. We credit this finding to a co-infection: the malware binary labeled *Vanbot* has been additionally infected by the malware *Virut*, a file infector.

3.4 Anomaly Detection

As final experiment, we evaluate the capabilities of ASAP in the fields of network intrusion detection. Anomaly detection is frequently applied as extension to signature-based intrusion detection systems, such as the Snort [1] and Bro [2] system, as it enables identification of unknown and novel network threats.

For evaluation of intrusion detection performance, we consider two datasets of network payloads: The first dataset (FIRST08) contains HTTP requests monitored at the web server of a research institute during a period of 60 days. The second dataset (FTP03) comprises FTP sessions recorded over 10 days at Lawrence Berkeley National Laboratory [23]. Additionally to this benign data, we inject network attacks into the traffic. The attacks are executed in a virtual environment using common tools for penetration testing, such as Metasploit, and are carefully adapted to match characteristics of the datasets [see 24].

For the experiment, we apply a detection method similar to the work of Rieck and Laskov [25]. A centroid model of normal network payloads is constructed using n-grams, $\mu_{full} = \frac{1}{N} \sum_{i=1}^{N} \phi(p_i)$, and used for identifying unusual network content. Additionally, we consider a second model in which the n-grams are refined using communication templates. Formally, after calculating the matrix factorization $X = BC$, we construct this model as follows: $\mu_{reduced} = B(\frac{1}{N} \sum_{i=1}^{N} c_i)$, where we calculate the centroid in the lower-dimensional space obtained by the first 20 base directions of NMF. The two models are trained on 1,000 randomly drawn payloads for each data set and anomaly detection is performed on 200,000 randomly chosen HTTP requests and 20,000 FTP sessions respectively.

Results are shown as Receiver Operating Characteristics (ROC) curves in Figure 4 (left). The performance of the full and reduced centroid model is identical on all three datasets. This demonstrates that the base directions identified by NMF capture semantic information of the underlying protocols accurately for detection of anomalies and attacks. Figure 4 (right) details the run-time performance attained by the different models. Reducing the analysis

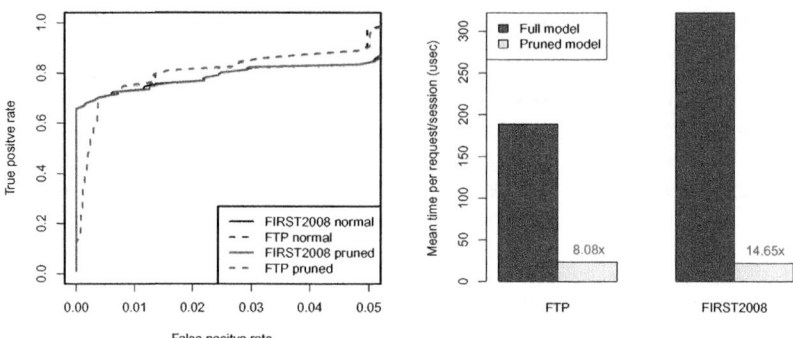

Fig. 4. ROC curves (left) and run-time (right) for network anomaly detection. Models are constructed using 4-grams and NMF for matrix factorization.

using communication templates provides a significant performance gain over regular anomaly detection. Speed-up factors of up to 15 can be observed and clearly indicate the utility of ASAP as a preprocessing step for anomaly detection.

4   Related Work

The problem of re-creating a certain structure based on data like network or execution traces has been extensively studied in the domain of protocol reverse engineering. The ultimate goal here is to reconstruct the grammar and also underlying state machines employed during communication. *Discoverer* [10] by Cui et al. works directly on recorded network traces to extract message formats by a combination of clustering of tokens and subsequent merging by sequence alignment. Wondracek et al. [11] are able to create grammar-like structures with the use of dynamic data tainting: a protocol is automatically constructed by monitoring data flow of protocol messages during request serving. This concept is further refined in *Prospex* [12] by Comparetti et al. which also incorporates the inference of the underlying state machine of the communication. All these approaches are orthogonal to the ASAP framework, since they try to extract the underlying syntax of the communication. With the ASAP method we address the extraction of semantics-aware components for a monitored application, which leads to different constraints and methods employed during the analysis.

A natural extension of protocol reverse engineering is to use the newly extracted protocol and communication state automaton and build an automated honeypot service, which is capable of mimicking the monitored application behavior. The work of Leita et al. [19, 20] target the honeyd platform: by examination of a tcpdump, which contains a sample interaction, they are able to generate a honeyd script, which can emulate to a certain extent the monitored application. In line with this work Cui et al. present *RolePlayer* [26], which is able to replay both the client and server side of a given communication. The *Replayer* [27] by Newsome et al. uses methods from program verification to build up a logical sound solution to the replaying problem. The ASAP framework in its current state does not incorporate any communication semantics apart from single message semantics. However, it would be a valuable extension to include communication behavior analysis by exploiting methods of time series analysis inside the ASAP framework.

Dimension reduction methods have been used before to visualize network traffic data [28] or track down traffic anomalies [29, 30]. While Principal Component Analysis and Non-negative Matrix Factorization (NMF) have been studied before, the ASAP framework analyzes the traffic both on the basis of tokens and n-grams in a unified way, which leads to a semantic-driven and easily comprehensible result. Furthermore NMF has also been used for intrusion detection by Wang et al. [31, 32] on system call traces and even for the task of document summarization [33] on a word level. This shows that the basis of the ASAP framework is well established even beyond analysis of structured network data.

5   Conclusions

We have introduced the ASAP framework, a new technique for automatic extraction of communication templates from recorded network traffic. The framework identifies components of network payloads by mapping them to a vector space and determining informative base directions using techniques of matrix factorization. This approach is orthogonal to existing techniques for network analysis based on protocol specifications, as it can be applied for analysis of unknown network protocols as well as network traces containing mixtures of protocols.

Empirically, we have demonstrated the utility of our framework in different security applications. For example, we have been able to automatically analyze data from a network honeypot and identify exploited vulnerabilities and attack sources—a task not attainable by sole means of specification-based analysis. Moreover, we have exemplarily dissected the communication of the malware *Vanbot*, demonstrating the ability of the ASAP framework to discover semantics in network traces of mixed protocols. Finally, we have applied our framework for preprocessing the input of a network anomaly detection method, realizing a speed-up factor of up to 15 while preserving an accurate detection of attacks.

Our analysis shows that base directions generated by our framework can be used to easily extract valuable details from a dataset, where nearly no information is available in advance. The ASAP framework is capable of analyzing network data even without knowledge about the underlying protocols. The flexibility of n-gram analysis paired with the structuring and summarization power of matrix factorization generates semantics-aware components, which enable fast and efficient insights for network traces at hand.

Besides applications presented in this work, the extracted base directions provide good candidates as input for other security methods: signature generation methods may use the concise representation of data as direct basis for constructing precise signatures, automatic construction of honeypot services could greatly profit from semantics-aware representations of communication and the process of forensic network analysis may be accelerated by taking these communication templates as starting points for further investigations. Finally, the incorporation of other matrix factorization methods like sparse NMF [34] or sparse PCA [35] and the evaluation of their respective performance in terms of data explanation and description would be a further extension of the ASAP framework.

Acknowledgments. The authors were supported by the BMBF grant FKZ 01-IS07007A (REMIND) and the FP7-ICT Programme of the European Community, under the PASCAL2 Network of Excellence, ICT-216886.

References

[1] Roesch, M.: Snort: Lightweight intrusion detection for networks. In: Proc. of USENIX Large Installation System Administration Conference LISA, pp. 229–238 (1999)

[2] Paxson, V.: Bro: A system for detecting network intruders in real-time. Computer Networks 31(23-24), 2435–2466 (1999)

[3] Vigna, G., Kemmerer, R.A.: NetSTAT: a network-based intrusion detection system. Journal of Computer Security 7(1), 37–71 (1999)

[4] Offutt, J., Liu, S., Abdurazik, A., Ammann, P.: Generating test data from state-based specifications. The Journal of Software Testing, Verification and Reliability 13, 25–53 (2003)

[5] McAllister, S., Kirda, E., Kruegel, C.: Leveraging user interactions for in-depth testing of web applications. In: Lippmann, R., Kirda, E., Trachtenberg, A. (eds.) RAID 2008. LNCS, vol. 5230, pp. 191–210. Springer, Heidelberg (2008)

[6] Abdelnur, H.J., State, R., Festor, O.: Advanced fuzzing in the voip space. Journal in Computer Virology 6(1), 57–64 (2010)

[7] Garfinkel, S.: Network Forensics: Tapping the Internet. O'Reilly, Sebastopol (2002)

[8] Moore, D., Shannon, C., Brown, J.: Code-Red: a case study on the spread and victims of an internet worm. In: Proc. of Internet Measurement Workshop (IMW), pp. 273–284 (2002)

[9] Gates, C., McHugh, J.: The contact surface: A technique for exploring internet scale emergent behaviors. In: Zamboni, D. (ed.) DIMVA 2008. LNCS, vol. 5137, pp. 228–246. Springer, Heidelberg (2008)

[10] Cui, W., Kannan, J., Wang, H.J.: Discoverer: automatic protocol reverse engineering from network traces. In: Proc. of 16th USENIX Security Symposium, pp. 1–14 (2007)

[11] Wondracek, G., Comparetti, P.M., Krügel, C., Kirda, E.: Automatic network protocol analysis. In: Proc. of Network and Distributed System Security Symposium, NDSS (2008)

[12] Comparetti, P.M., Wondracek, G., Kruegel, C., Kirda, E.: Prospex: Protocol specification extraction. In: Proc. of the 30th IEEE Symposium on Security and Privacy, pp. 110–125 (2009)

[13] Holm, S.: A simple sequentially rejective multiple test procedure. Scandinavian Journal of Statistics 6, 65–70 (1979)

[14] Rieck, K., Laskov, P.: Linear-time computation of similarity measures for sequential data. Journal of Machine Learning Research 9, 23–48 (2008)

[15] Jolliffe, I.: Principal Component Analysis. Springer, Heidelberg (2002)

[16] Schölkopf, B., Smola, A., Müller, K.R.: Nonlinear component analysis as a kernel eigenvalue problem. Neural Computation 10, 1299–1319 (1998)

[17] Lee, D.D., Seung, H.S.: Algorithms for non-negative matrix factorization. In: Advances in Neural Information Processing Systems, vol. 13, pp. 556–562 (2000)
[18] Baecher, P., Koetter, M., Holz, T., Dornseif, M., Freiling, F.C.: The nepenthes platform: An efficient approach to collect malware. In: Zamboni, D., Krügel, C. (eds.) RAID 2006. LNCS, vol. 4219, pp. 165–184. Springer, Heidelberg (2006)
[19] Leita, C., Mermoud, K., Dacier, M.: Scriptgen: an automated script generation tool for honeyd. In: Proc. of Annual Computer Security Applications Conference (ACSAC), pp. 203–214 (2005)
[20] Leita, C., Dacier, M., Massicotte, F.: Automatic handling of protocol dependencies and reaction to 0-day attacks with scriptGen based honeypots. In: Zamboni, D., Krügel, C. (eds.) RAID 2006. LNCS, vol. 4219, pp. 185–205. Springer, Heidelberg (2006)
[21] Bayer, U., Moser, A., Kruegel, C., Kirda, E.: Dynamic analysis of malicious code. Journal in Computer Virology 2(1), 67–77 (2006)
[22] Rieck, K., Schwenk, G., Limmer, T., Holz, T., Laskov, P.: Botzilla: Detecting the "phoning home" of malicious software. In: Proc. of 25th ACM Symposium on Applied Computing, SAC (2010)
[23] Paxson, V., Pang, R.: A high-level programming environment for packet trace anonymization and transformation. In: Proc. of ACM SIGCOMM, pp. 339–351 (2003)
[24] Krueger, T., Gehl, C., Rieck, K., Laskov, P.: TokDoc: A self-healing web application firewall. In: Proc. of 25th ACM Symposium on Applied Computing, SAC (2010)
[25] Rieck, K., Laskov, P.: Detecting unknown network attacks using language models. In: Büschkes, R., Laskov, P. (eds.) DIMVA 2006. LNCS, vol. 4064, pp. 74–90. Springer, Heidelberg (2006)
[26] Cui, W., Paxson, V., Weaver, N., Katz, R.H.: Protocol-independent adaptive replay of application dialog. In: Proc. of Network and Distributed System Security Symposium, NDSS (2006)
[27] Newsome, J., Brumley, D., Franklin, J., Song, D.: Replayer: automatic protocol replay by binary analysis. In: Conference on Computer and Communications Security (CCS), pp. 311–321 (2006)
[28] Patwari, N., Hero III, A.O., Pacholski, A.: Manifold learning visualization of network traffic data. In: Proc. of the ACM SIGCOMM Workshop on Mining Network Data, pp. 191–196 (2005)
[29] Lakhina, A., Crovella, M., Diot, C.: Diagnosing network-wide traffic anomalies. In: Proc. of ACM SIGCOMM, pp. 219–230 (2004)
[30] Ringberg, H., Soule, A., Rexford, J., Diot, C.: Sensitivity of PCA for traffic anomaly detection. In: Proc. of the ACM SIGMETRICS, pp. 109–120 (2007)
[31] Wang, W., Zhang, X., Gombault, S.: Constructing attribute weights from computer audit data for effective intrusion detection. J. Syst. Softw. 82(12), 1974–1981 (2009)
[32] Guan, X., Wang, W., Zhang, X.: Fast intrusion detection based on a non-negative matrix factorization model. J. Netw. Comput. Appl. 32(1) (2009)
[33] Wang, D., Li, T., Zhu, S., Ding, C.: Multi-document summarization via sentence-level semantic analysis and symmetric matrix factorization. In: Proc. of the 31st ACM SIGIR, pp. 307–314 (2008)
[34] Hoyer, P.O.: Non-negative matrix factorization with sparseness constraints. J. Mach. Learn. Res. 5, 1457–1469 (2004)
[35] Zou, H., Hastie, T., Tibshirani, R.: Sparse principal component analysis. Journal of Computational and Graphical Statistics 15, 2006–2035 (2004)

Temporal Defenses for Robust Recommendations

Neal Lathia, Stephen Hailes, and Licia Capra

Department of Computer Science
University College London
Gower Street, London WC1 E6BT, United Kingdom
{n.lathia,s.hailes,l.capra}@springer.com

Abstract. Recommender systems are vulnerable to attack: malicious users may deploy a set of sybils (pseudonymous, automated entities) to inject ratings in order to damage or modify the output of Collaborative Filtering (CF) algorithms. To protect against these attacks, previous work focuses on designing sybil profile classification algorithms, whose aim is to find and isolate sybils. These methods, however, assume that the full sybil profiles have already been input to the system. Deployed recommender systems, on the other hand, operate *over time*, and recommendations may be damaged while sybils are still injecting their profiles, rather than only after all malicious ratings have been input. Furthermore, system administrators do not know when their system is under attack, and thus when to run these classification techniques, thus risking to leave their recommender system vulnerable to attacks. In this work, we address the problem of *temporal* sybil attacks, and propose and evaluate methods for monitoring *global, user* and *item* behaviour over time, in order to detect rating anomalies that reflect an ongoing attack.

1 Introduction

Recommender systems based on Collaborative Filtering (CF) algorithms [1] have become important portals via which users access, browse, and interact with a plethora of web sites, ranging from e-commerce, to movie rentals, and music recommendation sites. These algorithms are built upon the assumption that users who have been like-minded in the past can provide insight into each other's future tastes. Like-mindedness is quantified by means of similarity metrics (e.g., Pearson correlation [1]) computed over users' profiles: the more items two users have rated in common, and the more similar the ratings they have associated to these items, the more like-minded they are considered. Unfortunately, the ratings that CF algorithms manipulate may not be honest depictions of user preferences, as they may have been fabricated by malicious users to damage or modify the recommendations the system outputs. Abusing recommender systems this way is referred to as *shilling, profile injection* or *sybil* attacks; Mobasher *et al.* provide an in-depth review of the problem [2].

To protect a recommender system from these attacks, a variety of classification algorithms [5] have been proposed, whose goal is to examine users' profiles,

C. Dimitrakakis et al. (Eds.): PSDML 2010, LNAI 6549, pp. 64–77, 2011.

determine whether they are honest or malicious, and isolate the latter. However, these approaches assume that the *full sybil profiles* have already been created (i.e., contained within the user-item matrix that CF algorithms operate on). In deployed recommender systems, such an assumption does not hold: sybil profiles may be inserted over an extended period of time, thus reducing their immediate detectability, while not necessarily reducing the damage they may inflict on the system. Furthermore, system administrators do not know when their system is under attack, so deciding when to run these computationally expensive classification algorithms becomes a fundamental issue.

In this work, we first demonstrate that attackers do have an incentive to spread their attack over time, as this makes it difficult for system administrators to know when to run classification algorithms and thus isolate them (Section 2). We provide a classification of *temporal sybil attacks* against which a deployed recommender system should defend itself (Section 3), and then propose and evaluate our *sybil detection technique*, which dynamically monitors the deployed recommender system to reveal anomalies in global, user, and item activity, with respect to normal user rating habits (Section 4). We then conclude the paper with a discussion of related work (Section 5) and future directions of research (Section 6).

2   From One-Shot to Temporal Attacks

In this section, we show that sybils have an incentive to spread their attack over time, as in so doing they reduce the risk of being detected and thus isolated. To begin with, we model a deployed recommender system as done in [6]: given a dataset at time t, and a window size $|w|$ (reflecting how often the system will be updated), we train the CF algorithm with any data input prior to t and predict any ratings input between t and $(t + |w|)$. The entire process is repeated at each update, with what was previously tested on becoming incorporated into the training data. To quantify the performance of the recommender system over time, we re-define the root mean squared error (RMSE) as follow:

$$RMSE_t = \sqrt{\frac{\sum_{\hat{r}_{u,i} \in R_t}^{N} (\hat{r}_{u,i} - r_{u,i})^2}{|R_t|}} \tag{1}$$

Given a set R_t of predictions made up to time t, the current error is simply the average of all predictions made to date.

The one-shot attack considered in the literature operates as follow: if we indicate with S the set of sybils in the system, and with X the set of ratings they inject, then all X would be input in the system within a single time window, that is, between time t and $(t + |w|)$. We visualise the effect of a one-shot attack with the following example: we consider five sub-samples of $10,000$ Netflix profiles[1], and weekly system updates ($|w| = 7$ days); for each of these sub-samples,

---

[1] http://www.netflixprize.com

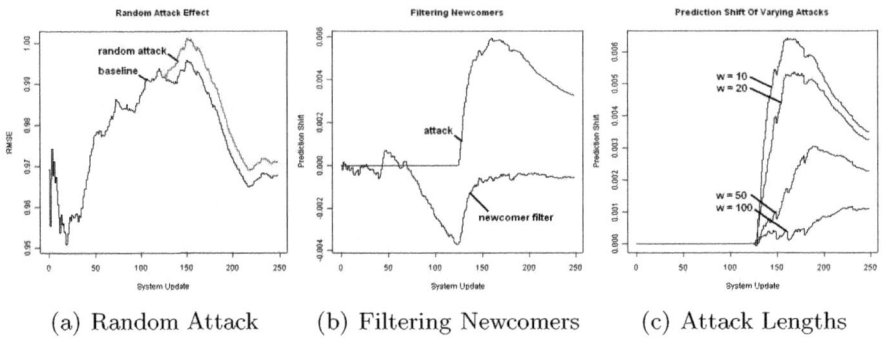

(a) Random Attack   (b) Filtering Newcomers   (c) Attack Lengths

Fig. 1. Time-Averaged RMSE Of One-Shot Attack; Prediction Shift When Pruning Newcomer's Ratings; Injecting Attacks Over Varying Time Windows

during the $125th$ week-long window we inserted 100 sybils who each rate approximately $10,000$ items (in this example, we limit ourselves to exploring the temporal effect of a *random* attack, where each sybil randomly picks one of the available items, and then rates it with a random value drawn uniformly from the rating scale). Figure 1(a) plots the impact that these ratings have on the time-averaged RMSE. As shown, the one-shot attack has a pronounced effect on the time-averaged RMSE: performance is consistently degraded over the rest of the updates.

However, this attack is very simple to detect: sybils appear all at once, rate high volumes of items within a single window length, and disappear. CF systems can easily defend against these attacks by *distrusting newcomers*: ratings coming from new users are considered *suspect* and excluded by the CF algorithm; if these users re-appear in future time windows, their ratings will be subsequently considered, otherwise they will never influence the recommender systems. We thus repeated the previous experiment, but excluded suspect ratings from the kNN CF algorithm. Note that, by excluding suspect ratings, we maintain our ability to formulate recommendations for all users (including sybil and new honest users), while removing the influence that suspect ratings exert. Figure 1(b) plots the difference in prediction (*prediction shift*) when exercising the same one-shot attack described above, with and without new ratings being suspected, against a baseline scenario of predictions computed when no sybils are inserted. Note that the technique not only eliminates the effect of the attack, but also *improves* upon the baseline RMSE in a number of windows prior to the attack taking place (the prediction shift is negative). Removing the ratings of users who rate and never return thus curbs these attacks and takes small steps towards de-noising the data [7].

Attackers may respond to this simple detection technique, by widening the number of windows taken to inject ratings. Sybils under the attacker's control would therefore appear in multiple windows and, after the first appearance, no longer be suspect. In order to explore the incentives that attackers have to rate quickly, we performed a number of random attacks, where a set of 100 sybils rated the same number of items over a varying number of sequential windows $W \in [10, 20, 50, 100]$. In each case, the *number* of malicious ratings remained the same, the only difference being the *time* taken to insert them; we compare attacks of the same magnitude that differ only in temporal spread (i.e., the ratings per sybil per window varies, as does the number of windows). The results in Figure 1(c) show that injecting ratings over longer time periods deviates the RMSE from the baseline less. This is likely to be an effect of the balance between sybil and non-sybil ratings: longer attacks have less of an effect since, during the time taken to operate the attack, there is a larger influx of non-sybil ratings.

Based on the above experiments, real sybils' behaviour is unlikely to follow the one shot pattern. Rather, we have observed that: (a) there is an incentive for attackers to inject ratings over more than one window, in order to not have their ratings be suspect and filtered out by simple detection schemes; and (b) attackers may attempt to displace the balance between sybil and non-sybil ratings, since higher volumes of sybil ratings per window have more pronounced effects. With this in mind, we provide next a classification of the types of temporal attacks that malicious users may undertake, before proposing a defence mechanisms capable of protecting a recommender system against them.

3   Temporal Attack Model

When enacting a sybil attack, there are two main factors that attackers can control: the *number of sybils* perpetrating the attack, and the *rate* at which they operate (i.e., number of ratings per sybil per window), for a predefined sequence of windows. We thus classify attacks according to how malicious users calibrate these two factors, and determine the four different attack types depicted in Figure 2(a). Protection mechanisms developed so far in the literature ignore these two factors and rather focus on another one: the *strategy* that attackers deploy in determining what items to rate (i.e, whether at random or targeted), as if the ratings were input all at once. We take a different stance and look at the attack while it unfolds: the strategy adopted is then treated as an orthogonal dimension, with respect to the temporal factors.

Our goal is to provide a monitoring and detection mechanism capable of alerting the system administrator when any of these attacks is in place. In order to assess the quality of our monitor, we will be measuring: *precision*, defined as the number of attacks that were flagged (true positives) over all flagged situations (true positives plus false positives); *recall*, defined as the number of attacks that were flagged, over all the attacks enacted (true positives plus false negatives); and *impact*, defined as the number of sybil ratings input at the current window, divided by the total number of ratings input in that window. Intuitively, the higher the precision, the lower the false alarms being raised; furthermore, the higher the recall, the lower the number of attacks that slip through. Finally, the impact gives an indication of the damage that an undetected attack (false negative) is causing; intuitively, the higher the number of malicious ratings that slip through, the higher the impact. Figure 2(b) illustrates the attack impact

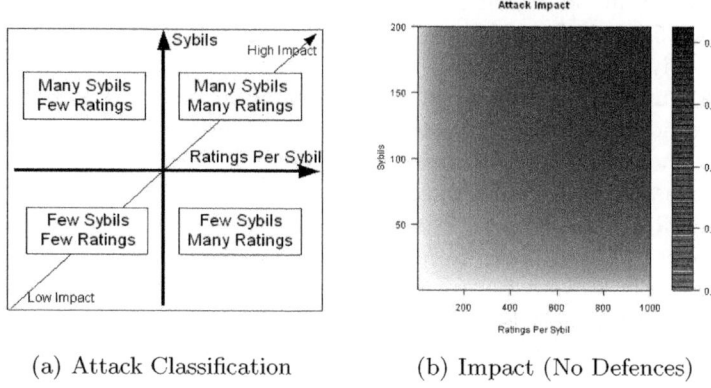

(a) Attack Classification   (b) Impact (No Defences)

Fig. 2. Attack Types and Impact With No Defences

for varying numbers of sybils and rating rates, when no defences are in place (and thus all attacks pass undetected). In this work, we place higher emphasis on reducing false negatives (finding all the attacks that we manually insert), rather than false positives. This is because we cannot know (and only assume) that the data we experiment with is the fruit of honest, well-intentioned users: false positives in the real data may very well be attacks that are likely to deserve further inspection; however, we note that the defences described below produced no false positives when run on the rating data with no attacks injected.

In the next section, we construct step by step a defence mechanism capable of defending a recommender system against the temporal attacks identified above. We do so by reasoning about factors that attackers cannot control, related to how the non-sybil users behave: how many non-sybil users there are, the number of ratings they input per window, what they rate, and how they rate.

4   A Temporal Defence

In this section, we focus on each type of attack in turn, and construct a comprehensive mechanism capable of detecting them all. The mechanism monitors different types of information to detect anomalies: global behaviour (Section 4.1), user behaviour (Section 4.2), and item behaviour (Section 4.3). The key to our proposal is the capturing of stable features in the rating data, so that anomalies introduced by attacks can be flagged.

4.1   Global Monitoring - Many Sybils/Many Ratings Scenario

The first perspective of system behaviour that we consider is at the *global*, or aggregate, level. While the number of ratings that users input varies over time, the average ratings per user per window (in the Netflix data) remains relatively flat: Figure 3(a) plots this value over time. From this, we see that the average user rates between $5-15$ movies per week. Since the mean is derived from

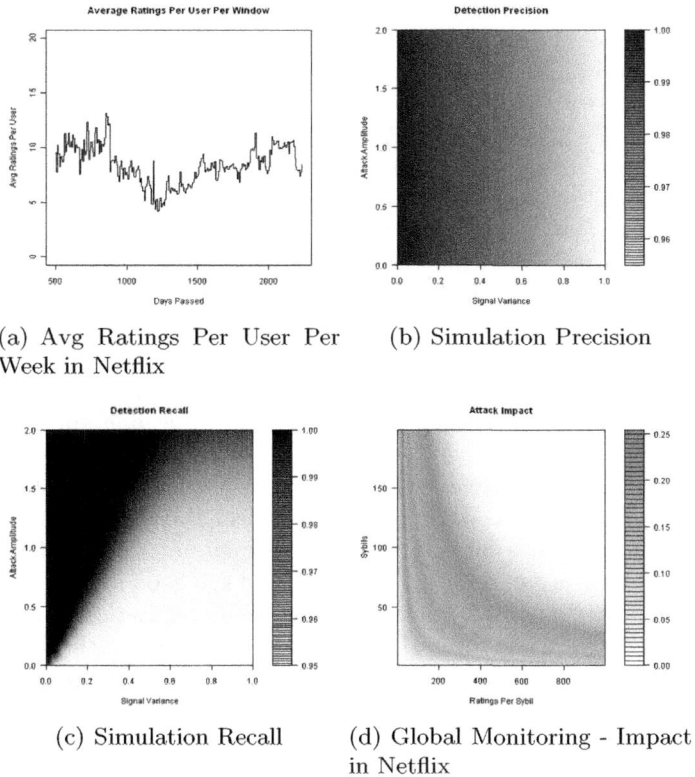

(a) Avg Ratings Per User Per   (b) Simulation Precision
Week in Netflix

(c) Simulation Recall   (d) Global Monitoring - Impact
in Netflix

Fig. 3. Global Monitoring

a long-tailed distribution, it is a skewed representation of the "average" user.
However, when an attacker deploys a large group of sybils, this aggregate value
changes: the first dimension of our defence thus aims at monitoring changes to
the average ratings per user MU_t over time. Given a window t, the current mean
ratings per user MU_t, standard deviation σ_t, the R_t ratings input by U_t users,
and a weighting factor β_t, an alarm is raised if the volume of incoming ratings
departs from the mean measured to date by an amount determined with a global
threshold $\alpha_t \geq 1$:

$$\frac{R_t}{U_t} \geq (MU_t + (\alpha_t \times \sigma_t)) \tag{2}$$

If an alarm is not raised, we update the current MU_t value as an exponentially
weighted moving average:

$$MU_t = (\beta_t \times MU_{t-|w|}) + ((1 - \beta_t) \times \frac{R_t}{U_t}) \tag{3}$$

MU_t is updated *conservatively*: if an attack is flagged, then it is not updated.
We also conservatively update both the α_t and β_t variables. The β_t variable
determines the weight that is given to historical data: relying too heavily on

historical data will not capture current fluctuations, while weighting current values too highly will disperse temporal trends. We therefore update β_t with the standard deviation measured to date:

$$\beta_{t+|w|} = min(|\sigma_{t-|w|} - \sigma_t|, 1) \tag{4}$$

The value is capped at 1, thus ensuring that when there is high variability in the data, β_t gives higher preference to current values, while a smaller standard deviation shifts β_t to give higher weight to historical values. The α_t variable determines the extent to which the current $\frac{R_t}{U_t}$ value can deviate from MU_t before an attack is flagged. When an attack is flagged, we reduce α_t, making it more difficult for attackers to learn the appropriate threshold. In this work, α_t jumps between pre-specified values (0.5 and 1.5). This parameter is sensitive to the context; we selected these values after examining our scenario (users rating movies). We leave a more in-depth investigation of scaling the threshold as a matter of future work.

Monitoring incoming ratings at the aggregate level is sensitive to two factors: how naturally variable the incoming ratings are, and the amount of variance that attacks introduce: a mechanism like this may not work if there is already high variance in the average ratings per user and sybils do not displace the mean value. We therefore evaluated this technique with two methods: in the first, we *simulate* a stream of incoming ratings (in order to control both the variance and size of attack); we then turned to *real data* where we could explore the effects of varying attacks in a more realistic setting.

In order to simulate a stream of incoming ratings, we draw a sequence of $\frac{R_t}{U_t}$ values from a normal distribution with mean μ and standard deviation $\sigma \in [0, \mu]$. Then, at random moments, we simulate an injected attack where a group of sybils shifts the incoming value by the attack *amplitude* $\gamma \in [0, (2 \times \mu)]$; in other words, at an attack time t, the window's value is $(\frac{R_t}{U_t} + \gamma)$. We then note whether an attack was flagged, and can compute the detection precision and recall with the results. When running the simulation, we assumed that, after a brief training phase, the system could be attacked at any time during a period of $1,000$ windows, for a pre-determined number of sequential attack windows (we used a value of 50, as this gives the attack high impact while being difficult to detect - see Figure 1(c)). We re-ran each simulation parameter setting $10,000$ times and present averaged results. Figure 3(b) shows the resulting precision, which fades as σ increases. The main point to note is that precision is dependent on σ (the variability in the ratings per user per window) rather than the attack amplitude γ. In other words, the number of false positives depends on how naturally variable the data is. Figure 3(c), instead, displays the detection recall. This plot highlights the trade-off between σ and γ: the best recall is when a small σ is modified with a large γ, while the worst values are found when a large σ is deviated by a small γ. Note that, in this simulated setting, the minimum precision is slightly below 0.90, and the minimum recall remains above approximately 0.95: we thus consistently get high precision and recall.

We returned to the Netflix dataset in order to test this method when injecting attacks on real data. To do so, we trained our monitor with all ratings per window until the attack time, and then measure the attack impact after injecting the attack. Since the attacker may unleash the sybils at any time, we repeated our experiments, starting attacks at each possible window, and plot average results across all windows. As Figure 3(d) shows, this method catches attacks where large groups of sybils inject their profiles at a very high rate; the top right corner of the plot is flattened to zero impact. However, two sensitive areas remain: first, where *many* sybils inject *few* ratings, and when *few* sybils inject *many* ratings. Attackers can thus respond by either reducing the size of the sybil group, or the sybil's rate. In Section 4.2 we address the former, while Section 4.3 describes how to detect the latter.

4.2   User Monitoring - Few Sybils/Many Ratings Scenario

The previous monitor cannot detect when *few* sybils rate *many* items each. We address this by designing a user monitor aimed at detecting these specific attacks. Figure 4(a) plots the distribution of ratings input per user in a sample window of the Netflix data; we find that the majority of users input a rather low number of ratings per week, while a minority of outliers rate a high volume of movies. An attack in this context would thus entail setting a small group of sybils to rate a high volume of content over a number of windows; detecting this behaviour focuses on examining *how many* high volume raters there are and *how much* these outliers are rating.

(a) How Much High Volume Raters Rate. Given the current mean value of ratings per user per window MU_t, we differentiate *high* from *low* volume raters based on the difference between the ratings that they have input in the current window and MU_t. Figure 4(b) plots the ratings per high volume user over time. The mean ratings per high volume user HM_t can then be monitored, in a similar way as we monitored the entire distribution in the previous section: an exponentially weighted moving average is regularly updated, and large deviations from the expected value flag an ongoing attack.

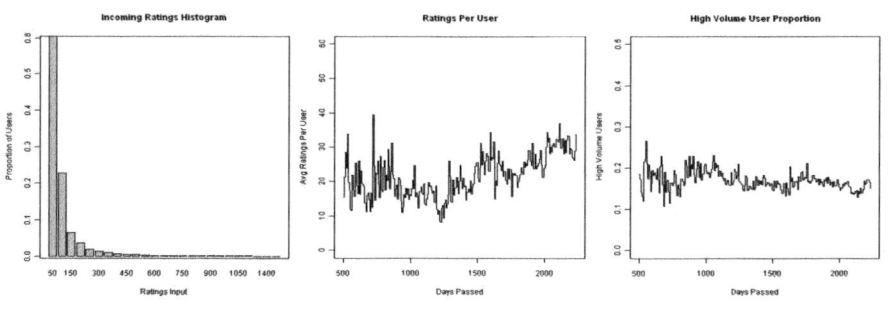

(a) Ratings Per User   (b) High Volume Raters (c) High Volume Proportion

Fig. 4. Analysis of Users' Behaviour in Netflix: (a) An example distribution of 1 week's ratings, (b) Ratings Per High Volume Raters Over Time and (c) the Proportion of High Volume Raters Over Time

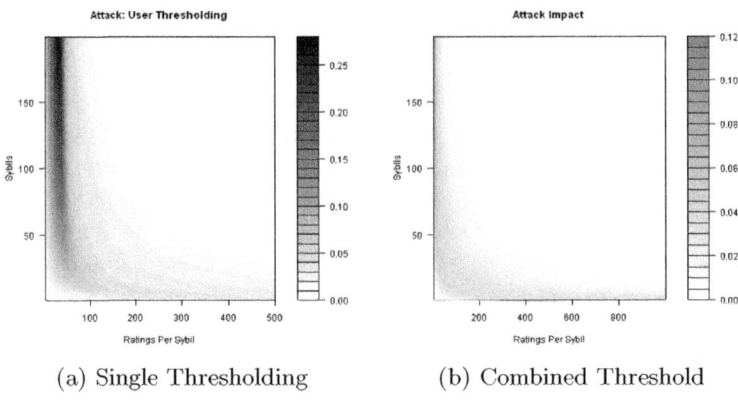

(a) Single Thresholding   (b) Combined Threshold

Fig. 5. User Monitoring

(b) How Many High Volume Raters. Beside the high volume ratings HM_t, we also keep track of how many users HU_t there are relative to all the users who have rated in the current window. A user becomes suspect if they are at the highest end of the user-rating distribution, and both the *size* of this group and *volume* of ratings they input may indicate an ongoing attack. As we plot in Figure 4(c), the size of this group of users, divided by the total number of high volume raters per window, tends to be relatively stable; injecting different forms of attacks upsets both this and the mean ratings per high volume user values. We take advantage of both pieces of information in order to amplify our detection mechanism: we create a *combined score* per window by multiplying the HM_t value by the proportion of suspect users HU_t. This way, we aim to capture fluctuations in both the *group size* and *rate* that a potential group of sybils will inflict when performing their attack.

We evaluated the user monitor with the Netflix subsets for cross-validated results with real data. We did so in two steps. First, Figure 5(a) shows the resulting impact if only part (a) of above is used to defend the system: this defence can overcome both scenarios similar to that addressed in the previous section, and also lessen the threat of smaller groups of high-volume rating sybils. This threat is not fully eliminated though: the top-left corner of the plot shows a remaining non-zero impact section (more precisely, impact is approximately $[0, 0.25]$). In Figure 5(b), we plot the impact of the *combined* defences: this time, the impact decreases to $[0, 0.12]$. There is now only one type of attack left, where *many* sybils rate *few* items. We tackle this scenario next.

4.3 Item Monitoring - Many Sybils/Few Ratings Scenario

The last scenario that we address is that of *many* sybils rating *few* items each. This form of attack would be undetected by the previously outlined defences: the sybils do not rate enough items each to be detected by the user monitor, and there are enough of them to not shift the rating per user temporal mean and flag their presence. To detect this kind of attack, we first reason on what items the group of sybils may be rating, and then design and evaluate an *item*-monitor to identify ongoing anomalous behaviour.

In order to have the greatest impact possible, sybils who inject very sparse profiles (by rating few items each) will tend to be rating a similar subgroup of items, rather than dispersing the ratings over a broad range of items, which would have a smaller effect. This strategy recalls the structure of *targeted* attacks [2], where injected profiles contain *filler*, *selected*, and *target* item ratings: for example, if an attack aims to promote a fantasy movie (target), the sybils will rate it, alongside famous fantasy movies (selected) that are likely to appear in the profiles of many honest users, together with a number of items (filler) to disguise each profile as a "normal" user profile. The difference between a random attack and a targeted one is thus determined by how profiles are populated: what the *selected, filler,* and *target* items are (in the case of a random attack, there is no target item) and how they are rated. We therefore turn to monitoring the items in a system to detect these kinds of attacks. We further assume that it is very unlikely for an item that is already popular to be subject to an attack that aims to promote it; similarly, it is unlikely that unpopular items be nuked. In other words, we assume that the purpose of attackers is to maliciously reverse an ongoing trend (rather than reinforce a pre-existing one). Given this, we design an item monitor to identify the target of attacks by focusing on three factors: (a) the *amount* that each item is being rated, (b) the distance the *mean* of the incoming ratings for each item has from an "average" item mean, and (c) a temporal mean *change detector*.

(a) The Item Is Rated By Many Users. In each window w, with R_t ratings input for I_t items, the average ratings per item MI_t (with standard deviation $\sigma_{i,t}$) can be computed. We can then select, from the available items, those that have been rated the most in the current window by selecting all those that received I_t ratings greater than the mean number of ratings per item MI_t.

(b) The Item is Rated With Extreme Ratings. Using only the ratings input in the current window w, we determine the *mean* score $\bar{r}_i$ for each item i, and then average these to produce the expected mean score v per item:

$$v = \frac{1}{I_t} \sum_{i \in I_t} \bar{r}_i \tag{5}$$

If an item has been targeted for attack (and either nuked or promoted by a group of sybils simultaneously), then the corresponding $\bar{r}_i$ will reflect this by being an outlier of the global average item mean v.

(c) The Item Mean Rating Shifts. We compare the item mean computed with historical ratings and the $\bar{r}_i$ value determined from the ratings in the current window. A successful attack will shift this value by some distance δ: in this work, since we are operating on the Netflix 5-star ratings scale, we set δ to slightly below 2.

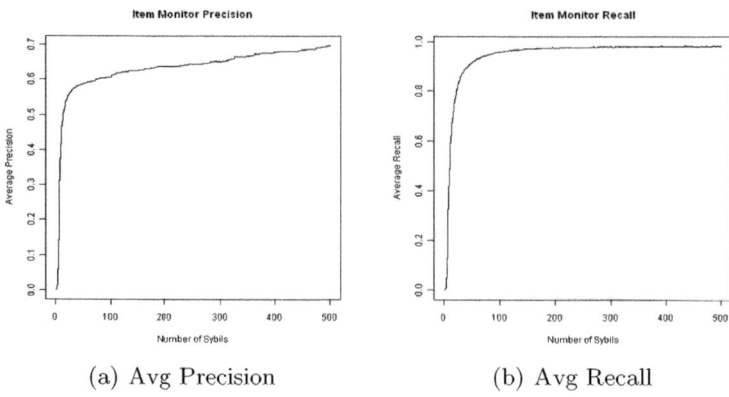

(a) Avg Precision   (b) Avg Recall

Fig. 6. Item Monitoring

An attack is flagged for an item if the above three conditions are met: it is rated more than average, the mean of the incoming ratings shows that it is not being rated in the same way as other items are, *and* a change from the historical value is being introduced. Our monitor therefore focuses on identifying the moments when groups (or subgroups) of sybils rate the *target* item. We therefore modified our evaluation mechanism to test how well we find *items* when they are attacked, depending on how many sybils push in the target rating at the same time.

We evaluated the monitor as follows: at time t, a group of sybils rates a randomly chosen target item. The sybils nuke the item if it is popular (it has mean greater than 3), and promote it otherwise. We do not discriminate on the number of ratings that movies currently have when determining whether to nuke or promote it; however, previous work shows that it is harder to protect sparsely rated items from attack [8], and our item selection process is biased toward selecting these items. We then check to see if the monitor flags any suspicious items, and measure the number of true/false positives and false negatives. We repeat the same run (i.e., group size and attack window) for 50 different items, and measure the resulting precision and recall. However, since an attack may begin in any of the available windows, we then repeat this process for each possible window, and average the results across time. Finally, we repeat this entire process with each Netflix subset to produce cross-validated results. The results therefore take into account the differences between sybil group size, target item, attack time, and honest user behaviour. The average precision and recall values are plotted in Figures 6(a) and 6(b). They highlight that these methods work best when *many* sybils are rating the same item, with recall near 99% and precision near 70%. The fact that the precision is not performing as well as the recall implies that there are a higher proportion of false positives rather than false negatives: when an item is under attack, it is likely to be flagged as such, but few items that are not attacked may be flagged as well. As with the user monitor, it remains unclear as to how to deal with items that are being rated anomalously by users who are not the sybils that we explicitly control in our experiments;

in fact, we can only be certain that users are malicious if we explicitly injected them. Otherwise, we have assumed that the users in the dataset are honest and well-intentioned, which may not be the case: it is therefore preferable, in this case, to have a monitor with higher recall than precision, since we are sure that the sybils we inject are being found.

5   Related Work

Anomaly detection algorithms have been used when securing a wide range of systems: they defend against financial fraud [9] and protect web servers from denial of service attacks [10]. These techniques are applicable to recommender systems too, the main problem being how to define what an anomaly is, and how to monitor the large volume of users and items. In this work, we have introduced novel methods that detect anomalies in various aspects of rating behaviour while learning what normal user behaviour is, thus liberating system administrators from these challenges. To do so, we leveraged the effect that honest users have on the temporal dynamics of the system. For example, we used the fact that majority of users rate very few items in order to identify the sybils who are rating a lot. The only way that sybils may dodge pushing the monitored variables over the detection thresholds is by *not rating*: our defences thus act as an incentive for attackers to draw out the length of their attack, thus reducing its overall effect (as seen in Section 2).

Anomaly detection has also been seen before in recommender system research. Bhaumik *et al.* [11] propose a method to monitor *items* as they are under attack, by looking at changes to an item's mean rating over time. Similarly, Yang *at al* [12] infer user trust values based on modelling the signal of incoming ratings. They use these techniques to monitor when *real users*, who each control 50 sybils, are attacking a system. To that extent, their system is under a variety of potentially conflicting attacks. Our work differs on two main points: first, we evaluate a system that iteratively updates and computes personalised recommendations for each user. We also propose methods that assume a large set of users and items, and flag attacks while monitoring all users and items (rather than simply monitoring users/items individually). We evaluate attacks that may not demonstrate anomalies within a single time window, but appear between system updates, and may be targeted to affect particular users' recommendations. We also explore a wide variety of attacks, ranging from the *random* to *targeted* scenarios, where a key aspect of the attacks is the fact that sybil groups of varying size are rating items.

The idea of temporality in attacks has also been explored from the point of view of user reputation; Resnick and Sami [13] prove a variety of properties of their reputation system, which takes into account the order that ratings are input. It remains unclear how these systems would work in practice: many reputation or trust-based systems assume that the ratings input by users are the ground truth, without taking into account that users are both naturally inconsistent when they rate [7] and what they rate will be influenced by what they are recommended. Furthermore, one of the most troubling problems that both monitoring techniques and reputation systems suffer from is *bootstrapping*; systems can be easily abused when the variables that monitor or reflect user behaviour have had little to no data. In this work, we use all ratings input prior to a pre-specified time ϵ to bootstrap each monitor. System administrators may opt to ask a controlled, closed group of trusted users to rate for varying lengths of time in order to bootstrap. Alternatively, if the system also offers social networking functionality, defences that identify sybils according to their location on the social graph can be applied [3]; in this work we assumed that no such graph was present. More generally, the breadth of work in this area reflects the tight coupling between the broader system design and particular defense mechanisms that are implemented. For example, DSybil [4] also explores temporal attacks, but for voting-based systems that do not provide personalised recommendations as we explore here.

6 Conclusion and Future Work

In this work, we have confronted the problem of sybil attacks to deployed recommender systems, where sybil groups (of varying size) inject item ratings (at varying rates) over time in order to either disrupt the system's recommendations (via a *random* attack) or modify the recommendations of a particular item (with a *targeted* attack). We introduced a windowed-view of temporal behaviour, defined a classification of temporal attacks, and then designed and evaluated a *global, user,* and *item* monitoring mechanism that flags when different forms of attack are taking place. Our work centred on the Netflix dataset: we captured a variety of features of this data that remain stable over time and are noticeably affected by a sybil attack. There are a number of other strategies that attackers may adopt, such as the bandwagon or average attacks strategies [2] when unleashing a set of sybils that we have not explored above. Our detection mechanism, in focusing on complimentary dimensions of attacks (the *group size* and *rate* of sybils as they attack), aims to detect attacks regardless of the adopted strategy.

Our ongoing and future work spans many directions: we have started broadening the range of datasets that we apply these defences to, in order to see how varying contexts (i.e., rating movies, music, places) change the stable factors that we take advantage of. We are also conducting experiments in less homogeneous settings, where different types of attacks are taking place simultaneously, to assess the precision, recall and impact of our monitors when combined. In this work, we assumed that the rate at which profiles are populated is roughly similar across sybils and constant in time; our future work aims to remove this assumption, thus addressing the case of attackers that *incrementally* change the rate of attack, to avoid exceeding the current thresholds and thus pass undetected. Note though that it is extremely difficult for attackers to know the values of current thresholds, as they vary with the updating of the exponentially weighted moving averages; experimenting, in order to discover the thresholds, would be difficult since avoiding detection in one window does not guarantee that the same rate will avoid detection in the next.

Acknowledgements

The research leading to these results has received funding from the European Community's Seventh Framework Programme (FP7-SST-2008-RTD-1) under Grant Agreement n. 234239. The authors are solely responsible for it, and this does not represent the opinion of the Community, nor is the Community responsible for any use that might be made of information contained therein.

References

1. Adomavicius, G., Tuzhilin, A.: Towards the Next Generation of Recommender Systems: A Survey of the State-of-the-Art and Possible Extensions. IEEE TKDE 17(6) (June 2005)
2. Mobasher, B., Burke, R., Bhaumik, R., Williams, C.: Toward Trustworthy Recommender Systems: An Analysis of Attack Models and Algorithm Robustness. In: ACM TOIT (2007)
3. Yu, H., Kaminsky, M., Gibbons, P., Flaxman, A.: SybilGuard: Defending Against Sybil Attacks Via Social Networks. In: ACM SIGCOMM, Pisa, Italy, vol. 4, pp. 267–278 (2006)
4. Yu, H., Shi, C., Kaminsky, M., Gibbons, P.B., Xiao, F.: DSybil: Optimal Sybil-Resistance for Recommendation Systems. In: IEEE Symposium on Security and Privacy, Oakland, CA (May 2009)
5. Williams, C., Mobasher, B., Burke, R.: Defending Recommender Systems: Detection of Profile Injection Attacks. Journal of Service Oriented Computing and Applications (August 2009)
6. Lathia, N., Hailes, S., Capra, L.: Temporal Collaborative Filtering With Adaptive Neighbourhoods. In: ACM SIGIR, Boston, USA (2009)
7. Amatriain, X., Pujol, J.M., Tintarev, N., Oliver, N.: Rate it Again: Increasing Recommendation Accuracy by User Re-Rating. In: ACM RecSys., New York, USA (2009)
8. Lam, S.K., Riedl, J.: Shilling Recommender Systems for Fun and Profit. In: Proceedings the 13th International Conference on World Wide Web, New York, USA (2004)
9. Wu, S.X., Banzhaf, W.: Combatting Financial Fraud: A Coevolutionary Anomaly Detection Approach. In: 10th Annual Conference on Genetic and Evolutionary Computation, Atlanta, GA, USA, pp. 1673–1680 (2008)
10. Siris, V.A., Papagalou, F.: Application of Anomaly Detection Algorithms for Detecting SYN Flooding Attacks. Computer Communications 29, 1433–1442 (2006)
11. Bhaumik, R., Williams, C., Mobasher, B., Burke, R.: Securing Collaborative Filtering Against Malicious Attacks Through Anomaly Detection. In: Proceedings of the 4th Workshop on Intelligent Techniques for Web Personalization (ITWP 2006), Boston (July 2006)
12. Yang, Y., Sun, Y., Kay, S., Yang, Q.: Defending Online Reputation Systems against Collaborative Unfair Raters through Signal Modeling and Trust. In: Proceedings of ACM SAC TRECK (2009)
13. Resnick, P., Sami, R.: The Influence Limiter: Provably Manipulation Resistant Recommender Systems. In: Proceedings of Recommender Systems (RecSys 2007), Minneapolis, USA (2007)

SBAD: Sequence Based Attack Detection via Sequence Comparison

Ching-Hao Mao[1], Hsing-Kuo Pao[1], Christos Faloutsos[2], and Hahn-Ming Lee[1,3]

[1] Dept. of Computer Science & Information Engineering,
National Taiwan University of Science & Technology, Taipei, Taiwan
{d9415004,pao,hmlee}@mail.ntust.edu.tw
[2] Dept. of Computer Science, Carnegie Mellon University, Pittsburgh, USA
christos@cs.cmu.edu
[3] Institute of Information Science, Academia Sinica, Taipei, Taiwan

Abstract. Given a stream of time-stamped events, like alerts in a network monitoring setting, how can we isolate a sequence of alerts that form a network attack? We propose a Sequence Based Attack Detection (*SBAD*) method, which makes the following contributions: (a) it automatically identifies groups of alerts that are frequent; (b) it summarizes them into a suspicious sequence of activity, representing them with graph structures; and (c) it suggests a novel graph-based dissimilarity measure. As a whole, *SBAD* is able to group suspicious alerts, visualize them, and spot anomalies at the sequence level. The evaluations from three datasets—two benchmark datasets (DARPA 1999, PKDD 2007) and a private dataset Acer 2007 gathered from a Security Operation Center in Taiwan—support our approach. The method performs well even without the help of the IP and payload information. No need for privacy information as the input makes the method easy to plug into existing system such as an intrusion detector. To talk about efficiency, the proposed method can deal with large-scale problems, such as processing 300K alerts within 20 mins on a regular PC.

1 Introduction

Given a long stream of events, such as network-intrusion alerts shown in Table. 1 or word tokens in HTTP request traffic, how can we spot subsequences inside it, that may correspond to an attack? Traditionally, such problem, known as anomaly detection or intrusion detection has been solved by methods that require considerable expertise. We propose a different approach which can automatically identify frequent groups of alerts, summarize them into suspicious sequences of activity, and represent them with graph structures. Based on the graphs, a *Sequence Based Attack Detection (SBAD)* method with a novel *Event Sequence Dissimilarity Measure (SeqD)* is proposed for separating the attack sequences from the normal ones. In the aspect of visualization for human analysis, the *SBAD* is also helpful for showing visualization in a low dimension space where human experts could easily identify attacks based on the clustered distribution.

C. Dimitrakakis et al. (Eds.): PSDML 2010, LNAI 6549, pp. 78–91, 2011.

Table 1. An example of alert sequence generated from Network Intrusion Detection System. Note that the IP information usually seen in the alert sequence is not included here.

Sequence of Attacks		
Event Type	Time Stamp (hh:mm)	Result
PortScan	June. 21 '09 10:00	True
PortSweep	June. 21 '09 10:10	True
PortScan	June. 21 '09 13:02	True
Open Port	June. 21 '09 13:10	True
Telnet Traffic Encrypted	June. 21 '09 13:13	True

Given HTTP request tokens, Fig. 1 shows the sequence-based 2-D *Isomap* embeddings, which belong to normal traffic and different Web attacks. For real application from security operation center, this 2-D map (rather then millions of HTTP traffic connection or IDS alerts) is convenient for domain experts to capture the attack behavior.

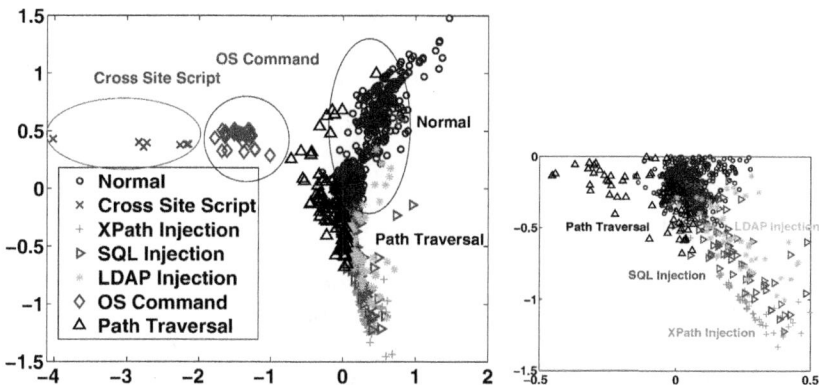

Fig. 1. The 2-D Isomap based on *SBAD*. Malicious behaviors are clustered together according to different classes. Each point represents a sequence within an interval, which is also associated with a correlation/attack graph. The figure on the right shows a "zoom in" of the dense area on the left figure.

The *behavior event*, or simply *event*, can be an alert for network data or a word token from HTTP request traffic. The *event stream* is a sequence of events. For example, Fig. 2 shows three alert sequences that represent different attack scenarios according to the alert occurrence and ordering. The sequence in Figs. 2(a) and (b) is the Web application attack that exploits the vulnerability of cross-site script, and the sequence in Fig. 2(c) is another type of attacks with successive attempts. Such attacks always consist of several steps. Given the event sequences, we aim at detecting these attacks.

Original Attack Sequence

B B C B C B B B C B B B

Original Pattern
F E D E

Original Pattern
F E D E

Closed Pattern
F E D E E D E

Interjection(Gap) Pattern
F E X X X D E

Interleaved Attack Sequence

B B A C G G B C B D B B

□ Thread 1   ○ Thread 2

(a) Pattern with variations   (b) Interjected pattern   (c) Interleaved attack sequence

Fig. 2. Challenges of this work in a real case from Acer07 data: (a) Web shell variation attack pattern for the same intention/goal, (b) interjected Web shell attack pattern by irrelevant alert events, (c) interleaved NMAP denial of service attack pattern by another event sequence. (A: protocol−command−decode, B: attempted recon, C: attempted user, D: attempted dos, E: Web application activity, F: possible SQL injection, G: bad unknown, and X: wild card alert event).

The challenges of this work are as follows:

- interleaving: alert events that belong to the same attack, are not necessarily consecutive; i.e., other alert events may intervene, as shown in Fig. 2(c)
- interjection: alert events might be interjected by other irrelevant background events, as shown in Fig. 2(b)
- missing alerts: the alert generation software may fail to generate some alerts, as shown in Fig. 2(a)
- variations in known attacks: intruders attempt to vary their methods, in order to evade detection, as shown in Fig. 2(a).

The problem definition is as follows:

Problem 0. Attack Detection

- **Given:** (1) a stream of events (alerts), some of which are labeled as "true attacks" and (2) a set of known attack graphs
- **Find:** which (unlabeled) alerts belong to the same sequence (attack) and give the attack id, if it is a known attack

Given an event stream, we propose a detection method *SBAD* on the basis of a sequence dissimilarity measure *SeqD*. First, the method spots fragments that appear often by constructing a transition matrix and looks for frequently-occurring transitions (allowing for a few variations). The novelty of the proposed method is the manner in which an exact measurement of the sequence dissimilarity is carried out on the basis of the dissimilarity between two slightly-different versions of a transition matrix. Such a dissimilarity measure opens the door for all the follow-up steps: we can perform clustering (of sequences); nearest-neighbor search/classification of a new sequence; visualization (e.g., using Fastmap [4] or Isomap [10]); outlier detection; and several other data mining operations.

We summarize the main contributions of our study as follows: First, we propose a novel dissimilarity measure for event sequences. Under this measure, not just sequence-to-sequence, but also sequence-to-template, or template-to-template comparisons can be carried out. Second, justified by some real case studies, our event analyzer can effectively deal with event sequences in the presence of noise, interleaving, interjection (long insertion) or interception contained sequences, sequences with missing alerts, etc. Last, we provide a visualization (Isomap) for an easy understanding of the properties of different malicious or normal behavior of event sequences. Providing the computable attack graphs by sequence comparison is the significant difference against to previewed graph-based alert analysis works [15,18]. The remainder of this paper is organized as follows: Sec. 2 contains a review of related work. In Sec. 3, we introduce our approach. In Sec. 4, our approach is evaluated by several series of experiments on the alert sequence dataset and the Web traffic dataset. Then, in Sec. 5, we conclude this work.

2   Related Work

Our objective is to detect intrusive or anomalous behavior from event sequences. In this section, we discuss some previous work on event mining, including a rich set of work on sequence alignment. One of the most widely used methods to describe the relationship of two sequences is *edit distance*. In the case of heavy interleaving, *interceptions* or interjections (long insertions) in the middle of a sequence, the edit distance is not appropriate to describe the relationship between two sequences. Likewise, various *sequence alignment* methods do not work either as they are considerably sensitive to the orders of one-by-one individual events. In particular, the finding of the *longest common subsequences* (LCS) does not contribute significantly toward solving this problem.

On the other hand, to speak of the complexity issue, the sequence comparison must be sufficiently efficient to be successfully applied to a considerably large amount of data like network streams. Ideally, we look for a strategy that can work in a *linear* or close-to-linear manner with respect to the number of event items. In this sense, edit distance and most alignment methods, if they attempt to solve a *global optimization* problem, will not be appropriate because their implementations rely mostly on a *quadratic* dynamic programming kernel. Overall, to effectively and efficiently solve the anomaly or intrusion detection problem, given an event stream, we need to identify the suspicious events or alerts from the stream with a low false alarm rate and the entire process is favorable to working in a linear or close to linear manner with respect to the number of events.

Toivonen et al. [14] processed events of Nokia routers, and report frequent subsequences, by extending the celebrated *a priori* algorithm [1]. In mining of frequent patterns with gapped constraint, Ji et al. [5] studied the minimal distinguishing sequences (MDSs) with a gapped constraint which occurs frequently in one class but infrequently in another class, and they developed an efficient algorithm named ConSGapMiner to prune the generated candidates patterns. Mining MDSs among sequences could be regarded as the enhancement of measuring the dissimilarity between sequences in order to alleviate the impact from none distinguishing sequences. Mining the frequent closed sequence is also a way to provide more compact result with better efficiency, Ding et al. [2] proposed an efficient approach for finding closed repetitive gapped subsequences which generates much smaller candidates of sub-sequences. All the above approaches intend to discover specific patterns in efficient way; but in our case for distinguishing intrinsic behavior from difference event sequence in network data with interleaving, interjection or high variance of patterns, it is unlikely that those methods can be helpful. In addition, a robust dissimilarity measure is required for this phenomenon to tolerance highly dynamic network environment.

Keogh et al. [7] looked for a parameter-free description of data. Pao et al. [16] studied the distance function between biological sequences. They followed the study of Li et al. [12] and attempted to use Kolmogorov complexity [13] to describe event sequences. Because of the difficulty of computing Kolmogorov complexity in general, some compression methods can be adopted for its approximation. Given two sequences, what is different in our approach is the consideration of the associated Markov chain models of the sequences and the measurement of how well one sequence is described by the model in association with another sequence in order to decide their distance/dissimilarity. Ke et al. [6] proposed an efficient algorithm, which mines the top-k correlative graphs by exploring only the candidate graphs. On the other hand, our measure is a graph-based one, which will be combined with geodesic distance estimation [17]. Lane and Brodley [9] gave an empirical study regarding instance-based learning and hidden Markov models approaches with sequence learning for anomaly detection.

3   Graph Based Dissimilarity Measure for Attack Detection

We propose an approach to identify the malicious behavior in sequences where a graph-based dissimilarity measure is computed for each pair of event sequences and the dissimilarity value will be used for intrusion or anomaly detection. In this section, we detail our approach. As discussed in Sec. 1, we would like to solve the attack detection problem, rigorously stated below:

Problem 1. Attack Detection in Event Sequences

- **Given:** (1) an event sequence e and (2) a set of known attack graphs (from domain experts) $\{\mathfrak{G}_1, \mathfrak{G}_2, \ldots, \mathfrak{G}_k\}$
- **Find:** (1) the most likely attack graphs $\mathfrak{G}$, (2) and give the attack-id, if it is a known attack

One input event example is the sequence of alerts each identified by the alert type, or also associated with several additional attributes such as source IP, target IP, and time stamp. The alerts can have up to 3000 different types, including Web-application-attack, misc-attack, etc., depending on the setting of IDS. The attributes such as source or target IPs are generally helpful to decide whether or not the network is under attack. However, in this work, we consider *only* the alert type for the detection, while the time stamp is used only to segregate alerts into groups. Another example is the sequence of HTTP request tokens.

The event types in this case can be words (alphanumerical tokens), symbols, script keywords, variables and so on. We would like to deal with mainly these two input sequences and detect attacks in these two sequences. To achieve the goal, we discuss the following three subproblems:

Problem 2. Graph Generation

- **Given:** a sequence of events **e**,
- **Find** the graph $\mathfrak{G}$ that best describes the sequence

Problem 3. Sequence Coding

- **Given:** a graph/model $\mathfrak{G}$ and a sequence **e**
- **Find** the best code to describe the sequence **e** given the known model $\mathfrak{G}$

Problem 4. Sequence Dissimilarity Measurement

- **Given:** two event sequences $\mathbf{e}_1$ and $\mathbf{e}_2$,
- **Find** the dissimilarity measure of the two sequences

Our algorithm consists of three modules: (1) *Correlation Graph Construction*, (2) *Sequence Coding*, and (3) *Sequence Comparison* from our Dissimilarity Measure *SeqD* where each tries to solve the Problems 2, 3, 4 just mentioned respectively. After the dissimilarity measurement is done for each pair of sequences, ideally we can plug-in any supervised, unsupervised or even semi-supervised schemes for intrusion detection or anomaly detection. The complete algorithm is shown in Algorithm 1. Below we discuss all the modules in turn in the following sections. Before doing so, let us introduce our notations used in this work.

Notations. We use lower case bold letters for vectors or sequences and capital bold letters for matrices. Given the event sequence $\mathbf{e} = (e_1, \ldots, e_t, \ldots, e_T)$, the goal is to find out the subsequence with abnormal behavior. In the alert sequence, e_t is simply alert type while in the HTTP token sequence, e_t is chosen one of the token types. Given the event sequence, we define the *correlation window* of size W_c to indicate the range of (directly) related events. Informally, two events that are within the distance W_c may be related, such as one attack action leads to another attack action. For instance, the probing is always the prerequisite for "Buffered Overflow Attack" or "Denial of Service Attack" for finding the system's vulnerability. Formally, two correlated events indicate the possible transition in our Markov chain model. The correlation window is operated in a sliding fashion. On the other hand, we segregate the event sequence into several *scenario interval* of size $W_s \geq W_c$ and assume that a complete attack or network behavior can be observed in this interval, or we can have enough information to judge the event flow belonging to an attack or a normal behavior within the interval. The typical choice of the interval is from several hours to several days. In a supervised problem, we have labels $y_i = \{1, -1\} = \{\text{attack}, \text{normal}\}$ to describe the intention of network actions for an interval i. In interval i, we construct correlation graph $\mathfrak{G}_i(V, E, \theta)$ to describe the relation of events where V is the

Algorithm 1. SBAD algorithm (batch version)

> **Input**: $\{e_i\} := \{e^*\} \cup \{e_\ell\}$, the new event seq. e^* and a set of labeled event
>   sequences $\{e_\ell\}$
> **Output**: associated graphs $\{\mathfrak{G}_i\} := \{\mathfrak{G}^*\} \cup \{\mathfrak{G}_\ell\}$, dissimilarity matrix $\mathbf{D}$, label
>   of e^*
> ```
> /* step 1: Construction of Correlation Graph            */
> ```
> 1 **for** *each sequence* e *in* $\{e_i\}$ **do**
> 2 $\quad$ Find the event sets V and relations E of e for graph $\mathfrak{G}$;
> 3 $\quad$ $\mathbf{A} \leftarrow$ the frequency counts in all pairs of events within window W_c ;
> 4 $\quad$ $\mathbf{A} \leftarrow \mathbf{A} + \epsilon$ (Laplace smoothing factor) ;
> 5 **end**
> ```
> /* step 2: Sequence Coding                              */
> ```
> 6 **for** *each pair of* $(e, \mathfrak{G}) \in \{(e_i, \mathfrak{G}_i)\}$ **do**
> 7 $\quad$ Encode the sequence e given $\mathfrak{G}$ as $c(e \mid \mathfrak{G})$ **(Eq.1)** ;
> 8 **end**
> ```
> /* step 3: Dissimilarity Measurement                    */
> ```
> 9 Compute dissimilarity matrix $\mathbf{D}_{ij} := d(e_i, e_j)$ for each pair of event sequences
> e_i, e_j **(Eq. 3)** ;
> ```
> /* step 4: Attack Labeling                              */
> ```
> 10 Given $\mathbf{D}$, adopt any dissimilarity-based clustering or classification algorithm for
>   identifying attacks in e^*

Table 2. Notations

Notation	Definition and Description
T	the total number of entire event instances
W_c	the size of correlation window
W_s	the size of scenario interval
S	the number of different event types
$e(t : u)$	the event sequence where $e(t : u) = (e_t, e_{t+1}, \ldots, e_u)$
y_i	the label of interval i
$\mathfrak{G}(V, E, \theta)$	the Markov chain-based correlation graph with vertex set V, edge set E and θ as the model parameters; one graph for each scenario interval
$\mathbf{A}$	the transition matrix

set of all event types, and the edge set E as well as the corresponding transition probabilities θ describes the transition between pair of events, if within window size W_c. The model parameters θ can be written in a matrix form, known as the transition matrix, denoted by $\mathbf{A}$ of dimension $S \times S$, with the number of states or event types equal to S. Table 2 summarizes all of our notations.

3.1 Construction of Correlation Graph

Given an event sequence e, we look for the graph $\mathfrak{G}$ that is the most appropriate one to describe the sequence. We consider correlation graph in this study. A correlation graph $\mathfrak{G}(V, E, \theta)$ has its vertices V belonging to the event types, either the alert or token types; while its edges E are the possible transitions between those event types; and the model parameters θ record all transitions, or in matrix form the $S \times S$ transition matrix $\mathbf{A}$ with $\mathbf{A}_{ij}$ denotes the probability[1] of jumping from state (alert or token type) i at some time to state j at a later time. To be specific, if two events $e_t = i$ at time t and $e_u = j$ at time u are directly correlated, such transition should contribute to $\mathbf{A}_{ij}$. The goal of correlation graph is intended to model the correlations between pairs of events. We build a graph for each partial sequence in a scenario interval of length W_s.

Given *interleaved* inputs like network data, we consider the pair of events to be the possible related events if they are within the distance of W_c. Trying *all* the event pairs within the time stamp distance W_c is because we have no clue whether two events indeed form a correlated event pair. This design may give an overestimated result. However, we can assume that the event pairs not considered to be the true correlated pairs contribute randomly to each of the transitions. Hopefully, the Laplace smoothing shall give us nothing but the bias of uniform prior.

3.2 Sequence Coding

We would like to study the coding scheme of a sequence given some background knowledge of a model. In our design, each sequence $\mathbf{e}(t_0 : t_0 + W_s)$ has an associated correlation graph $\mathfrak{G}(V, E, \theta)$ with a set of transition parameters and states (types) decided by the sequence. The code of sequence $\mathbf{e}$ given $\mathfrak{G}$ can be chosen to be the Shannon code, with the code length equal to the negation of log-likelihood $\ell(\mathbf{e}; \mathfrak{G}) = \log L(\mathbf{e}; \mathfrak{G}) = \log P(\mathbf{e} \mid \mathfrak{G})$. The code length is given by

$$c(\mathbf{e} \mid \mathfrak{G}) = -\ell(\mathbf{e}; \mathfrak{G}) = -\log L(\mathbf{e}; \mathfrak{G}). \tag{1}$$

The alert sequence is likely to be heavily interleaved. We consider all the pairs to be the possible transitions. That is, we compute

$$\tilde{\ell}(\mathbf{e}; \mathfrak{G}) = \log \tilde{L}(\mathbf{e}; \mathfrak{G}) = \log \left(P(e_{t_0}) \prod_{0 < u - t \leq W_c} P(e_u \mid e_t) \right)$$

$$= \log P(e_{t_0}) + \sum_{0 < u - t \leq W_c} \log P(e_u \mid e_t). \tag{2}$$

where L is the likelihood function. We assume the initial probability $P(e_{t_0})$ to be constant in this work and therefore can be avoided in later computations.

Suppose we try bi-gram counts for heavily interleaved inputs, *because the consecutive events are less likely to be correlated, we may encounter a lot of transitions that are not existed in the model.* The consequence is to obtain a low likelihood or long code length. Opposed to that, choosing Eq. 2 can "smooth out" such defect and give us reasonable result. We justify our conjecture in Fig. 3(c), where an all-pair design is compared to a bi-gram strategy and the experiment shows that the all-pair strategy is superior to the bi-gram strategy.

---

[1] In this study, we assume $\mathbf{A}$ to be stationary, that is, not changing through the time.

3.3   Sequence Comparison and Dissimilarity Measure

Given two event sequences $\mathbf{e}_1$ and $\mathbf{e}_2$ and their associated graphs $\mathfrak{G}_1$, $\mathfrak{G}_2$, the dissimilarity between the two sequences depends on how well one sequence is described by the model for another sequence. We define the dissimilarity of two event sequences $\mathbf{e}_1$ and $\mathbf{e}_2$ as

$$d(\mathbf{e}_1, \mathbf{e}_2) = \frac{c(\mathbf{e}_1 \mid \mathfrak{G}_2) + c(\mathbf{e}_2 \mid \mathfrak{G}_1)}{c(\mathbf{e}_{12} \mid \mathfrak{G}_{12})} , \tag{3}$$

where $\mathbf{e}_{12}$ is the new sequence formed by concatenating sequences $\mathbf{e}_1$ and $\mathbf{e}_2$ together, and $\mathfrak{G}_{12}$ is the associated correlation graph of the concatenated[2] sequence $\mathbf{e}_{12}$. In the end, we have pairwise dissimilarities for all pairs of event sequences.

Embedding and Attack Detection. The last goal is attack detection. Given the dissimilarity for each pair of sequences, sequence embedding seeks to represent the event sequences in an space so that the distance in the space well represents the relation of those sequences. It provides the interpretable insight for further investigation from domain experts. We need to emphasize that the "distance" in Eq. 3 is not exactly distance if the triangle inequality does not hold. However, with the sequences embedded by Isomap, the triangle inequality naturally holds as it finds shortest paths between pairs of event sequences.

With the sequence embedding, in principle we can plug in any classifiers for signature-based detection or any clustering methods for anomaly detection. In this study, we adopt smooth SVM (SSVM), which tries to solve an unconstrained minimization problem [11], and kNN for most of our evaluation.

4   Experiment Result

In this section, we compare our proposed method to other approaches and illustrate the experiment results to justify our method and the dataset and SBAD code are available at http://neuron.csie.ntust.edu.tw/sbad. The evaluation metrics are described for evaluating the perfromance of proposed approach in teh aspect of attack detection are given in Sec. 4.2. The applied data and the parameters for our experiments are introduced in Sec. 4.1, followed by the results on the datasets in Sec. 4.3 and Sec. 4.4.

4.1   Datasets

We use three different datasets in our experiments, summarized in Table 3 . We test our proposed *SBAD* on DARPA 1999 (DARPA99)[3], iCAST/Acer eDC07

---

[2] We can treat $\mathbf{e}_{12}$ and $\mathbf{e}_{21}$ as virtually the same to generate similar correlation graphs between $\mathfrak{G}_{12}$ or $\mathfrak{G}_{21}$. The only thing to make the difference is the transition at concatenating point between $\mathbf{e}_1$ and $\mathbf{e}_2$.

[3] DARPA intrusion detection evaluation, in http://www.ll.mit.edu/ The proposed method in this study just considers the alert sequences and time stamps, some problematic features are not adopted.

Table 3. Dataset Description (T:F denotes the ratio between True and False Events)

	Duration	Total Events (T:F)	Correlation Graphs (T:F)
DARPA99	5 weeks	55473 (1:1.9)	442 (1:6.3)
Acer07	9 days	302434 (1:58.5)	2062 (1:5.8)
PKDD07	—	50116 (1:2.3)	50116 (1:2.3)

dataset (Acer07) [4], and ECML-PKDD 2007's "Analyzing Web Traffic challenge" (PKDD07) for the evaluation. For DARPA99 and Acer07, alerts are generated using Snort[5].

Other than IDS alert datasets, PKDD07 is for determining whether or not a given HTTP request contains attack(s). PKDD07 extracted from HTTP query logs consists of 50116 examples including one valid (normal query) category and seven attack categories. Each example in the dataset is completely independent from others and has a unique id, context (describing what environment the query was run), class (the sample category classified by experts), and the content of the query itself. Additionally, there is an important attribute called "attackInterval" which indicates the location of attack sequences. We grouped the tokens into 40 pre-specified token categories, such as "Scripts Word", "SQL syntax" and so on, as event types.

4.2   Evaluation Metrics

In our evaluation, we regard each alert event as an instance for detection; that is, our evaluation is *sequence-based* rather than *alert-based*. We identify attacks based on a series of alerts/events and the correlations between them. Given a series of alerts/events, we construct an associated graph and predict its label as either an attack or normal traffic/HTTP request.

To evaluate the effectiveness of proposed method, we use a confusion matrix [8] to measure the *precision* and *recall* in our experiments. Here, let TP (true positive) be the number of alert sequences with true alarms (attacks) that are correctly detected; FN (false negative) be the number of attacks that are not detected; let TN (true negative) be the number of alert sequences without true alarms (normal sequences) that are correctly classified; and let FP (false positive) be the number of normal sequences that are incorrectly detected as malicious sequences. The accuracy is defined by as follows: the precision (P) is defined by

$$Precision = \frac{TP}{TP + FP},\tag{4}$$

and the recall rate (R) is defined by

$$recall = \frac{TP}{TP + FN}.\tag{5}$$

---

[4] http://www.accsi.net/english/index.html
[5] Snort, the open source network intrusion system, in http://www.snort.org

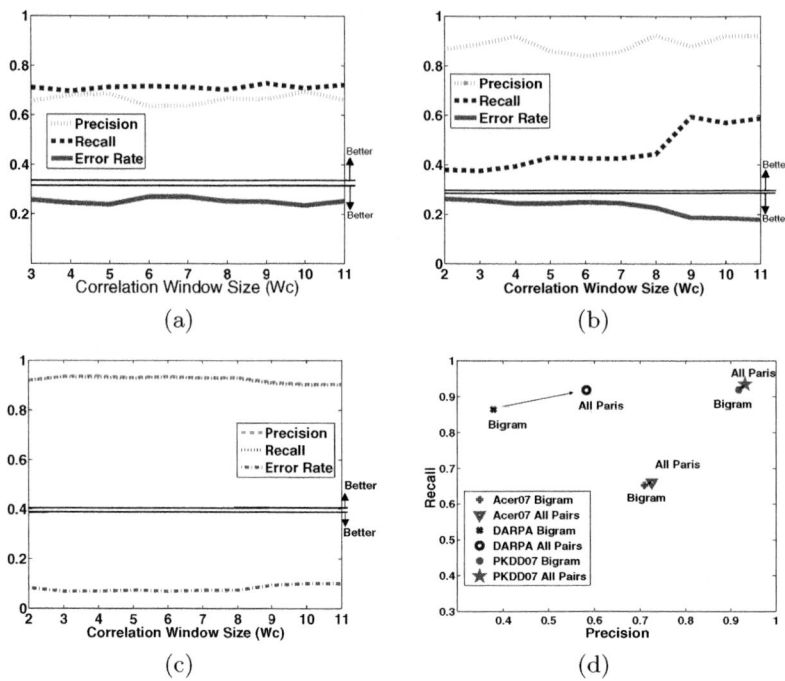

Fig. 3. Sensitivity analysis of correlation window W_c with its size equal to $2, 3, \ldots$ to 11 events (W_s is 60 mins) for (a) Acer07, (b) DARPA99 and (c) PKDD07. It gives relatively stable result. However, all-pair approach still performs better than bi-gram approach, as shown in (d). It shows the comparison of precision and recall for Acer07, DARPA99 and PKDD07 in both bi-gram ($W_c = 2$) and all-pair ($W_c > 7$) settings.

We use the above evaluation metrics to assess the efficacy of proposed method.

4.3   Sensitivity Analysis and Robustness

The first series is the sensitivity study of *SBAD* based on different choices of correlation windows. As shown in Fig. 3(a) or (b), choosing the window size from 2 to 11 gives relatively stable performance according to error rate, false positive rate and false negative rate. In Fig. 3(c), all-pair did not perform significant better than bi-gram due to without interleaving situation in HTTP traffics (easily separated by HTTP Request/Response protocol). However, *SBAD* with a correlation window larger than 2 (bi-gram) always performs better, as shown in (d). It confirms our conjecture that all-pair approach suits better for network data than bi-gram approach where we have interleaved data, or data contains interjections or variations. That means when the data is highly interleaved, to count frequencies from all pairs as correlated events makes more sense than counting only the consecutive bi-gram pairs ($W_c = 2$). As discussed before, even with

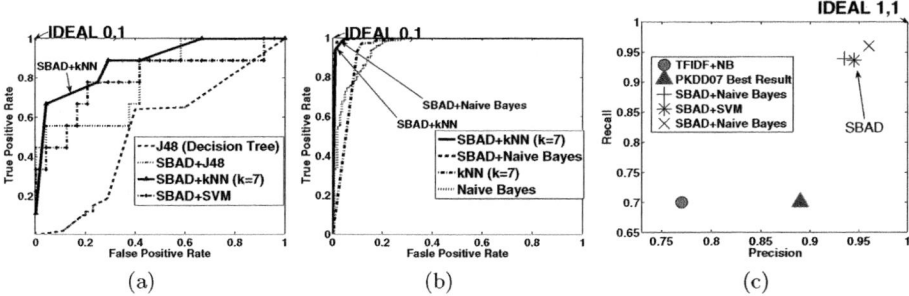

Fig. 4. Capability of detection, evaluated by ROC curves for both Acer07 and PKDD07 datasets: (a) shows the Acer07 data, with AUC values equal to 0.882, 0.796, 0.792 and 0.530 for the methods of *SBAD*+*k*NN, *SBAD*+DT(decision tree), *SBAD*+SVM, and DT respectively; (b) shows the ROC curves of several methods when they work on the PKDD07 data. As shown, *SBAD*+*k*NN and *SBAD*+Naïve Bayes work better. For PKDD07 data, (c) is the precision vs. recall plot of *SBAD* compared with various other methods. *SBAD*'s are in "+", "×" and "*", all closest to the ideal $(1, 1)$.

the overestimation on the frequency counts, the counts are likely uniformly and randomly distributed to all the different state transitions and give little negative impact to our detection.

4.4   Effectiveness Analysis

In this part of experiments, we show that our *SBAD* is indeed superior to other methods in several different aspects. Three datasets, DARPA99 and Acer07 for alert analysis and PKDD07 for Web access analysis are used to demonstrate the effectiveness of our proposed approach on solving the Problem 1. In the evaluation of DARPA99 and Acer07 alert data, as binary classification problems (identifying true alarm from false alarm), *SBAD* can achieve 90% or higher accuracies, as shown in Fig. 4 (DARPA result is not shown due to space limitation). In the comparisons, *SBAD* is superior to other baseline approach (e.g., decision tree), even *without using the IP information*.

For PKDD07, there is no IP information involved. Note that HTTP traffic dataset in PKDD07 is a multi-class dataset, and several methods including the method from [3] and conventional TF-IDF method are compared. As shown in Fig. 4(b) and (c), our *SBAD* combined with either *k*NN, Naïve Bayes, or SVM works the best among all the other methods, including the PKDD07 best result which is a kind of generalized signature-based approach.

4.5   Real Case for Dissimilarity

Based on Acer07's ground truth, we provide an example to demonstrate the use of our constructed knowledge base. Figure 5(a) shows a query ACG comprised of an alert thread and its frequency computation. We apply our dissimilarity measure to find the alert sequences that are in close proximity, as shown in

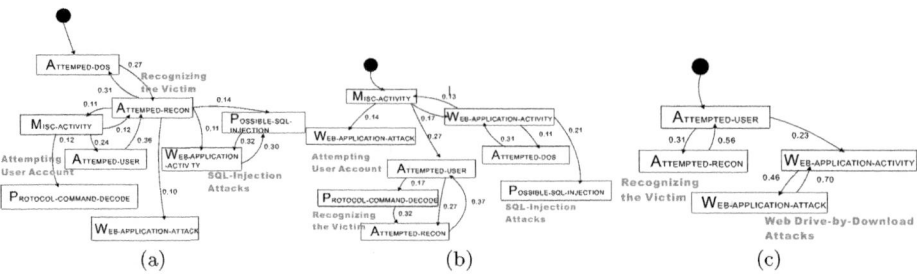

Fig. 5. Examples of correlation graphs and similarity measurement by proposed approach, (a) alert correlation graph query, (b) similar malicious correlation graph graph, (c) dissimilar graph

Figure 5(b). An example of an irrelevant sequences extracted from the dataset is shown in Figure 5(c). The dissimilarity measure can be easily validated by checking the alert types and the structure of the correlation graph. Through the dissimilarity measuring for two arbitrary event sequences, the different event occurrence and ordering were considered in the same time.

5 Conclusion

We proposed a fully implemented method for event sequence analysis. Our method can automatically extract frequent transition sets from interleaving sequences and give effective detection result on data with malicious or anomaly behavior, even in the cases where attack sequences may hide themselves by adding noise or be with missing alerts. Moreover, we showed that it can provide meaningful insights and good visualization for domain experts, all these merits are attributed to our carefully designed dissimilarity measure (Eq. 3). The results show that our method consistently matched or outperformed the competitors in terms of precision and recall, or ROC curve, even without the help of IP information.

Acknowledgements

This work was supported in part by the Taiwan Information Security Center (TWISC), the National Science Council under grants NSC 99-2219-E-011-004, and also by the National Science Council NSC 97-2221-E-011-105 and NSC 96-2221-E-011-064-MY3. This work was also supported in part by ChunghwaTelecom Laboratories under grants TL-99-7401. The authors would like to express their gratitude to Mr. Chi-Dong Chen for his helpful analysis and suggestions. The authors also gratefully acknowledge the helpful comments and suggestions of the reviewers, which have improved the presentation.

References

1. Agrawal, R., Imielinski, T., Swami, A.: Database mining: a performance perspective. IEEE Trans. on Knowledge and Data Engineering 5(6), 914–925 (1993)
2. Ding, B., Lo, D., Han, J., Khoo, S.-C.: Efficient mining of closed repetitive gapped subsequences from a sequence database. In: ICDE 2009 (March 2009)
3. Exbrayat, M.: ECML/PKDD challenge: analyzing web traffic a boundaries signature approach. In: PKDD 2007, pp. 17–29 (2007)
4. Faloutsos, C., Lin, K.-I.D.: Fastmap: A fast algorithm for indexing, data-mining and visualization of traditional and multimedia datasets. In: ACM SIGMOD, May 23-25, pp. 163–174 (1995)
5. Ji, X., Bailey, J., Dong, G.: Mining minimal distinguishing subsequence patterns with gap constraints. In: ICDM 2005 (2005)
6. Ke, Y., Cheng, J., Yu, J.X.: Top-k correlative graph mining. In: SDM, pp. 1038–1049 (2009)
7. Keogh, E., Lonardi, S., Ratanamahatana, C.A.: Towards parameter-free data mining. In: KDD 2004, pp. 206–215 (2004)
8. Kohavi, R., Provost, F.: Glossary of terms. Editorial for the Special Issue on Applications of Machine Learning and the Knowledge Discovery Process 30, 271–274 (1998)
9. Lane, T., Brodley, C.E.: An empirical study of two approaches to sequence learning for anomaly detection. Machine Learning 51(1), 73–107 (2004)
10. Law, M.H.C., Zhang, N., Jain, A.K.: Nonlinear manifold learning for data stream. In: Jonker, W., Petković, M. (eds.) SDM 2004. LNCS, vol. 3178. Springer, Heidelberg (2004)
11. Lee, Y.-J., Mangasarian, O.L.: SSVM: A smooth support vector machine for classification. Comput. Optim. Appl. 20(1), 5–22 (2001)
12. Li, M., Badger, J.H., Chen, X., Kwong, S., Kearney, P., Zhang, H.: An information-based sequence distance and its application to whole mitochondrialgenome phylogeny. Bioinformatics 17(2), 149–154 (2001)
13. Li, M., Vitányi, P.: An Introduction to Kolmogorov Complexity and Its Applications, 2nd edn. Springer, New York (1997)
14. Mannila, H., Toivonen, H., Verkamo, A.I.: Discovering frequent episodes in sequences. In: Fayyad, U.M., Uthurusamy, R. (eds.) KDD 1995 (1995)
15. Ning, P., Cui, Y., Reeves, D., Xu, D.: Techniques and tools for analyzing intrusion alerts. ACM Trans. Inf. Sys. Secur. 7(2), 274–318 (2004)
16. Pao, H.-K., Case, J.: Computing entropy for ortholog detection. In: International Conference on Computational Intelligence, pp. 89–92 (2004)
17. Tenenbaum, J.B., de Silva, V., Langford, J.C.: A global geometric framework for nonlinear dimensionality reduction. Science 290(5500), 2319–2323 (2000)
18. Zhou, J., Heckman, M., Reynolds, B., Carlson, A., Bishop, M.: Modeling network intrusion detection alerts for correlation. ACM Trans. Inf. Sys. Secur. 10(1), 1–31 (2007)

Classifier Evasion: Models and Open Problems

Blaine Nelson[1], Benjamin I.P. Rubinstein[2], Ling Huang[3],
Anthony D. Joseph[1,3], and J.D. Tygar[1]

[1] UC Berkeley
[2] Microsoft Research
[3] Intel Labs Berkeley

Abstract. As a growing number of software developers apply machine learning to make key decisions in their systems, adversaries are adapting and launching ever more sophisticated attacks against these systems. The near-optimal evasion problem considers an adversary that searches for a low-cost negative instance by submitting a minimal number of queries to a classifier, in order to effectively evade the classifier. In this position paper, we posit several open problems and alternative variants to the near-optimal evasion problem. Solutions to these problems would significantly advance the state-of-the-art in secure machine learning.

Keywords: Query Algorithms, Evasion, Reverse Engineering, Adversarial Learning.

1 Introduction

A number of systems and security engineers have proposed the use of machine learning techniques for detecting or filtering miscreant activities in a variety of applications, *e.g.*, spam, intrusion, virus, and fraud detection. All known detection algorithms have *blind spots*: classes of miscreant activity that fail to be detected. While learning enables the detector to adapt, adversaries can still exploit blind spots to evade detection. A significant challenge is to quantify how effectively an adversary can discover blind spots by querying the detector.

Consider, for example, a spammer who wishes to minimally modify a spam message so it is not classified as spam by a public webmail system's spam classifier. His cost is measured by the change in the value of the modified message. The spammer can observe the classifier's behavior by creating a dummy account on the webmail system. By observing the responses of the spam detector to queries, the spammer can search for a minimal modification. Similarly for host-based intrusion detection, an intruder may be forced to obfuscate an attack to avoid detection. The attacker can alter their exploit by inserting *no-ops*, using synonymous system calls, or even choosing between one of several possible exploits. Successful intrusions can also be observed by the attacker.

While instances have associated costs to the adversary, he also incurs a cost for the queries needed to search for evading instances. Sending a large number of queries requires additional resources and may arouse suspicion to the malicious

C. Dimitrakakis et al. (Eds.): PSDML 2010, LNAI 6549, pp. 92–98, 2011.

behavior. In practice, adversaries employ a number of techniques to mitigate this second cost, such as opening multiple webmail accounts or rate-limiting spam or worm probing attacks; these strategies require the attacker to use increased sophistication and computational resources.

Here we revisit the near-optimal evasion problem—a theoretical formulation that quantifies how effectively a classifier can be evaded through querying. We outline open problems and introduce novel variants of the original formulation.

1.1   The Near-Optimal Evasion Problem

The *Near-Optimal Evasion Problem* is a formulation of adversarial evasion that quantifies the hardness of search for low-cost negative instances in terms of the number of queries used. As first posed by Lowd and Meek [6] under the name *adversarial classifier reverse-engineering*, the near-optimal evasion problem quantifies the query complexity required by an adversary to find a negative instance with near-minimal cost in terms of the size of the feature space and the desired accuracy. By analyzing the query complexity for a family of classifiers, near-optimal evasion provides a notion of how hard that family is to evade; *e.g.*, if a spammer must send exponentially-many queries in the dimensionality of the feature space, it is difficult for the spammer to successfully improve his spam.

In this setting, we assume instances are represented in a D-dimensional feature space (*e.g.*, $\mathcal{X} \subseteq \mathbb{R}^D$) and the target classifier f belongs to a family $\mathcal{F}$ of binary classifiers where each classifier $f \in \mathcal{F}$ is a mapping from feature space $\mathcal{X}$ to a label in $\{'-', '+'\}$. A deterministic $f \in \mathcal{F}$ partitions $\mathcal{X}$ into two sets—the positive class $\mathcal{X}_f^+ = \{\mathbf{x} \in \mathcal{X} \mid f(\mathbf{x}) = '+'\}$ and the analogous negative class $\mathcal{X}_f^-$, which we take to be the *normal* instances. We assume that the adversary is aware of at least one instance in each class, $\mathbf{x}^- \in \mathcal{X}_f^-$ and $\mathbf{x}^A \in \mathcal{X}_f^+$, knows $\mathcal{F}$ and not f, and can observe $f(\mathbf{x})$ for any $\mathbf{x} \in \mathcal{X}$ by issuing a *membership query*.

Adversarial Cost. We assume the adversary has a cost function $A : \mathcal{X} \to \mathbb{R}^{0+}$; *e.g.*, for a spammer this could be edit distance on messages. The adversary wishes to optimize A over the negative class $\mathcal{X}_f^-$; *e.g.*, the spammer wants to send spam that will be classified as normal email ('−'). Typically the cost function is a distance to a target instance $\mathbf{x}^A \in \mathcal{X}_f^+$ that is most desirable to the adversary; *e.g.*, an ℓ_p distance induces cost $A_p(\mathbf{x}) = \|\mathbf{x} - \mathbf{x}^A\|_p$.

Lowd and Meek [6] define *minimal adversarial cost (MAC)* of a classifier f to be the best lower bound on the cost that any negative instance obtains

$$MAC(f, A) \triangleq \inf_{\mathbf{x} \in \mathcal{X}_f^-} [A(\mathbf{x})] \quad . \tag{1}$$

They further define a data point to be an ϵ-approximate *instance of minimal adversarial cost (ϵ-IMAC)* if it is a negative instance with cost no more than a factor of $(1 + \epsilon)$ times the *MAC*; *i.e.*, every ϵ-IMAC is a member of the set

$$\epsilon\text{-}IMAC(f, A) \triangleq \left\{ \mathbf{x} \in \mathcal{X}_f^- \mid A(\mathbf{x}) \leq (1 + \epsilon) \cdot MAC(f, A) \right\} \quad . \tag{2}$$

The goal of the *Near-Optimal Evasion Problem* is to quantify the worst-case query complexity required for an adversary to infer an ϵ-*IMAC*, depending on the richness of the family of classifiers. Finding an ϵ-*IMAC* for a singleton family can be achieved offline without any queries, whereas if the family is large, many more queries will be necessary to find an ϵ-*IMAC*. Formally,

> A family of classifiers $\mathcal{F}$ is ϵ-*IMAC searchable* under a family of cost functions $\mathcal{A}$ if for all $f \in \mathcal{F}$ and $A \in \mathcal{A}$, there is an algorithm that finds $\mathbf{x} \in \epsilon$-*IMAC* (f, A) using polynomially many membership queries in D and $L_\epsilon = \log \frac{1}{\epsilon}$. We will refer to such an algorithm as *efficient*.

1.2   Security and the Near-Optimal Evasion Problem

The near-optimal evasion problem sheds light on several real-world security issues. The problem abstracts the scenario of an adversary who wishes to launch a specific attack that is blocked by a classifier-based defense. The attacker has a limited number of probing opportunities after which he must send an attack as close as possible to his originally intended attack—a *near-optimal attack*.

In the case of email spam, the spammer may originally have a message that will be detected as spam. He probes, finds a near-optimal message that evades the filter, and sends this message instead. In the case of an intruder, he has a preferred sequence of system calls that will be detected as intrusions. He probes, finds and executes a near-optimal sequence that evades the detector.

With this framework in mind, we now clearly see the role of a defender: to provide a classifier that resists near-optimal evasion. Practical implementation requires careful selection of costs and realistic bounds on the number of probes an adversary can perform. Resulting lower-bounds on the number of probes required for near-optimal evasion provide significant evidence of effective security.

1.3   Previous Work

Lowd and Meek [6] first introduced near-optimal evasion and developed efficient methods that reverse-engineer linear classifiers in both real-valued and Boolean feature spaces for ℓ_1 costs. Nelson *et al.* [7] generalized the result from linear classifiers to the family of *convex-inducing classifiers* that partition the space of instances into two sets one of which is convex. In generalizing to this family, they showed that near-optimal evasion does not require an estimate of the classifier's decision boundary or state. Nelson *et al.* [8] further explored general ℓ_p costs and found not all are ϵ-*IMAC* searchable for convex-inducing classifiers.

Dalvi *et al.* use a cost-sensitive game-theoretic approach to preemptively patch a classifier's blind spots [5]. They construct a modified classifier designed to detect optimally modified instances. Biggio *et al.* [3] extend this game-theoretic approach and propose hiding information or randomization as additional defense mechanisms for this setting. However, they do not explore near-optimal evasion for randomized classifiers as we propose in Section 3.3.

2 Open Problems in the Theory of Near-Optimal Evasion

A number of unanswered questions remain about the near-optimal evasion problem. Here we motivate these problems and suggest potential directions.

QUESTION 1: *Can we find matching upper and lower bounds for evasion algorithms? Is there a deterministic strategy with polynomial query complexity for all convex-inducing classifiers?* In previous work, linear and convex-inducing classifiers were shown to be ϵ-*IMAC* searchable for ℓ_1 costs by demonstrating algorithms with polynomial query complexity. Currently, it is known that for convex positive class, $\mathcal{O}\left(L_\epsilon + \sqrt{L_\epsilon}D\right)$ queries are sufficient to find a near-optimal instance, although the tightest known lower bound in this case is $\mathcal{O}\left(L_\epsilon + D\right)$. In the case of convex $\mathcal{X}_f^-$, the best known algorithm is a randomized ellipsoid approach (*cf.* [2]) that finds a near-optimal instance with high probability using $\mathcal{O}^*\left(D^5\right)$ queries (ignoring logarithmic terms).

QUESTION 2: *Is there some family larger than the convex-inducing classifiers that is ϵ-IMAC searchable? Are there families outside of the convex-inducing classifiers for which near-optimal evasion is efficient?* Existing approaches to near-optimality have built on the machinery of convex optimization. However, many interesting classifiers are not convex-inducing classifiers. Currently, the only such known result (due to Lowd and Meek) is that linear classifiers on Boolean instance space are 2-*IMAC* searchable.

QUESTION 3: *Is some family of SVMs (e.g., with a known kernel) ϵ-IMAC searchable for some ϵ? Can an adversary incorporate the structure of a non-convex classifier into the ϵ-IMAC search?* Consider SVMs with non-linear kernels. The classifier is non-convex in the original feature space, while the classifier is linear in its Reproducing Kernel Hilbert Space but the cost function may no longer be easy to minimize in that space. However SVMs have other properties that may facilitate near-optimal evasion. For instance, in cases where there are few support vectors, one only needs to find these instances to reconstruct the classifier.

QUESTION 4: *Are there characteristics of non-convex, contiguous bodies that are indicative of the hardness of the body for near-optimal evasion? What about non-contiguous bodies?* It appears that the family of contiguous bodies (*i.e.*, the set of all classifiers for which either $\mathcal{X}_f^+$ or $\mathcal{X}_f^-$ is a contiguous set) cannot be generally ϵ-*IMAC* searchable since this family includes members with many locally minimal cost regions which are hard for local search or binary search procedures to avoid, but perhaps some subsets of this family are ϵ-*IMAC* searchable. For families of non-contiguous bodies, ϵ-*IMAC* searchability seems impossible to achieve (disconnected components could be arbitrarily close to $\mathbf{x}^A$) unless the classifiers' structure can be exploited; *e.g.*, as we discuss for SVMs above.

QUESTION 5: *For what classes of classifiers is reverse-engineering as easy as evasion?* Reverse-engineering is the process of querying to learn the decision boundary, and is sufficient for solving the evasion problem. It is now known that the query complexity of reverse-engineering linear classifiers is identical to that of evasion, while reverse-engineering is strictly more difficult for general convex-inducing classifiers [8]. It is unknown whether there exists a class in between linear and convex-inducing classifiers on which the two tasks are equivalent.

QUESTION 6: *Is there a relationship between the query complexity required for evasion and traditional measures of classifier complexity such as the* VC-dimension? Currently, there is no known relationship between these complexity measures for a family of classifiers. Finding such a relationship could answer many of the previous questions about what classifiers can be evaded.

3   Alternative Models for Evasion

Here we suggest a number of variants of near-optimal evasion that generalize or reformulate the original problem to capture new aspects of the overall challenge.

3.1   Additional Information about Training Data Distribution

Consider an adversary that knows the training algorithm and obtains samples drawn from a natural distribution. A few interesting settings include:

1. The adversary's samples are a subset of the training data.
2. The adversary's samples are from the same distribution as the training data.
3. The adversary's samples are from a perturbation of the training distribution.

With this additional information, the adversary may estimate their own classifier $\tilde{f}$ and analyze it offline. Some open questions include:

QUESTION 7: *What can be learned from $\tilde{f}$ about f? How can $\tilde{f}$ best be used to guide search? Can the sample data be directly incorporated into ϵ-IMAC-search?* Relationships between between f and $\tilde{f}$ can build on existing results in learning theory. A possibility is to bound the difference between $MAC(f, A)$ and $MAC(\tilde{f}, A)$ in one of the above settings. If the difference is sufficiently small with high probability, then a search for an ϵ-IMAC could use $MAC(\tilde{f}, A)$ to initially lower bound $MAC(f, A)$. This should reduce query complexity since lower bounds on the MAC are typically harder to obtain than upper bounds.

3.2   Beyond the Membership Oracle

QUESTION 8: *What types of additional feedback may be available to the adversary and how do they impact the query complexity of ϵ-IMAC-search?* In this scenario, the adversary receives more from the classifier than just a '+'/'−' label. For instance, suppose the classifier is defined as $f(\mathbf{x}) = \mathbb{I}\{g(\mathbf{x}) > 0\}$ for some real-valued function g (as is the case for SVMs) and the adversary receives $g(\mathbf{x})$ for every query instead of $f(\mathbf{x})$. If g is linear, the adversary can use $D + 1$ queries and solve a linear regression problem to reverse-engineer g. This additional information may also be useful for approximating the support of an SVM.

3.3   Evading Randomized Classifiers

In this variant of near-optimal evasion, we consider randomized classifiers that generate random responses from a distribution conditioned on the query $\mathbf{x}$. To analyze the query complexity of such a classifier, we must first generalize our concept of the MAC. We propose the following candidate generalization:

$$RMAC\,(f, A) = \inf_{\mathbf{x} \in \mathcal{X}_f^-} \{A\,(\mathbf{x}) + \lambda \mathbb{P}\,(f\,(\mathbf{x}) = {}'-') \} \ .$$

If f is deterministic, we need $\lambda \geq MAC\,(f, A)$ for this definition to be equivalent to Eq. (1) (e.g., $\lambda = A\,(\mathbf{x}^A) + 1$ is sufficient); otherwise, a trivial minimizer for $\lambda < MAC\,(f, A)$ is $\mathbf{x}^A$. For a randomized classifier, λ balances cost with probability of success.

QUESTION 9: *Given access to the membership oracle only, how difficult is near-optimal evasion of randomized classifiers? Are there families of randomized classifiers that are ϵ-IMAC searchable?* Potential randomized families include:

1. Classifiers with fuzzy boundary of width δ around a deterministic boundary
2. Classifiers based on the class-conditional densities for a pair of Gaussians, a logistic regression model, or other members of the exponential family.

Evasion of randomized classifiers seems to be more difficult than for deterministic classifiers as each query provides limited information about the query probabilities. Based on this argument, Biggio *et al.* promote randomized classifiers as a defense against evasion [3]. However, the query complexity for evasion of randomized classifiers is currently unknown.

3.4   Querying with Real-World Objects

QUESTION 10: *How can the feature mapping be inverted to design real-world instances to map to desired queries? How can query algorithms be adapted for approximate querying?* In the original model of evasion, it was assumed that the attacker could observe $f\,(\mathbf{x})$ for any $\mathbf{x} \in \mathcal{X}$. This capability implicitly assumes that the attacker has knowledge of the feature mapping from real-world objects (*e.g.*, emails or packets) into the learner's feature space. Not only is this mapping often unknown, it also need not be one-to-one or onto: multiple emails may map to the same bag-of-words vector, and some instances in feature space may not correspond to *any* real-world object. This significantly complicates evasion for real-world adversaries.

3.5   Evading an Adaptive Classifier

Finally we consider a classifier that periodically retrains on queries. This variant is a multi-fold game between the attacker and learner, with the adversary now able to issue queries that degrade the learner's performance. Techniques from game-theoretic online learning should be well-suited to this setting [4].

QUESTION 11: *Given a set of adversarial queries (and possibly additional innocuous data) will the learning algorithm converge to the true boundary or can the adversary deceive the learner and evade it simultaneously? If the algorithm does converge, at what rate?* To properly analyze retraining, it is important to have an oracle that labels the points sent by the adversary since the adversary can also query in $\mathcal{X}_f^-$. If all points sent by the adversary are labeled '+', the classifier may prevent effective evasion, but with a large number of false positives due to the adversary's queries in $\mathcal{X}_f^-$; this itself would constitute an attack against the learner [1].

4   Conclusion

The intersection of security, systems, and machine learning research has yielded significant advances in decision-making for complex systems, but has also introduced new challenges in protecting against malicious users. While earlier research laid the groundwork for understanding the near-optimal evasion problem, fundamental problems remain unaddressed. In this paper, we discussed several of these problems and variants, and proposed potential avenues for future research.

References

1. Barreno, M., Nelson, B., Joseph, A.D., Tygar, J.D.: The security of machine learning. Machine Learning 81(2), 121–148 (2010)
2. Bertsimas, D., Vempala, S.: Solving convex programs by random walks. J. ACM 51(4), 540–556 (2004)
3. Biggio, B., Fumera, G., Roli, F.: Multiple classifier systems under attack. In: El Gayar, N., Kittler, J., Roli, F. (eds.) MCS 2010. LNCS, vol. 5997, pp. 74–83. Springer, Heidelberg (2010)
4. Cesa-Bianchi, N., Lugosi, G.: Prediction, Learning, and Games. Cambridge University Press, Cambridge (2006)
5. Dalvi, N., Domingos, P., Sanghai, S., Verma, D.: Adversarial classification. In: Proc. KDD 2004, pp. 99–108 (2004)
6. Lowd, D., Meek, C.: Adversarial learning. In: Pro. KDD 2005, pp. 641–647 (2005)
7. Nelson, B., Rubinstein, B.I.P., Huang, L., Joseph, A.D., Lau, S., Lee, S., Rao, S., Tran, A., Tygar, J.D.: Near-optimal evasion of convex-inducing classifiers. In: Proc. AISTATS 2010, pp. 549–556 (2010)
8. Nelson, B., Rubinstein, B.I.P., Huang, L., Joseph, A.D., Lee, S.J., Rao, S., Tygar, J.D.: Query strategies for evading convex-inducing classifiers (2010) report arXiv:1007.0484v1 available at, http://arxiv.org/abs/1007.0484

Large Margin Multiclass Gaussian Classification with Differential Privacy

Manas A. Pathak and Bhiksha Raj

Carnegie Mellon University, Pittsburgh, PA 15213, USA
{manasp,bhiksha}@cs.cmu.edu

Abstract. As increasing amounts of sensitive personal information is aggregated into data repositories, it has become important to develop mechanisms for processing the data without revealing information about individual data instances. The differential privacy model provides a framework for the development and theoretical analysis of such mechanisms. In this paper, we propose an algorithm for learning a discriminatively trained multiclass Gaussian classifier that satisfies differential privacy using a large margin loss function with a perturbed regularization term. We present a theoretical upper bound on the excess risk of the classifier introduced by the perturbation.

1 Introduction

In recent years, vast amounts of personal data is being aggregated in the form of medical, financial records, social networks, and government census data. As these often contain sensitive information, a database curator interested in releasing a function such as a statistic evaluated over the data is faced with the prospect that it may lead to a breach of privacy of the individuals who contributed to the database. It is therefore important to develop techniques for retrieving desired information from a dataset without revealing any information about individual data instances. *Differential privacy* [1] is a theoretical model proposed to address this issue. A query mechanism evaluated over a dataset is said to satisfy differential privacy if it is likely to produce the same output on a dataset differing by at most one element. This implies that an adversary having complete knowledge of all data instances but one along with *a priori* information about the remaining instance, is not likely to be able to infer any more information about the remaining instance by observing the output of the mechanism.

One of the most common applications for such large data sets such as the ones mentioned above is for training classifiers that can be used to categorize new data. If the training data contains private data instances, an adversary should not be able to learn anything about the individual training dataset instances by analyzing the output of the classifier. Recently, mechanisms for learning differentially private classifiers have been proposed for logistic regression [2]. In this method, the objective function which is minimized by the classification algorithm is modified by adding a linear perturbation term. Compared to the original classifier, there is an additional error introduced by the perturbation term in the

C. Dimitrakakis et al. (Eds.): PSDML 2010, LNAI 6549, pp. 99–112, 2011.

differentially private classifier. It is important to have an upper bound on this error as a cost of preserving privacy.

The work mentioned above is largely restricted to binary classification, while multi-class classifiers are more useful in many practical situations. In this paper, we propose an algorithm for learning multi-class Gaussian classifiers which satisfies differential privacy. Gaussian classifiers that model the distributions of individual classes as being generated from Gaussian distribution or a mixture of Gaussian distributions [3] are commonly used as multi-class classifiers. We use a large margin discriminative algorithm for training the classifier introduced by Sha and Saul [4]. To ensure that the learned multi-class classifier preserves differential privacy, we modify the objective function by introducing a perturbed regularization term.

2   Differential Privacy

In recent years, the differential privacy model proposed by Dwork, *et al.* [1] has emerged as a robust standard for data privacy. It originated from the statistical database model, where the dataset D is a collection of elements and a randomized *query mechanism* M produces a response when performed on a given dataset. Two datasets D and D' differing by at most one element are said to be *adjacent*. There are two proposed definitions for adjacent datasets one based on symmetric difference – D' containing of one entry less than D, and one based on substitution – one entry of D' differs in value from D. We use the substitution definition of adjacency previously used by [5,2], where the one entry of the dataset $D = \{x_1, \ldots, x_{n-1}, x_n\}$ is modified to result in an adjacent dataset $D' = \{x_1, \ldots, x_{n-1}, x'_n\}$. The query mechanism M is said to satisfy differential privacy if the probability of M resulting in a solution S when performed on a dataset D is very close to the probability of M resulting in the same solution S when executed on an adjacent dataset D'. Assuming the query mechanism to be a function $M : D \mapsto \text{range}(M)$ with a probability function P defined over the space of M, differential privacy is formally defined as follows.

Definition 1. *A randomized function M satisfies ϵ-differential privacy if for all adjacent datasets D and D' and for any $S \in \text{range}(M)$,*

$$\left| \log \frac{P\left(M(D) = S\right)}{P\left(M(D') = S\right)} \right| \leq \epsilon.$$

The value of the ϵ parameter, which is referred to as *leakage*, determines the degree of privacy. As there is always a trade-off between privacy and utility, the choice of ϵ is motivated by the requirements of the application.

In a machine learning setting, the query mechanism can be thought of as an algorithm learning the classification, regression or density estimation rule which is evaluated over the training dataset. The output of an algorithm satisfying differential privacy is likely to be same when the value of any single dataset instance is modified, and therefore, no additional information can be obtained about any individual training data instances with certainty by observing the output of the learning algorithm, beyond what is already known to an adversary. Differential privacy is a strong definition of privacy – it provides *ad omnia* guarantee as opposed to most other models that provide *ad hoc* guarantees against specific set of attacks and adversarial behaviors.

2.1   Related Work

The earlier work on differential privacy was related to functional approximations for simple data mining tasks and data release mechanisms [6,7,8,9]. Although many of these works have connection to machine learning problems, more recently the design and analysis of machine learning algorithms satisfying differential privacy has been actively studied. Kasiviswanathan, *et al.* [5] present a framework for converting a general agnostic PAC learning algorithm to an algorithm that satisfies privacy constraints. Chaudhuri and Monteleoni [2] use the exponential mechanism [10] to create a differentially private logistic regression classifier by adding Laplace noise to the estimated parameters. They propose another differentially private formulation which involves modifying the objective function of the logistic regression classifier by adding a linear term scaled by Laplace noise. The second formulation is advantageous because it does not require the classifier sensitivity which is difficult to calculate in general. Also, it can be shown that using a perturbed objective function introduces a lower error as compared to the exponential mechanism.

However, the above mentioned differentially private classification algorithms only address the problem of binary classification. Although it is possible to extend binary classification algorithms to multi-class using techniques like one-vs-all, it is much more expensive to do so as compared to a naturally multi-class classification algorithm. Jagannathan, *et al.* [11] present a differentially private random decision tree learning algorithm which can be applied to multi-class classification. Their approach involves perturbing leaf nodes using the sensitivity method, and they do not provide theoretical analysis of excess risk of the perturbed classifier. In this paper, we propose a modification to the naturally multi-class large margin Gaussian classification algorithm [4,12].

3   Large Margin Gaussian Classifiers

We investigate the large margin multi-class classification algorithm introduced by Sha and Saul [4]. The training dataset $(\boldsymbol{x}, \boldsymbol{y})^1$ contains n d-dimensional iid training data instances $\boldsymbol{x}_i \in \mathbb{R}^d$ each with labels $y_i \in \{1, \ldots, C\}$. We consider the setting where each class is modeled as a single Gaussian ellipsoid. Each class ellipsoid is parametrized by the centroid $\boldsymbol{\mu}_c \in \mathbb{R}^d$, the inverse covariance matrix $\boldsymbol{\Psi}_c \in \mathbb{R}^{d \times d}$, and a scalar offset $\theta_c \geq 0$. The decision rule is to assign an instance $\boldsymbol{x}_i$ to the class having smallest Mahalanobis distance [13] with the scalar offset from $\boldsymbol{x}_i$ to the centroid of that class.

---

[1] Notation: vectors and matrices are denoted by **boldface**.

$$y_i = \operatorname*{argmin}_c \, (\boldsymbol{x}_i - \boldsymbol{\mu}_c)^T \boldsymbol{\Psi}_c (\boldsymbol{x}_i - \boldsymbol{\mu}_c) + \theta_c. \tag{1}$$

To simplify the notation, we expand $(\boldsymbol{x}_i - \boldsymbol{\mu}_c)^T \boldsymbol{\Psi}_c (\boldsymbol{x}_i - \boldsymbol{\mu}_c)$ and collect the parameters for each class as the following $(d+1) \times (d+1)$ *positive semidefinite* matrix

$$\boldsymbol{\Phi}_c = \begin{bmatrix} \boldsymbol{\Psi}_c & -\boldsymbol{\Psi}_c \boldsymbol{\mu}_c \\ -\boldsymbol{\mu}_c^T \boldsymbol{\Psi}_c & \boldsymbol{\mu}_c^T \boldsymbol{\Psi}_c \boldsymbol{\mu}_c + \theta_c \end{bmatrix} \tag{2}$$

and append a unit element to each d-dimensional vector $\boldsymbol{x}_i$. The decision rule for a data instance $\boldsymbol{x}_i$ simplifies to

$$y_i = \operatorname*{argmin}_c \, \boldsymbol{x}_i^T \boldsymbol{\Phi}_c \boldsymbol{x}_i. \tag{3}$$

The discriminative training procedure involves estimating a set of positive semidefinite matrices $\{\boldsymbol{\Phi}_1, \ldots, \boldsymbol{\Phi}_C\}$ from the training data $\{(\boldsymbol{x}_1, y_1), \ldots, (\boldsymbol{x}_n, y_n)\}$ which optimize the performance on the decision rule mentioned above. We apply the large margin intuition about the classifier maximizing the distance of training data instances from the decision boundaries having a lower error. This leads to the classification algorithm being robust to outliers with provably strong generalization guarantees. Formally, we require that for each training data instance $\boldsymbol{x}_i$ with label y_i, the distance from $\boldsymbol{x}_i$ to the centroid of class y_i is at least less than its distance from centroids of all other classes by one.

$$\forall c \neq y_i : \boldsymbol{x}_i^T \boldsymbol{\Phi}_c \boldsymbol{x}_i \geq 1 + \boldsymbol{x}_i^T \boldsymbol{\Phi}_{y_i} \boldsymbol{x}_i.$$

Analogous to support vector machines, the training algorithm is an optimization problem minimizing the *hinge loss* denoted by $[f]_+ = \max(0, f)$, with a linear penalty for incorrect classification. We use the sum of traces of inverse covariance matrices for each classes as a *regularization* term. The regularization requires that if we can learn a classifier which labels every training data instance correctly, we choose the one with the lowest inverse covariance or highest covariance for each class ellipsoid as this prevents the classifier from over-fitting. The parameter λ controls the trade off between the loss function and the regularization.

$$J(\boldsymbol{\Phi}, \boldsymbol{x}, \boldsymbol{y}) = \sum_i \sum_{c \neq y_i} \left[1 + \boldsymbol{x}_i^T (\boldsymbol{\Phi}_{y_i} - \boldsymbol{\Phi}_c) \boldsymbol{x}_i \right]_+ + \lambda \sum_c \operatorname{trace}(\boldsymbol{\Psi}_c). \tag{4}$$

The inverse covariance matrix $\boldsymbol{\Psi}_c$ is contained in the upper left size $d \times d$ block of the matrix $\boldsymbol{\Phi}_c$. We replace it with $\mathbf{I}_{\boldsymbol{\Phi}} \boldsymbol{\Phi}_c \mathbf{I}_{\boldsymbol{\Phi}}$, where $\mathbf{I}_{\boldsymbol{\Phi}}$ is the truncated size $(d+1) \times (d+1)$ identity matrix with the last diagonal element $I_{\boldsymbol{\Phi}_{d+1,d+1}}$ set to zero. The optimization problem becomes

$$\begin{aligned} J(\boldsymbol{\Phi}, \boldsymbol{x}, \boldsymbol{y}) &= \sum_i \sum_{c \neq y_i} \left[1 + \boldsymbol{x}_i^T (\boldsymbol{\Phi}_{y_i} - \boldsymbol{\Phi}_c) \boldsymbol{x}_i \right]_+ + \lambda \sum_c \operatorname{trace}(\mathbf{I}_{\boldsymbol{\Phi}} \boldsymbol{\Phi}_c \mathbf{I}_{\boldsymbol{\Phi}}) \\ &= L(\boldsymbol{\Phi}, \boldsymbol{x}, \boldsymbol{y}) + N(\boldsymbol{\Phi}). \end{aligned} \tag{5}$$

The hinge loss being non-differentiable is not convenient for our analysis; we replace it with a surrogate loss function called Huber loss l_h [14] which has similar characteristics as the hinge loss for small values of h.

$$\ell_h(\mathbf{\Phi}_c, \boldsymbol{x}_i, y_i) = \begin{cases} 0 & \text{if } \boldsymbol{x}_i^T(\mathbf{\Phi}_c - \mathbf{\Phi}_{y_i})\boldsymbol{x}_i > h, \\ \frac{1}{4h}\left[h - \boldsymbol{x}_i^T(\mathbf{\Phi}_{y_i} - \mathbf{\Phi}_c)\boldsymbol{x}_i\right]^2 & \text{if } |\boldsymbol{x}_i^T(\mathbf{\Phi}_c - \mathbf{\Phi}_c)\boldsymbol{x}_i| \leq h \\ -\boldsymbol{x}_i^T(\mathbf{\Phi}_{y_i} - \mathbf{\Phi}_c)\boldsymbol{x}_i & \text{if } \boldsymbol{x}_i^T(\mathbf{\Phi}_c - \mathbf{\Phi}_{y_i})\boldsymbol{x}_i < -h. \end{cases} \quad (6)$$

The objective function is convex function of positive semidefinite matrices $\mathbf{\Phi}_c$. The optimization can be formulated as a semidefinite programming problem [15] and be solved efficiently using interior point methods.

The large margin classification framework can be easily extended to modeling each class with a mixture of Gaussians. Similar to support vector machines, when training with non-separable data, we can introduce slack parameters to permit margin violations. These extensions do not change the basic characteristics of the learning algorithm. The optimization problem remains a convex semidefinite program with piecewise linear terms and is equally tractable. For simplicity, we restrict our discussion to single Gaussians and hard margins in this paper. As we shall see, it is easy to extend our proposed modifications to these cases.

4   Differentially Private Large Margin Gaussian Classifiers

We modify the large margin Gaussian classification formulation to satisfy differential privacy by introducing a perturbation term in the objective function. As we will see in Section 5.2, this modification leads to a classifier that preserves differential privacy.

We generate the size $(d + 1) \times (d + 1)$ perturbation matrix $\mathbf{b}$ with density

$$P(\mathbf{b}) \propto \exp\left(-\frac{\epsilon}{2}\|\mathbf{b}\|\right), \quad (7)$$

where $\|\cdot\|$ is the Frobenius norm (element-wise ℓ_2 norm) and ϵ is the privacy parameter. One method of generating such a $\mathbf{b}$ matrix is to sample the norm $\|\mathbf{b}\|$ from $\Gamma\left((d+1)^2, \frac{2}{\epsilon}\right)$ and the direction of $\mathbf{b}$ at random.

Our proposed learning algorithm minimizes the following objective function $J_p(\mathbf{\Phi}, \boldsymbol{x}, \boldsymbol{y})$, where the subscript p denotes privacy.

$$J_p(\mathbf{\Phi}, \boldsymbol{x}, \boldsymbol{y}) = L(\mathbf{\Phi}, \boldsymbol{x}, \boldsymbol{y}) + \lambda \sum_c \text{trace}(\mathbf{I}_{\mathbf{\Phi}} \mathbf{\Phi}_c \mathbf{I}_{\mathbf{\Phi}}) + \sum_c \sum_{ij} b_{ij} \Phi_{cij}$$

$$= J(\mathbf{\Phi}, \boldsymbol{x}, \boldsymbol{y}) + \sum_c \sum_{ij} b_{ij} \Phi_{cij}. \quad (8)$$

As the dimensionality of the perturbation matrix $\mathbf{b}$ is same as that of the classifier parameters $\mathbf{\Phi}_c$, the parameter space of $\mathbf{\Phi}$ does not change after perturbation. In other words, given two datasets $(\boldsymbol{x}, \boldsymbol{y})$ and $(\boldsymbol{x}', \boldsymbol{y}')$, if $\mathbf{\Phi}^P$ minimizes $J_p(\mathbf{\Phi}, \boldsymbol{x}, \boldsymbol{y})$, it is always possible to have $\mathbf{\Phi}^P$ minimize $J_p(\mathbf{\Phi}, \boldsymbol{x}', \boldsymbol{y}')$. This is a necessary condition for the classifier $\mathbf{\Phi}^P$ satisfying differential privacy.

Furthermore, as the perturbation term is convex and positive semidefinite, the perturbed objective function $J_p(\boldsymbol{\Phi}, \boldsymbol{x}, \boldsymbol{y})$ has the same properties as the unperturbed objective function $J(\boldsymbol{\Phi}, \boldsymbol{x}, \boldsymbol{y})$. Also, the perturbation does not introduce any additional computational cost as compared to the original algorithm.

5   Theoretical Analysis

5.1   Proof of Differential Privacy

We prove that the classifier minimizing the perturbed optimization function $J_p(\boldsymbol{\Phi}, \boldsymbol{x}, \boldsymbol{y})$ satisfies ϵ-differential privacy in the following theorem. Given a dataset $(\boldsymbol{x}, \boldsymbol{y}) = \{(\boldsymbol{x}_1, y_1), \ldots, (\boldsymbol{x}_{n-1}, y_{n-1}), (\boldsymbol{x}_n, y_n)\}$, the probability of learning the classifier $\boldsymbol{\Phi}^p$ is close to the the probability of learning the same classifier $\boldsymbol{\Phi}^p$ given an adjacent dataset $(\boldsymbol{x}', \boldsymbol{y}') = \{(\boldsymbol{x}_1, y_1), \ldots, (\boldsymbol{x}_{n-1}, y_{n-1}), (\boldsymbol{x}'_n, y'_n)\}$ differing wlog on the nth instance. As we mentioned in the previous section, it is always possible to find such a classifier $\boldsymbol{\Phi}^p$ minimizing both $J_p(\boldsymbol{\Phi}, \boldsymbol{x}, \boldsymbol{y})$ and $J_p(\boldsymbol{\Phi}, \boldsymbol{x}', \boldsymbol{y}')$ due to the perturbation matrix being in the same space as the optimization parameters.

Our proof requires a strictly convex perturbed objective function resulting in a unique solution $\boldsymbol{\Phi}^p$ minimizing it. This in turn requires that the loss function $L(\boldsymbol{\Phi}, \boldsymbol{x}, \boldsymbol{y})$ is strictly convex and differentiable, and the regularization term $N(\boldsymbol{\Phi})$ is convex. These seemingly strong constraints are satisfied by many commonly used classification algorithms such as logistic regression, support vector machines, and our general perturbation technique can be extended to those algorithms. In our proposed algorithm, the Huber loss is by definition a differentiable function and the trace regularization term is convex and differentiable. Additionally, we require that the difference in the gradients of $L(\boldsymbol{\Phi}, \boldsymbol{x}, \boldsymbol{y})$ calculated over for two adjacent training datasets is bounded. We prove this property in Lemma 1 given in the appendix.

Theorem 1. *For any two adjacent training datasets $(\boldsymbol{x}, \boldsymbol{y})$ and $(\boldsymbol{x}', \boldsymbol{y}')$, the classifier $\boldsymbol{\Phi}^p$ minimizing the perturbed objective function $J_p(\boldsymbol{\Phi}, \boldsymbol{x}, \boldsymbol{y})$ satisfies differential privacy.*

$$\left| \log \frac{P(\boldsymbol{\Phi}^p | \boldsymbol{x}, \boldsymbol{y})}{P(\boldsymbol{\Phi}^p | \boldsymbol{x}', \boldsymbol{y}')} \right| \leq \epsilon',$$

where $\epsilon' = \epsilon + k$ for a constant factor $k = \log\left(1 + \frac{2\alpha}{n\lambda} + \frac{\alpha^2}{n^2\lambda^2}\right)$ with a constant value of α.

Proof. As $J(\boldsymbol{\Phi}, \boldsymbol{x}, \boldsymbol{y})$ is convex and differentiable, there is a unique solution $\boldsymbol{\Phi}^*$ that minimizes it. As the perturbation term $\sum_c \sum_{ij} b_{ij} \Phi_{cij}$ is also convex and differentiable, the perturbed objective function $J_p(\boldsymbol{\Phi}, \boldsymbol{x}, \boldsymbol{y})$ also has a unique solution $\boldsymbol{\Phi}^p$ that minimizes it. Differentiating $J_p(\boldsymbol{\Phi}, \boldsymbol{x}, \boldsymbol{y})$ wrt $\boldsymbol{\Phi}_c$, we have

$$\frac{\partial}{\partial \boldsymbol{\Phi}_c} J_p(\boldsymbol{\Phi}, \boldsymbol{x}, \boldsymbol{y}) = \frac{\partial}{\partial \boldsymbol{\Phi}_c} L(\boldsymbol{\Phi}, \boldsymbol{x}, \boldsymbol{y}) + \lambda \mathbf{I}_{\boldsymbol{\Phi}} + \mathbf{b}. \tag{9}$$

Substituting the optimal $\boldsymbol{\Phi}_c^p$ in the derivative gives us

$$\lambda \mathbf{I}_\Phi + \mathbf{b} = -\frac{\partial}{\partial \boldsymbol{\Phi}_c} L(\boldsymbol{\Phi}^p, \boldsymbol{x}, \boldsymbol{y}).$$

This relation shows that two different values of $\mathbf{b}$ cannot result in the same optimal $\boldsymbol{\Phi}^p$. As the perturbed objective function $J_p(\boldsymbol{\Phi}, \boldsymbol{x}, \boldsymbol{y})$ is also convex and differentiable, there is a bijective map between the perturbation $\mathbf{b}$ and the unique $\boldsymbol{\Phi}^p$ minimizing $J_p(\boldsymbol{\Phi}, \boldsymbol{x}, \boldsymbol{y})$.

Let $\mathbf{b_1}$ and $\mathbf{b_2}$ be the two perturbations applied when training with the adjacent datasets $(\boldsymbol{x}, \boldsymbol{y})$ and $(\boldsymbol{x'}, \boldsymbol{y'})$, respectively. Assuming that we obtain the same optimal solution $\boldsymbol{\Phi}^p$ while minimizing both $J_p(\boldsymbol{\Phi}, \boldsymbol{x}, \boldsymbol{y})$ with perturbation $\mathbf{b_1}$ and $J_p(\boldsymbol{\Phi}, \boldsymbol{x}, \boldsymbol{y})$ with perturbation $\mathbf{b_2}$,

$$\lambda \mathbf{I}_\Phi + \mathbf{b_1} = -\frac{\partial}{\partial \boldsymbol{\Phi}_c} L(\boldsymbol{\Phi}^p, \boldsymbol{x}, \boldsymbol{y}),$$

$$\lambda \mathbf{I}_\Phi + \mathbf{b_2} = -\frac{\partial}{\partial \boldsymbol{\Phi}_c} L(\boldsymbol{\Phi}^p, \boldsymbol{x'}, \boldsymbol{y'}),$$

$$\mathbf{b_1} - \mathbf{b_2} = \frac{\partial}{\partial \boldsymbol{\Phi}_c} L(\boldsymbol{\Phi}^p, \boldsymbol{x'}, \boldsymbol{y'}) - \frac{\partial}{\partial \boldsymbol{\Phi}_c} L(\boldsymbol{\Phi}^p, \boldsymbol{x}, \boldsymbol{y}). \tag{10}$$

We take the Frobenius norm of both sides and apply the bound on the the RHS as given by Lemma 1.

$$\|\mathbf{b_1} - \mathbf{b_2}\| = \left\| \frac{\partial}{\partial \boldsymbol{\Phi}_c} L(\boldsymbol{\Phi}^p, \boldsymbol{x'}, \boldsymbol{y'}) - \frac{\partial}{\partial \boldsymbol{\Phi}_c} L(\boldsymbol{\Phi}^p, \boldsymbol{x}, \boldsymbol{y}) \right\|$$

$$= \left\| \sum_{i=1}^{n-1} \frac{\partial}{\partial \boldsymbol{\Phi}_c} L(\boldsymbol{\Phi}^p, \boldsymbol{x}_i, y_i) + \frac{\partial}{\partial \boldsymbol{\Phi}_c} L(\boldsymbol{\Phi}^p, \boldsymbol{x'}_n, y'_n) \right.$$

$$\left. - \sum_{i=1}^{n-1} \frac{\partial}{\partial \boldsymbol{\Phi}_c} L(\boldsymbol{\Phi}^p, \boldsymbol{x}_i, y_i) - \frac{\partial}{\partial \boldsymbol{\Phi}_c} L(\boldsymbol{\Phi}^p, \boldsymbol{x}_n, y_n) \right\|$$

$$= \left\| \frac{\partial}{\partial \boldsymbol{\Phi}_c} L(\boldsymbol{\Phi}^p, \boldsymbol{x'}_n, y'_n) - \frac{\partial}{\partial \boldsymbol{\Phi}_c} L(\boldsymbol{\Phi}^p, \boldsymbol{x}_n, y_n) \right\| \leq 2.$$

Using this property, we can calculate the ratio of densities of drawing the perturbation matrices $\mathbf{b_1}$ and $\mathbf{b_2}$ as

$$\frac{P(\mathbf{b} = \mathbf{b_1})}{P(\mathbf{b} = \mathbf{b_2})} = \frac{\frac{1}{\text{surf}(\|\mathbf{b_1}\|)} \|\mathbf{b_1}\|^d \exp\left[-\frac{\epsilon}{2}\|\mathbf{b_1}\|\right]}{\frac{1}{\text{surf}(\|\mathbf{b_2}\|)} \|\mathbf{b_2}\|^d \exp\left[-\frac{\epsilon}{2}\|\mathbf{b_2}\|\right]},$$

where $\text{surf}(\|\mathbf{b}\|)$ is the surface area of the $(d+1)$-dimensional hypersphere with radius $\|\mathbf{b}\|$. As $\text{surf}(\|\mathbf{b}\|) = \text{surf}(1)\|\mathbf{b}\|^d$, where $\text{surf}(1)$ is the area of the unit $(d+1)$-dimensional hypersphere, the ratio of the densities becomes

$$\frac{P(\mathbf{b} = \mathbf{b_1})}{P(\mathbf{b} = \mathbf{b_2})} = \exp\left[\frac{\epsilon}{2}(\|\mathbf{b_2}\| - \|\mathbf{b_1}\|)\right] \leq \exp\left[\frac{\epsilon}{2}\|\mathbf{b_2} - \mathbf{b_1}\|\right] \leq \exp(\epsilon). \tag{11}$$

The ratio of the densities of learning $\mathbf{\Phi}^p$ using the adjacent datasets $(\boldsymbol{x}, \boldsymbol{y})$ and $(\boldsymbol{x}', \boldsymbol{y}')$ is given by

$$\frac{P(\mathbf{\Phi}^p | \boldsymbol{x}, \boldsymbol{y})}{P(\mathbf{\Phi}^p | \boldsymbol{x}', \boldsymbol{y}')} = \frac{P(\mathbf{b} = \mathbf{b}_1)}{P(\mathbf{b} = \mathbf{b}_2)} \frac{|\det(\mathbf{J}(\mathbf{\Phi}^p \to \mathbf{b}_1 | \boldsymbol{x}, \boldsymbol{y}))|^{-1}}{|\det(\mathbf{J}(\mathbf{\Phi}^p \to \mathbf{b}_2 | \boldsymbol{x}', \boldsymbol{y}'))|^{-1}}, \tag{12}$$

where $\mathbf{J}(\mathbf{\Phi}^p \to \mathbf{b}_1 | \boldsymbol{x}, \boldsymbol{y})$ and $\mathbf{J}(\mathbf{\Phi}^p \to \mathbf{b}_2 | \boldsymbol{x}', \boldsymbol{y}')$ are the Jacobian matrices of the bijective mappings from $\mathbf{\Phi}^p$ to $\mathbf{b}_1$ and $\mathbf{b}_2$, respectively. Following a procedure identical to Theorem 2 of [16] (omitted due to lack of space), it can be shown that the ratio of Jacobian determinants is upper bounded by a constant factor $\exp(k) = 1 + \frac{2\alpha}{n\lambda} + \frac{\alpha^2}{n^2\lambda^2}$ for a constant value of α. Therefore, the ratio of the densities of learning $\mathbf{\Phi}^p$ using the adjacent datasets becomes

$$\frac{P(\mathbf{\Phi}^p | \boldsymbol{x}, \boldsymbol{y})}{P(\mathbf{\Phi}^p | \boldsymbol{x}', \boldsymbol{y}')} \leq \exp(\epsilon + k) = \exp(\epsilon'). \tag{13}$$

Similarly, we can show that the probability ratio is lower bounded by $\exp(-\epsilon')$, which together with Equation (13) satisfies the definition of differential privacy. □

5.2 Analysis of Excess Error

In the remainder of this section, we denote the terms $J(\mathbf{\Phi}, \mathbf{x}, \mathbf{y})$ and $L(\mathbf{\Phi}, \mathbf{x}, \mathbf{y})$ by $J(\mathbf{\Phi})$ and $L(\mathbf{\Phi})$, respectively for conciseness. The objective function $J(\mathbf{\Phi})$ contains the loss function $L(\mathbf{\Phi})$ computed over the training data $(\mathbf{x}, \mathbf{y})$ and the regularization term $N(\mathbf{\Phi})$ – this is known as the regularized *empirical risk* of the classifier $\mathbf{\Phi}$. In the following theorem, we establish a bound on the regularized empirical excess risk of the differentially private classifier minimizing the perturbed objective function $J_p(\mathbf{\Phi})$ over the classifier minimizing the unperturbed objective function $J(\mathbf{\Phi})$. We use the strong convexity of the objective function $J(\mathbf{\Phi})$ as given by Lemma 2.

Theorem 2. *With probability at least $1 - \delta$, the regularized empirical excess risk of the classifier $\mathbf{\Phi}^p$ minimizing the perturbed objective function $J_p(\mathbf{\Phi})$ over the classifier $\mathbf{\Phi}^*$ minimizing the unperturbed objective function $J(\mathbf{\Phi})$ is bounded as*

$$J(\mathbf{\Phi}^p) \leq J(\mathbf{\Phi}^*) + \frac{8(d+1)^4 C}{\epsilon^2 \lambda} \log^2 \left(\frac{d}{\delta}\right).$$

Proof. We use the definition of $J_p(\mathbf{\Phi}) = J(\mathbf{\Phi}) + \sum_c \sum_{ij} b_{ij} \Phi_{cij}$ and the optimality of $\mathbf{\Phi}^p$, i.e., $J_p(\mathbf{\Phi}^p) \leq J_p(\mathbf{\Phi}^*)$.

$$J(\mathbf{\Phi}^p) + \sum_c \sum_{ij} b_{ij} \Phi_{cij}^p \leq J(\mathbf{\Phi}^*) + \sum_c \sum_{ij} b_{ij} \Phi_{cij}^*,$$

$$J(\mathbf{\Phi}^p) \leq J(\mathbf{\Phi}^*) + \sum_c \sum_{ij} b_{ij}(\Phi_{cij}^* - \Phi_{cij}^p). \tag{14}$$

Using the strong convexity of $J(\mathbf{\Phi})$ as given by Lemma 2 and the optimality of $J(\mathbf{\Phi}^*)$, we have

$$J(\mathbf{\Phi}^*) \leq J\left(\frac{\mathbf{\Phi}^p + \mathbf{\Phi}^*}{2}\right) \leq \frac{J(\mathbf{\Phi}^p) + J(\mathbf{\Phi}^*)}{2} - \frac{\lambda}{8}\sum_c \|\mathbf{\Phi}_c^* - \mathbf{\Phi}_c^p\|^2,$$

$$J(\mathbf{\Phi}^p) - J(\mathbf{\Phi}^*) \geq \frac{\lambda}{4}\sum_c \|\mathbf{\Phi}_c^* - \mathbf{\Phi}_c^p\|^2. \tag{15}$$

Similarly, using the strong convexity of $J_p(\mathbf{\Phi})$ and the optimality of $J_p(\mathbf{\Phi}^p)$,

$$J_p(\mathbf{\Phi}^p) \leq J_p\left(\frac{\mathbf{\Phi}^p + \mathbf{\Phi}^*}{2}\right) \leq \frac{J_p(\mathbf{\Phi}^p) + J_p(\mathbf{\Phi}^*)}{2} - \frac{\lambda}{8}\sum_c \|\mathbf{\Phi}_c^p - \mathbf{\Phi}_c^*\|^2,$$

$$J_p(\mathbf{\Phi}^*) - J_p(\mathbf{\Phi}^p) \geq \frac{\lambda}{4}\sum_c \|\mathbf{\Phi}_c^p - \mathbf{\Phi}_c^*\|^2.$$

Substituting the definition $J_p(\mathbf{\Phi}) = J(\mathbf{\Phi}) + \sum_c \sum_{ij} b_{ij}\Phi_{cij}$,

$$J(\mathbf{\Phi}^*) + \sum_c \sum_{ij} b_{ij}\Phi_{cij}^* - J(\mathbf{\Phi}^p) - \sum_c \sum_{ij} b_{ij}\Phi_{cij}^p \geq \frac{\lambda}{4}\sum_c \|\mathbf{\Phi}_c^* - \mathbf{\Phi}_c^p\|^2$$

$$\sum_c \sum_{ij} b_{ij}(\Phi_{cij}^* - \Phi_{cij}^p) - (J(\mathbf{\Phi}^p) - J(\mathbf{\Phi}^*)) \geq \frac{\lambda}{4}\sum_c \|\mathbf{\Phi}_c^* - \mathbf{\Phi}_c^p\|^2.$$

Substituting the lower bound on $J(\mathbf{\Phi}^p) - J(\mathbf{\Phi}^*)$ given by Equation (15),

$$\sum_c \sum_{ij} b_{ij}(\Phi_{cij}^* - \Phi_{cij}^p) \geq \frac{\lambda}{2}\sum_c \|\mathbf{\Phi}_c^* - \mathbf{\Phi}_c^p\|^2,$$

$$\left[\sum_c \sum_{ij} b_{ij}(\Phi_{cij}^* - \Phi_{cij}^p)\right]^2 \geq \frac{\lambda^2}{4}\left[\sum_c \|\mathbf{\Phi}_c^* - \mathbf{\Phi}_c^p\|^2\right]^2. \tag{16}$$

Using the Cauchy-Schwarz inequality, we have,

$$\left[\sum_c \sum_{ij} b_{ij}(\Phi_{cij}^* - \Phi_{cij}^p)\right]^2 \leq C\|\mathbf{b}\|^2 \sum_c \|\mathbf{\Phi}_c^* - \mathbf{\Phi}_c^p\|^2. \tag{17}$$

Combining this with Equation (16) gives us

$$C\|\mathbf{b}\|^2 \sum_c \|\mathbf{\Phi}_c^* - \mathbf{\Phi}_c^p\|^2 \geq \frac{\lambda^2}{4}\left[\sum_c \|\mathbf{\Phi}_c^* - \mathbf{\Phi}_c^p\|^2\right]^2,$$

$$\sum_c \|\mathbf{\Phi}_c^* - \mathbf{\Phi}_c^p\|^2 \leq \frac{4C}{\lambda^2}\|\mathbf{b}\|^2. \tag{18}$$

Combining this with Equation (17) gives us

$$\sum_c \sum_{ij} b_{ij}(\Phi^*_{cij} - \Phi^p_{cij}) \le \frac{2C}{\lambda}\|\mathbf{b}\|^2.$$

We bound $\|\mathbf{b}\|^2$ with probability at least $1 - \delta$ as given by Lemma 4.

$$\sum_c \sum_{ij} b_{ij}(\Phi^*_{cij} - \Phi^p_{cij}) \le \frac{8(d + 1)^4 C}{\epsilon^2 \lambda} \log^2\left(\frac{d}{\delta}\right). \tag{19}$$

Substituting this in Equation (14) proves the theorem.   □

The upper bound on the regularized empirical risk is in $O(\frac{C}{\epsilon^2})$. The bound increases for smaller values of ϵ which implies tighter privacy and therefore suggests a trade off between privacy and utility.

The regularized empirical risk of a classifier is calculated over a given training dataset. In practice, we are more interested in how the classifier will perform on new test data which is assumed to be generated from the same source as the training data. The expected value of the loss function computed over the data is called the *true risk* $\tilde{L}(\boldsymbol{\Phi}) = \mathbb{E}[L(\boldsymbol{\Phi})]$ of the classifier $\boldsymbol{\Phi}$. In the following theorem, we establish a bound on the true excess risk of the differentially private classifier minimizing the perturbed objective function and the classifier minimizing the original objective function.

Theorem 3. *With probability at least $1 - \delta$, the true excess risk of the classifier $\boldsymbol{\Phi}^p$ minimizing the perturbed objective function $J_p(\boldsymbol{\Phi})$ over the classifier $\boldsymbol{\Phi}^*$ minimizing the unperturbed objective function $J(\boldsymbol{\Phi})$ is bounded as*

$$\tilde{L}(\boldsymbol{\Phi}^p) \le \tilde{L}(\boldsymbol{\Phi}^*) + \frac{4\sqrt{d}(d+1)^2 C}{\epsilon \lambda} \log\left(\frac{d}{\delta}\right)$$
$$+ \frac{8(d+1)^4 C}{\epsilon^2 \lambda} \log^2\left(\frac{d}{\delta}\right) + \frac{16}{\lambda n}\left[32 + \log\left(\frac{1}{\delta}\right)\right].$$

Proof. Let the expected value of the regularized empirical risk be

$$\tilde{J}(\boldsymbol{\Phi}) = \tilde{L}(\boldsymbol{\Phi}) + \lambda \sum_c \text{trace}(\mathbf{I}_\Phi \boldsymbol{\Phi}_c \mathbf{I}_\Phi). \tag{20}$$

Let $\boldsymbol{\Phi}^r$ be the classifier minimizing $\tilde{J}(\boldsymbol{\Phi})$, *i.e.*, $\tilde{J}(\boldsymbol{\Phi}^r) \le \tilde{J}(\boldsymbol{\Phi}^*)$. Rearranging the terms, we have

$$\tilde{J}(\boldsymbol{\Phi}^p) = \tilde{J}(\boldsymbol{\Phi}^*) + [\tilde{J}(\boldsymbol{\Phi}^p) - \tilde{J}(\boldsymbol{\Phi}^r)] + [\tilde{J}(\boldsymbol{\Phi}^r) - \tilde{J}(\boldsymbol{\Phi}^*)]$$
$$\le \tilde{J}(\boldsymbol{\Phi}^*) + [\tilde{J}(\boldsymbol{\Phi}^p) - \tilde{J}(\boldsymbol{\Phi}^r)].$$

Substituting the definition of $\tilde{J}(\boldsymbol{\Phi})$,

$$\tilde{L}(\boldsymbol{\Phi}^p) + \lambda \sum_c \text{trace}(\mathbf{I}_\Phi \boldsymbol{\Phi}^p_c \mathbf{I}_\Phi) \le \tilde{L}(\boldsymbol{\Phi}^*) + \lambda \sum_c \text{trace}(\mathbf{I}_\Phi \boldsymbol{\Phi}^*_c \mathbf{I}_\Phi) + [\tilde{J}(\boldsymbol{\Phi}^p) - \tilde{J}(\boldsymbol{\Phi}^r)],$$

$$\tilde{L}(\boldsymbol{\Phi}^p) \le \tilde{L}(\boldsymbol{\Phi}^*) + \lambda \sum_c \text{trace}[\mathbf{I}_\Phi(\boldsymbol{\Phi}^*_c - \boldsymbol{\Phi}^p_c)\mathbf{I}_\Phi] + [\tilde{J}(\boldsymbol{\Phi}^p) - \tilde{J}(\boldsymbol{\Phi}^r)]. \tag{21}$$

From Lemma 3 and Equation (18), we have,

$$\left[\sum_c \text{trace}[\mathbf{I}_\Phi(\Phi_c^* - \Phi_c^p)\mathbf{I}_\Phi]\right]^2 \leq dC \sum_c \|\Phi_c - \Phi_c'\|^2$$

$$\leq \frac{4dC^2}{\lambda^2}\|\mathbf{b}\|^2 = \frac{16d(d+1)^4 C^2}{\epsilon^2 \lambda^2} \log^2\left(\frac{d}{\delta}\right).$$

Taking the square root,

$$\sum_c \text{trace}[\mathbf{I}_\Phi(\Phi_c^* - \Phi_c^p)\mathbf{I}_\Phi] \leq \frac{4\sqrt{d}(d+1)^2 C}{\epsilon\lambda} \log\left(\frac{d}{\delta}\right). \qquad (22)$$

Sridharan, *et al.* [17] present a bound on the true excess risk of any classifier as an expression of the bound on the regularized empirical excess risk for that classifier. With probability at least $1 - \delta$,

$$\tilde{J}(\Phi^p) - \tilde{J}(\Phi^r) \leq 2[J(\Phi^p) - J(\Phi^*)] + \frac{16}{\lambda n}\left[32 + \log\left(\frac{1}{\delta}\right)\right].$$

Substituting the bound from Theorem 2,

$$\tilde{J}(\Phi^p) - \tilde{J}(\Phi^r) \leq \frac{8(d+1)^4 C}{\epsilon^2 \lambda} \log^2\left(\frac{d}{\delta}\right) + \frac{16}{\lambda n}\left[32 + \log\left(\frac{1}{\delta}\right)\right]. \qquad (23)$$

Substituting the results from Equations (22) and (23) into Equation (21) proves the theorem. □

Similar to the bound on the regularized empirical excess risk, the bound on the true excess risk is also inversely proportional to ϵ reflecting the privacy-utility trade-off. The bound is linear in the number of classes C, which is a consequence of the multi-class classification. The classifier learned using a higher value of the regularization parameter λ will have a higher covariance for each class ellipsoid. This would also make the classifier less sensitive to the perturbation. This intuition is confirmed by the fact that the true excess risk bound is inversely proportional to λ.

6   Conclusion

In this paper, we present a discriminatively trained Gaussian classification algorithm that satisfies differential privacy. Our proposed technique involves adding a perturbation term to the objective function. We prove that the proposed algorithm satisfies differential privacy and establish a bound on the excess risk of the classifier learned by the algorithm which is directly proportional to the number of classes and inversely proportional to the privacy parameter ϵ reflecting a trade-off between privacy and utility.

In the future, we plan to extend this work along two main directions: extending our perturbation technique for a general class of learning algorithms and applying results from theory of large margin classifiers to arrive at tighter excess risk bounds for the differentially private large margin classifiers. Our intuition is that compared to other classification algorithms, a large margin classifier should be much more robust to perturbation. This would also give us insights into designing low error inducing mechanisms for differentially private classifiers.

Acknowledgements

We would like to thank the anonymous reviewers for their insightful comments.

References

1. Dwork, C.: Differential privacy. In: Bugliesi, M., Preneel, B., Sassone, V., Wegener, I. (eds.) ICALP 2006. LNCS, vol. 4052, pp. 1–12. Springer, Heidelberg (2006)
2. Chaudhuri, K., Monteleoni, C.: Privacy-preserving logistic regression. In: Neural Information Processing Systems, pp. 289–296 (2008)
3. McLachlan, G., Peel, D.: Finite Mixture Models. Wiley series in probability and statistics. Wiley-Interscience, Hoboken (2000)
4. Sha, F., Saul, L.K.: Large margin gaussian mixture modeling for phonetic classification and recognition. In: IEEE International Conference on Acoustics, Speech and Signal Processing, pp. 265–268 (2006)
5. Kasiviswanathan, S.P., Lee, H.K., Nissim, K., Raskhodnikova, S., Smith, A.: What can we learn privately? In: IEEE Symposium on Foundations of Computer Science, pp. 531–540 (2008)
6. Dinur, I., Nissim, K.: Revealing information while preserving privacy. In: Symposium on Principles of Database Systems (2003)
7. Dwork, C., Nissim, K.: Privacy-preserving datamining on vertically partitioned databases. In: Franklin, M. (ed.) CRYPTO 2004. LNCS, vol. 3152, pp. 528–544. Springer, Heidelberg (2004)
8. Blum, A., Dwork, C., McSherry, F., Nissim, K.: Practical privacy: The suLQ framework. In: Symposium on Principles of Database Systems (2005)
9. Barak, B., Chaudhuri, K., Dwork, C., Kale, S., McSherry, F., Talwar, K.: Privacy, accuracy, and consistency too: a holistic solution to contingency table release. In: Symposium on Principles of Database Systems, pp. 273–282 (2007)
10. Dwork, C., McSherry, F., Nissim, K., Smith, A.: Calibrating noise to sensitivity in private data analysis. In: Halevi, S., Rabin, T. (eds.) TCC 2006. LNCS, vol. 3876, pp. 265–284. Springer, Heidelberg (2006)
11. Jagannathan, G., Pillaipakkamnatt, K., Wright, R.N.: A practical differentially private random decision tree classifier. In: ICDM Workshop on Privacy Aspects of Data Mining, pp. 114–121 (2009)
12. Sha, F., Saul, L.K.: Large margin hidden markov models for automatic speech recognition. In: Neural Information Processing Systems, pp. 1249–1256 (2007)
13. Mahalanobis, P.C.: On the generalised distance in statistics. Proceedings of the National Institute of Sciences of India 2, 49–55 (1936)
14. Chapelle, O.: Training a support vector machine in the primal. Neural Computation 19(5), 1155–1178 (2007)

15. Vandenberghe, L., Boyd, S.: Semidefinite programming. SIAM Review 38, 49–95 (1996)
16. Chaudhuri, K., Monteleoni, C., Sarwate, A.D.: Differentially private empirical risk minimization. arXiv:0912.0071v4 [cs.LG] (2010)
17. Sridharan, K., Shalev-Shwartz, S., Srebro, N.: Fast rates for regularized objectives. In: Neural Information Processing Systems, pp. 1545–1552 (2008)

Appendix

Lemma 1. *Assuming all the data instances to lie within a unit ℓ_2 ball, the difference in the derivative of Huber loss function $L(\mathbf{\Phi}, \boldsymbol{x}, y)$ calculated over two data instances $(\boldsymbol{x}_i, y_i)$ and $(\boldsymbol{x}_i', y_i')$ is bounded.*

$$\left\| \frac{\partial}{\partial \mathbf{\Phi}_c} L(\mathbf{\Phi}, \boldsymbol{x}_i, y_i) - \frac{\partial}{\partial \mathbf{\Phi}_c} L(\mathbf{\Phi}, \boldsymbol{x}_i', y_i') \right\| \leq 2.$$

Proof. The derivative of the Huber loss function for the data instance $\boldsymbol{x}_i$ with label y_i is

$$\frac{\partial}{\partial \mathbf{\Phi}_c} L(\mathbf{\Phi}, \boldsymbol{x}_i, y_i) = \begin{cases} 0 & if \ \boldsymbol{x}_i^T(\mathbf{\Phi}_c - \mathbf{\Phi}_{y_i})\boldsymbol{x}_i > h, \\ \frac{1}{2h}[h - \boldsymbol{x}_i^T(\mathbf{\Phi}_{y_i} - \mathbf{\Phi}_c)\boldsymbol{x}_i]\boldsymbol{x}_i\boldsymbol{x}_i^T & if \ |\boldsymbol{x}_i^T(\mathbf{\Phi}_c - \mathbf{\Phi}_{y_i})\boldsymbol{x}_i| \leq h, \\ \boldsymbol{x}_i\boldsymbol{x}_i^T & if \ \boldsymbol{x}_i^T(\mathbf{\Phi}_c - \mathbf{\Phi}_{y_i})\boldsymbol{x}_i < -h. \end{cases}$$

The data points lie in a ℓ_2 ball of radius 1, $\forall i : \|\boldsymbol{x}_i\|_2 \leq 1$. Using linear algebra, it is easy to show that the Frobenius norm of the matrix $\boldsymbol{x}_i\boldsymbol{x}_i^T$ is same as the ℓ_2 norm of the vector $\boldsymbol{x}_i$, $\|\boldsymbol{x}_i\boldsymbol{x}_i^T\| = \|\boldsymbol{x}_i\|_2 \leq 1$.

As the term $\frac{1}{2h}[h - \boldsymbol{x}_i^T(\mathbf{\Phi}_{y_i} - \mathbf{\Phi}_c)\boldsymbol{x}_i]$ is at most one when $|\boldsymbol{x}_i^T(\mathbf{\Phi}_c - \mathbf{\Phi}_{y_i})\boldsymbol{x}_i| \leq h$, the Frobenius norm of the derivative of the Huber loss function is at most one in all cases, $\left\| \frac{\partial}{\partial \mathbf{\Phi}_c} L(\mathbf{\Phi}, \boldsymbol{x}_i, y_i) \right\| \leq 1$. Using a similar argument for data instance $\boldsymbol{x}_i'$ with label y_i', we have $\left\| \frac{\partial}{\partial \mathbf{\Phi}_c} L(\mathbf{\Phi}, \boldsymbol{x}_i', y_i') \right\| \leq 1$.

Finally, using the triangle inequality $\|\boldsymbol{a} - \boldsymbol{b}\| = \|\boldsymbol{a} + (-\boldsymbol{b})\| \leq \|\boldsymbol{a}\| + \|\boldsymbol{b}\|$,

$$\left\| \frac{\partial}{\partial \mathbf{\Phi}_c} L(\mathbf{\Phi}, \boldsymbol{x}_i, y_i) - \frac{\partial}{\partial \mathbf{\Phi}_c} L(\mathbf{\Phi}, \boldsymbol{x}_i', y_i') \right\|$$

$$\leq \left\| \frac{\partial}{\partial \mathbf{\Phi}_c} L(\mathbf{\Phi}, \boldsymbol{x}_i, y_i) \right\| + \left\| \frac{\partial}{\partial \mathbf{\Phi}_c} L(\mathbf{\Phi}, \boldsymbol{x}_i', y_i') \right\| \leq 2.$$

$\square$

Lemma 2. *The objective function $J(\mathbf{\Phi})$ is λ-strongly convex. For $0 \leq \alpha \leq 1$,*

$$J(\alpha\mathbf{\Phi} + (1 - \alpha)\mathbf{\Phi}') \leq \alpha J(\mathbf{\Phi}) + (1 - \alpha)J(\mathbf{\Phi}') - \frac{\lambda\alpha(1 - \alpha)}{2} \sum_c \|\mathbf{\Phi}_c - \mathbf{\Phi}_c'\|^2.$$

Proof. By definition, Huber loss is λ-strongly convex, *i.e.*

$$L\left(\alpha\boldsymbol{\Phi} + (1-\alpha)\boldsymbol{\Phi}'\right) \leq \alpha L(\boldsymbol{\Phi}) + (1-\alpha)L(\boldsymbol{\Phi}') - \frac{\lambda\alpha(1-\alpha)}{2}\left\|\boldsymbol{\Phi} - \boldsymbol{\Phi}'\right\|^2. \quad (24)$$

where the Frobenius norm of the matrix set $\boldsymbol{\Phi} - \boldsymbol{\Phi}'$ is the sum of norms of the component matrices $\boldsymbol{\Phi}_c - \boldsymbol{\Phi}'_c$,

$$\left\|\boldsymbol{\Phi} - \boldsymbol{\Phi}'\right\|^2 = \sum_c \left\|\boldsymbol{\Phi}_c - \boldsymbol{\Phi}'_c\right\|^2. \quad (25)$$

As the regularization term $N(\boldsymbol{\Phi})$ is linear,

$$N(\alpha\boldsymbol{\Phi} + (1-\alpha)\boldsymbol{\Phi}') = \lambda\sum_c \text{trace}(\alpha\mathbf{I}_\Phi\boldsymbol{\Phi}_c\mathbf{I}_\Phi + (1-\alpha)\mathbf{I}_\Phi\boldsymbol{\Phi}'_c\mathbf{I}_\Phi) \quad (26)$$

$$= \alpha\lambda\sum_c \text{trace}(\mathbf{I}_\Phi\boldsymbol{\Phi}_c\mathbf{I}_\Phi) + (1-\alpha)\lambda\sum_c \text{trace}(\mathbf{I}_\Phi\boldsymbol{\Phi}'_c\mathbf{I}_\Phi)$$

$$= \alpha N(\boldsymbol{\Phi}) + (1-\alpha)N(\boldsymbol{\Phi}').$$

The lemma follows directly from the definition $J(\boldsymbol{\Phi}) = L(\boldsymbol{\Phi}) + N(\boldsymbol{\Phi})$. $\qquad\square$

Lemma 3

$$\frac{1}{dC}\left[\sum_c trace[\mathbf{I}_\Phi(\boldsymbol{\Phi}_c - \boldsymbol{\Phi}'_c)\mathbf{I}_\Phi]\right]^2 \leq \sum_c \left\|\boldsymbol{\Phi}_c - \boldsymbol{\Phi}'_c\right\|^2.$$

Proof. Let $\Phi_{c,i,j}$ be the $(i,j)^{\text{th}}$ element of the size $(d+1)\times(d+1)$ matrix $\boldsymbol{\Phi}_c - \boldsymbol{\Phi}'_c$. By the definition of the Frobenius norm, and using the identity $N\sum_{i=1}^N x_i^2 \geq (\sum_{i=1}^N x_i)^2$,

$$\sum_c \left\|\boldsymbol{\Phi}_c - \boldsymbol{\Phi}'_c\right\|^2 = \sum_c \sum_{i=1}^{d+1}\sum_{j=1}^{d+1} \Phi_{c,i,j}^2 \geq \sum_c \sum_{i=1}^{d+1} \Phi_{c,i,i}^2 \geq \sum_c \sum_{i=1}^{d} \Phi_{c,i,i}^2$$

$$\geq \frac{1}{dC}\left(\sum_c \sum_{i=1}^{d} \Phi_{c,i,i}\right)^2 = \frac{1}{dC}\left[\sum_c \text{trace}[\mathbf{I}_\Phi(\boldsymbol{\Phi}_c - \boldsymbol{\Phi}'_c)\mathbf{I}_\Phi]\right]^2.$$

$\qquad\square$

Lemma 4

$$P\left[\|\mathbf{b}\| \geq \frac{2(d+1)^2}{\epsilon}\log\left(\frac{d}{\delta}\right)\right] \leq \delta.$$

Proof. Follows from the union bound argument used in Lemma 5 of [2].

Privacy Preserving Protocols
for Eigenvector Computation

Manas Pathak and Bhiksha Raj

Carnegie Mellon University, Pittsburgh, PA 15213, USA
{manasp,bhiksha}@cs.cmu.edu

Abstract. In this paper, we present a protocol for computing the principal eigenvector of a collection of data matrices belonging to multiple semi-honest parties with privacy constraints. Our proposed protocol is based on secure multi-party computation with a semi-honest arbitrator who deals with data encrypted by the other parties using an additive homomorphic cryptosystem. We augment the protocol with randomization and oblivious transfer to make it difficult for any party to estimate properties of the data belonging to other parties from the intermediate steps. The previous approaches towards this problem were based on expensive QR decomposition of correlation matrices, we present an efficient algorithm using the power iteration method. We present an analysis of the correctness, security, and efficiency of protocol.

1 Introduction

Eigenvector computation is one of the most basic tools of data analysis. In any multivariate dataset, the eigenvectors provide information about key trends in the data, as well as the relative importance of the different variables. These find use in a diverse set of applications, including principal component analysis [6], collaborative filtering [3] and PageRank [7]. Not all eigenvectors of the data are equally important; only those corresponding to the highest eigenvalues are used as representations of trends in the data. The most important eigenvector is the *principal* eigenvector corresponding to the maximum eigenvalue.

In many scenarios, the entity that actually computes the eigenvectors is different from the entities that possess the data. For instance, a data mining agency may desire to compute the eigenvectors of a distributed set of records, or an enterprise providing recommendations may want to compute eigenvectors from the personal ratings of subscribers to facilitate making recommendations to new customers. We will refer to such entities as *arbitrators*. Computation of eigenvectors requires the knowledge of either the data from the individual parties or the correlation matrix derived from it. The parties that hold the data may however consider them private and be unwilling to expose any aspect of their individual data to either the arbitrator or to other parties, while being agreeable, in principle, to contribute to the computation of a global trend. As a result, we require a privacy preserving algorithm that can compute the eigenvectors of the aggregate data while maintaining the necessary privacy of the individual data providers.

C. Dimitrakakis et al. (Eds.): PSDML 2010, LNAI 6549, pp. 113–126, 2011.
© Springer-Verlag Berlin Heidelberg 2011

The common approach to this type of problem is to obfuscate individual data through controlled randomization [2]. However, since we desire our estimates to be exact, simple randomization methods that merely ensure accuracy in the mean cannot be employed. Han *et al.* [5] address the problem by computing the complete QR decomposition [4] of privately shared data using cryptographic primitives. This enables all parties to collaboratively compute the complete set of global eigenvectors but does not truly hide the data from individual sources. Given the complete set of eigenvectors and eigenvalues provided by the QR decomposition, any party can reverse engineer the correlation matrix for the data from the remaining parties and compute trends among them. Canny [1] present a different distributed approach that does employ an arbitrator, in their case a *blackboard*, however although individual data instances are hidden, both the arbitrator and individual parties have access to all aggregated individual stages of the computation and the final result is public, which is much less stringent than our privacy constraints.

In this paper, we propose a new privacy-preserving protocol for shared computation of the principal eigenvector of a distributed collection of privately held data. The algorithm is designed such that the individual parties, whom we will refer to as "Alice" and "Bob" learn nothing about each others' data, and only learn the degree to which their own data follow the global trend indicated by the principal eigenvector. The arbitrator, who we call "Trent", coordinates the computation but learns nothing about the data of the individual parties besides the principal eigenvector which he receives at the end of the computation. In our presentation, for simplicity, we initially consider two parties having a share of data. Later we show that the protocol can be naturally generalized to N parties. The data may be split in two possible ways: along data instances or features. In this work, we principally consider the data-split case. However, as we show, our algorithm is easily applied to feature split data as well.

We primarily use the power iteration method [4] to compute the principal eigenvector. We will use a combination of randomization, homomorphic encryption [8] and oblivious transfer (OT) [10] to enforce privacy on the computation. The algorithm assumes the parties to be *semi-honest*. While they are assumed to follow the protocol correctly and refrain from using falsified data as input, they may record and analyze the intermediate results obtained while following the protocol in order to to gain as much information as possible. It is also assumed that no party collude with Trent as this will give Trent access to information.

The computational requirements of the algorithm are the same as that of the power iteration method. In addition, each iteration requires the encryption and decryption of two k dimensional vectors, where k is the dimensionality of the data, as well as transmission of the encrypted vectors to and from Trent. Nevertheless, the encryption and transmission overhead, which is linear in k, may be expected to be significantly lower than the calculating the QR decomposition or similar methods which require repeated transmission of entire matrices. In general, the computational cost of the protocol is dependent on the degree of security we desire as required by the application.

2   Preliminaries

2.1   Power Iteration Method

The power iteration method [4] is an algorithm to find the principal eigenvector and its associated eigenvalue for square matrices. To simplify explanation, we assume that the matrix is diagonalizable with real eigenvalues, although the algorithm is applicable to general square matrices as well [11]. Let A be a size $N \times N$ matrix whose eigenvalues are $\lambda_1, \ldots, \lambda_N$.

The power iteration method computes the principal eigenvector of A through the iteration

$$x_{n+1} = \frac{Ax_n}{\|Ax_n\|},$$

where x_n is a N dimensional vector. If the principal eigenvalue is unique, the series $\omega_n = A^n x_0$ is guaranteed to converge to a scaling of the principal eigenvector. In the standard algorithm, ℓ_2 normalization is used to prevent the magnitude of the vector from overflow and underflow. Other normalization factors can also be used if they do not change the limit of the series.

We assume wlog that $|\lambda_1| \geq \cdots \geq |\lambda_N| \geq 0$. Let v_i be the normalized eigenvector corresponding to λ_i. Since A is assumed to be diagonalizable, the eigenvectors $\{v_1, \ldots, v_N\}$ create a basis for $\mathbb{R}^N$. For unique values of $c_i \in \mathbb{R}^N$, any vector $x_0 \in \mathbb{R}^N$ can be written as $x_0 = \sum_{i=1}^N c_i v_i$. It can be shown that $\frac{1}{|\lambda_1|^n} A^n x_0$ is asymptotically equal to $c_1 v_1$ which forms the basis of the power iteration method and the convergence rate of the algorithm is $\left| \frac{\lambda_2}{\lambda_1} \right|$. The algorithm converges quickly when there is no eigenvalue close in magnitude to the principal eigenvalue.

2.2   Homomorphic Encryption

A homomorphic encryption algorithm allows for operations to be perform on the encrypted data without requiring to know the unencrypted values. If $\cdot$ and $+$ are two operators and x and y are two plaintext elements, a homomorphic encryption function E satisfies

$$E[x] \cdot E[y] = E[x + y].$$

In this work, we use the additive homomorphic Paillier asymmetric key cryptosystem [8].

3   Privacy Preserving Protocol

3.1   Data Setup and Privacy Conditions

We formally define the problem, in which multiple parties, try to compute the principal eigenvector over their collectively held datasets without disclosing any information to each other. For simplicity, we describe the problem with two parties, Alice and Bob; and later show that the algorithm is easily extended to multiple parties.

The parties Alice and Bob are assumed to be *semi-honest* which means that the parties will follow the steps of the protocol correctly and will not try to cheat by passing falsified data aimed at extracting information about other parties. The parties are assumed to be curious in the sense that they may record the outcomes of all intermediate steps of the protocol to extract any possible information. The protocol is coordinated by the semi-honest arbitrator Trent. Alice and Bob communicate directly with Trent rather than each other. Trent performs all the intermediate computations and transfers the results to each party. Although Trent is trusted not to collude with other parties, it is important to note that the parties do not trust Trent with their data and intend to prevent him from being able to see it. Alice and Bob hide information by using a shared key cryptosystem to send only encrypted data to Trent.

We assume that both the datasets can be represented as matrices in which columns and rows correspond to the data samples and the features, respectively. For instance, the individual email collections of Alice and Bob are represented as matrices A and B respectively, in which the columns correspond to the emails, and the rows correspond to the words. The entries of these matrices represent the frequency of occurrence of a given word in a given email. The combined dataset may be split between Alice and Bob in two possible ways. In a *data* split, both Alice and Bob have a disjoint set of data samples with the same features. The aggregate dataset is obtained by concatenating columns given by the data matrix $M = \begin{bmatrix} A & B \end{bmatrix}$ and correlation matrix $M^T M$. In a *feature* split, Alice and Bob have different features of the same data. The aggregate data matrix M is obtained by concatenating rows given by the data matrix $M = \begin{bmatrix} A \\ B \end{bmatrix}$ and correlation matrix $M M^T$. If v is an eigenvector of $M^T M$ with a non-zero eigenvalue λ, we have

$$M^T M v = \lambda v \;\Rightarrow\; M M^T M v = \lambda M v.$$

Therefore, $Mv \neq 0$ is the eigenvector of MM^T with eigenvalue λ. Similarly, any eigenvector of horizontally split data MM^T associated with a non-zero eigenvalue is an eigenvector of vertically split data $M^T M$ corresponding to the same eigenvalue. Hence, we mainly deal with calculating the principal eigenvector of the vertically split data. In practice the correlation matrix that has the smaller size should be used to reduce the computational cost of eigen-decomposition algorithms.

For vertical data split, if Alice's data A is of size $k \times m$ and Bob's data B is of size $k \times n$, the combined data matrix will be $M_{k \times (m+n)}$. The correlation matrix of size $(m + n) \times (m + n)$ is given by

$$M^T M = \begin{bmatrix} A^T A & A^T B \\ B^T A & B^T B \end{bmatrix}.$$

3.2   The Basic Protocol

The power iteration algorithm computes the principal eigenvector of $M^T M$ by updating and normalizing the vector x_t until convergence. Starting with a random vector x_0, we calculate

$$x_{i+1} = \frac{M^T M \ x_i}{\| M^T M \ x_i \|}.$$

For privacy, we split the vector x_i into two parts, α_i and β_i. α_i corresponds to the first m components of x_i and β_i corresponds to the remaining n components. In each iteration, we need to securely compute

$$M^T M x_i = \begin{bmatrix} A^T A & A^T B \\ B^T A & B^T B \end{bmatrix} \begin{bmatrix} \alpha_i \\ \beta_i \end{bmatrix} = \begin{bmatrix} A^T (A\alpha_i + B\beta_i) \\ B^T (A\alpha_i + B\beta_i) \end{bmatrix} = \begin{bmatrix} A^T u_i \\ B^T u_i \end{bmatrix} \quad (1)$$

where $u_i = A\alpha_i + B\beta_i$. After convergence, α_i and β_i will represent shares held by Alice and Bob of the principal eigenvector of $M^T M$.

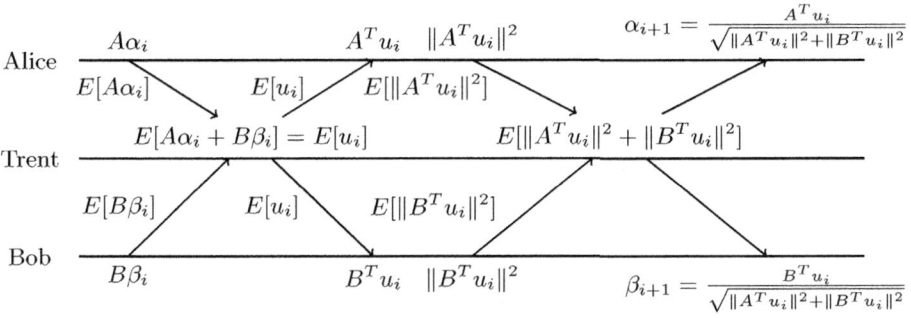

Fig. 1. Visual description of the protocol

This now lays the groundwork for us to define a distributed protocol in which Alice and Bob work only on their portions of the data, while computing the principal eigenvector of the combined data in collaboration with a third party Trent. An iteration of the algorithm proceeds as illustrated in Fig. 1. At the outset Alice and Bob randomly generate component vectors α_0 and β_0 respectively. At the beginning of the ith iteration, Alice and Bob possess component vectors α_i and β_i respectively. They compute the product of their data and their corresponding component vectors as $A\alpha_i$ and $B\beta_i$. To compute u_i, Alice and Bob individually transfer these products to Trent. Trent adds the contributions from Alice and Bob by computing

$$u_i = A\alpha_i + B\beta_i.$$

He then transfers u_i back to Alice and Bob, who then individually compute $A^T u_i$ and $B^T u_i$, without requiring data from one other. For normalization, Alice and Bob also need to securely compute the term

$$\|M^T M \; x_i\| = \sqrt{\|A^T u_i\|^2 + \|B^T u_i\|^2}. \tag{2}$$

Again, Alice and Bob compute the individual terms $\|A^T u_i\|^2$ and $\|B^T u_i\|^2$ respectively and transfer it to Trent. As earlier, Trent computes the sum

$$\|A^T u_i\|^2 + \|B^T u_i\|^2$$

and transfers it back to Alice and Bob. Finally, Alice and Bob respectively update α and β vectors as

$$u_i = A\alpha_i + B\beta_i,$$

$$\alpha_{i+1} = \frac{A^T u_i}{\sqrt{\|A^T u_i\|^2 + \|B^T u_i\|^2}},$$

$$\beta_{i+1} = \frac{B^T u_i}{\sqrt{\|A^T u_i\|^2 + \|B^T u_i\|^2}}. \tag{3}$$

The algorithm terminates when the α and β vectors converge.

3.3   Making the Protocol More Secure

The basic protocol described above is provably correct. After convergence, Alice and Bob end up with the principal eigenvector of the row space of the combined data, as well as concatenative shares of the column space which Trent can gather to compute the principal eigenvector. However the protocol is not completely secure; Alice and Bob obtain sufficient information about properties of each others' data matrices, such as their column spaces, null spaces, and correlation matrices. We present a series of modifications to the basic protocol so that such information is not revealed.

Homomorphic Encryption: Securing the data from Trent. The central objective of the protocol is to prevent Trent from learning anything about either the individual data sets or the combined data other than the principal eigenvector of the combined data. Trent receives a series of partial results of the form $AA^T u$, $BB^T u$ and $MM^T u$. By analyzing these results, he can potentially determine the entire column spaces of Alice and Bob as well as the combined data. To prevent this, we employ an additive homomorphic cryptosystem introduced in Section 2.2.

At the beginning of the protocol, Alice and Bob obtain a shared public key/private key pair for an additive homomorphic cryptosystem from an authenticating authority. The public key is also known to Trent who, however, does not know the private key; While he can encrypt data, he cannot decrypt it. Alice and Bob encrypt all transmissions to Trent, at the first transmission step of each iteration Trent receives the encrypted inputs $E[A\alpha_i]$ and $E[B\beta_i]$. He multiplies the two element by element to compute $E[A\alpha_i] \cdot E[B\beta_i] = E[A\alpha_i + B\beta_i] = E[u_i]$. He returns $E[u_i]$ to both Alice and Bob who decrypt it with their private key to obtain u_i. In the second transmission step of each iteration, Alice and Bob send $E[\|A^T u_i\|^2]$ and $E[\|B^T u_i\|^2]$ respectively to Trent, who computes the encrypted sum

$$E\left[\|A^T u_i\|^2\right] \cdot E\left[\|B^T u_i\|^2\right] = E\left[\|A^T u_i\|^2 + \|B^T u_i\|^2\right]$$

and transfers it back to Alice and Bob, who then decrypt it to obtain $\|A^T u_i\|^2 + \|B^T u_i\|^2$, which is required for normalization.

This modification does not change the actual computation of the power iterations in any manner. Thus the procedure remains as correct as before, except that Trent now no longer has any access to any of the intermediate computations. At the termination of the algorithm he can now receive the converged values of α and β from Alice and Bob, who will send it in clear text.

Random Scaling: Securing the Column Spaces. After Alice and Bob receive $u_i = A\alpha_i + B\beta_i$ from Trent, Alice can calculate $u_i - A\alpha_i = B\beta_i$ and Bob can calculate $u_i - B\beta_i = A\alpha_i$. After a sufficient number of iterations, particularly in the early stages of the computation (when u_i has not yet converged) Alice can find the column space of B and Bob can find the column space of A. Similarly, by subtracting their share from the normalization term returned by Trent, Alice and Bob are able to find $\|B^T u_i\|^2$ and $\|A^T u_i\|^2$ respectively.

In order to prevent this, Trent multiplies u_i with a randomly generated scaling term r_i that he does not share with anyone. Trent computes

$$(E[A\alpha_i] \cdot E[B\beta_i])^{r_i} = E[r_i(A\alpha_i + B\beta_i)] = E[r_i u_i]$$

by performing element-wise exponentiation of the encrypted vector by r_i and transfers $r_i u_i$ to Alice and Bob. By using a different value of r_i at each iteration, Trent ensures that Alice and Bob are not able to calculate $B\beta_i$ and $A\alpha_i$ respectively. In the second step, Trent scales the normalization constant by r_i^2,

$$\left(E\left[\|A^T u_i\|^2\right] \cdot E\left[\|B^T u_i\|^2\right]\right)^{r_i^2} = E\left[r_i^2\left(\|A_i^T u\|^2 + \|B_i^T u\|^2\right)\right].$$

Normalization causes the r_i factor to cancel out and the update rules remain unchanged.

$$u_i = A\alpha_i + B\beta_i,$$
$$\alpha_{i+1} = \frac{r_i A^T u_i}{\sqrt{r_i^2\left(\|A^T u_i\|^2 + \|B^T u_i\|^2\right)}} = \frac{A^T u_i}{\sqrt{\|A^T u_i\|^2 + \|B^T u_i\|^2}},$$
$$\beta_{i+1} = \frac{r_i B^T u_i}{\sqrt{r_i^2\left(\|A^T u_i\|^2 + \|B^T u_i\|^2\right)}} = \frac{B^T u_i}{\sqrt{\|A^T u_i\|^2 + \|B^T u_i\|^2}}. \qquad (4)$$

The random scaling does not affect the final outcome of the computation, and the algorithm remains correct as before.

Data Padding: Securing null spaces. In each iteration, Alice observes one vector $r_i u_i = r_i(A\alpha_i + B\beta_i)$ in the column space of $M = [A\ B]$. Alice can calculate the *null space* $H(A)$ of A, given by

$$H(A) = \{x \in \mathbb{R}^m | Ax = 0\}$$

and pre-multiply a non-zero vector $x \in H(A)$ with $r_i u_i$ to calculate

$$x r_i u_i = r_i x(A\alpha_i + B\beta_i) = r_i x B\beta_i.$$

This is a projection of $B\beta_i$, a vector in the column space of B into the null space $H(A)$. Similarly, Bob can find projections of $A\alpha_i$ in the null space $H(B)$. While considering the projected vectors separately will not give away much information, after several iterations Alice will have a projection of the column space of B on the null space of A, thereby learning about the component's of Bob's data that lie in her null space. Bob can similarly learn about the component's of Alice's data that lie in his null space.

In order to prevent this, Alice *pads* her data matrix A by concatenating it with a random matrix $P_a = r_a I_{k \times k}$, to obtain $\begin{bmatrix} A\ P_a \end{bmatrix}$ where r_a is a positive scalar chosen by Alice. Similarly, Bob pads his data matrix B with $P_b = r_b I_{k \times k}$ to obtain $\begin{bmatrix} B\ P_b \end{bmatrix}$ where r_b is a different positive scalar chosen by Bob. This has the effect of hiding the null spaces in both their data sets. In the following lemma, we prove that the eigenvectors of the combined data do not change after padding, while every eigenvalue λ of MM^T is now modified to $\lambda + r_a + r_b$. Please refer to appendix for the proof.

Lemma 1. *Let* $\bar{M} = \begin{bmatrix} M\ P \end{bmatrix}$ *where M is a $s \times t$ matrix, and P is a $s \times s$ orthogonal matrix. If* $\bar{v} = \begin{bmatrix} v_{t \times 1} \\ v'_{s \times 1} \end{bmatrix}$ *is an eigenvector of $\bar{M}^T \bar{M}$ corresponding to an eigenvalue λ, then v is an eigenvector of $M^T M$.*

While the random factors r_a and r_b prevent Alice and Bob from estimating the eigenvalues of the data, the computation of principal eigenvector remains correct as before.

Oblivious Transfer: Securing Krylov spaces. For a constant c, we can show that the vector $u_i = A\alpha_i + B\beta_i$ is equal to $cMM^T u_{i-1}$. The sequence of vectors $U = \{u_1, u_2, u_3, \ldots\}$ form the Krylov subspace $(MM^T)^n u_1$ of the matrix MM^T. Knowledge of this series of vectors can reveal all eigenvectors of MM^T. Consider $u_0 = c_1 v_1 + c_2 v_2 + \cdots$, where v_i is the ith eigenvector. If λ_j is the jth eigenvalue, we have $u_i = c_1 \lambda_1 v_1 + c_2 \lambda_2 v_2 + \cdots$. We assume wlog that the eigenvalues λ are in a descending order, *i.e.*, $\lambda_j \geq \lambda_k$ for $j < k$. Let u_{conv} be the normalized converged value of u_i which is equal to the normalized principal eigenvector v_1.

Let $w_i = u_i - (u_i \cdot u_{conv})u_i$ which can be shown to be equal to $c_2 \lambda_2 v_2 + c_3 \lambda_3 v_3 + \cdots$, *i.e.*, a vector with no component along v_1. If we perform power iterations with initial vector w_1, the converged vector w_{conv} will be equal to the eigenvector corresponding to the second largest eigenvalue. Hence, once Alice has the converged value, u_{conv}, she can subtract it out of all the stored u_i values and determine the second principal eigenvector of MM^T. She can repeat the process iteratively to obtain all eigenvectors of MM^T, although in practice the estimates become noisy very quickly. As we will show in Section 4, the following modification prevents Alice and Bob from identifying the Krylov space with any certainty and they are thereby unable to compute the additional eigenvectors of the combined data.

We introduce a form of oblivious transfer (OT) [10] in the protocol. We assume that Trent stores the encrypted results of intermediate steps at every iteration. After computing $E[r_iu_i]$, Trent either sends this quantity to Alice and Bob with a probability p or sends a random vector $E[u_i']$ of the same size ($k \times 1$) with probability $1 - p$. As the encryption key of the cryptosystem is publicly known, Trent can encrypt the vector u_i'. Alice and Bob do not know whether they are receiving r_iu_i or u_i'. If a random vector is sent, Trent continues with the protocol, but ignores the terms Alice and Bob return in the next iteration, $E[A\alpha_{i+1}]$ and $E[B\beta_{i+1}]$. Instead, he sends the result of a the last non-random iteration j, $E[r_ju_j]$, thereby restarting that iteration.

This sequence of data sent by Trent is an example of a Bernoulli Process [9]. An illustrative example of the protocol is shown in Fig. 2. In the first two iterations, Trent sends valid vectors r_1u_1 and r_2u_2 back to Alice and Bob. In the beginning of the third iteration, Trent receives and computes $E[r_3u_3]$ but sends a random vector u_3'. He ignores what Alice and Bob send him in the fourth iteration and sends back $E[r_3u_3]$ instead. Trent then stores the vector $E[r_4u_4]$ sent by Alice and Bob in the fifth iteration and sends a random vector u_2'. Similarly, he ignores the computed vector of the sixth iteration and sends u_3'. Finally, he ignores the computed vector of the seventh iteration and sends $E[r_4u_4]$.

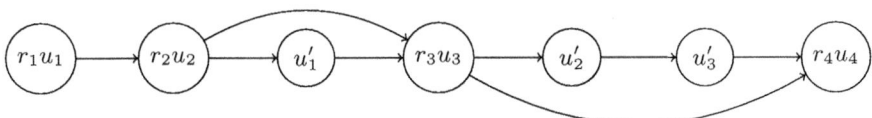

Fig. 2. An example of the protocol execution with oblivious transfer

This modification has two effects – firstly it prevents Alice and Bob from identifying the Krylov space with certainty. As a result, they are now unable to obtain additional Eigenvectors from the data. Secondly, oblivious transfer essentially obfuscates the projection of the column space of B on to the null space of A for Alice, and analogously for Bob by introducing random vectors. As Alice and Bob do not know which vectors are random, they cannot completely calculate the true projection of each others data on the null spaces. This is rendered less important if Alice and Bob pad their data as suggested in the previous subsection.

Alice and Bob can store the vectors they receive from Trent in each iteration. By analyzing the distribution of the normalized vectors, Alice and Bob can identify the random vectors using a simple outlier detection technique. To prevent this, one possible solution is for Trent to pick a previously computed value of $r_j u_j$ and add zero mean noise e_i, for instance, sampled from the Gaussian distribution.

$$u_i' = r_j u_j + e_i, \quad e_i \sim \mathcal{N}(0, \sigma^2).$$

Instead of transmitting a perturbation of a previous vector, Trent can also use perturbed mean of a few previous $r_j u_j$ with noise. Doing this will create a random vector with the same distributional properties as the real vectors. The noise variance parameter σ controls the error in identifying the random vector from the valid vectors and how much error do we want to introduce in the projected column space.

Oblivious transfer has the effect of increasing the total computation as every iteration in which Trent sends a random vector is wasted. In any secure multiparty computation, there is an inherent trade-off between computation time and the degree of security. The parameter p which is the probability of Trent sending a non-random vector allows us to control this at a fine level based on the application requirements. As before, introducing oblivious transfer does not affect the correctness of the computation – it does not modify the values of the non-random vectors u_i.

3.4   Extension to Multiple Parties

As we mentioned before, the protocol can be naturally extended to multiple parties. Let us consider the case of N parties: $P_1, \ldots, P_N$ each having data $A_1, \ldots, A_N$ of sizes $k \times n_1, \ldots, k \times n_N$ respectively. The parties are interested in computing the principal eigenvector of the combined data without disclosing anything about their data. We make the same assumption about the parties and the arbitrator Trent being *semi-honest*. All the parties except Trent share the decryption key to the additive homomorphic encryption scheme and the encryption key is public.

In case of a data split, for the combined data matrix $M = \begin{bmatrix} A_1 & A_2 & \cdots & A_N \end{bmatrix}$, the correlation matrix is

$$M^T M = \begin{bmatrix} A_1^T A_1 & \cdots & A_1^T A_N \\ \vdots & \ddots & \vdots \\ A_N^T A_1 & \cdots & A_N^T A_N \end{bmatrix}.$$

We split the eigenvector into N parts, $\alpha_1, \ldots, \alpha_N$ of size $n_1, \ldots, n_N$ respectively, each corresponding to one party. For simplicity, we describe the basic protocol with homomorphic encryption; randomization and oblivious transfer can be easily added by making the same modifications as we saw in Sections 3.3. One iteration of the protocol starts with the ith party computing $A_i \alpha_i$ and transferring to Trent the encrypted vector $E[A_i \alpha_i]$. Trent receives this from each party and computes

$$\prod_i E\left[A_i\alpha_i\right] = E\left[\sum_i A_i\alpha_i\right] = E[u]$$

where $u = \sum_i A_i\alpha_i$, and product is an element-wise operation. Trent sends the encrypted vector $E[u]$ back to $P_1, \ldots, P_N$ who decrypt it and individually compute $A_i^T u$. The parties individually compute $\|A_i^T u\|^2$ and send its encrypted value to Trent. Trent receives N encrypted scalars $E\left[\|A_i^T u\|^2\right]$ and calculates the normalization term

$$\prod_i E\left[\|A_i^T u\|^2\right] = E\left[\sum_i \|A_i^T u\|^2\right]$$

and sends it back to the parties. At the end of the iteration, the party P_i updates α_i as

$$u = \sum_i A_i\alpha_i^{(old)},$$

$$\alpha_i^{(new)} = \frac{A_i^T u}{\sqrt{\sum_i \|A_i^T u\|^2}}. \tag{5}$$

The algorithm terminates when any one party P_i converges on α_i.

4   Analysis

4.1   Correctness

The protocol outlined in Section 3.2 is provably correct. The steps introduced in Section 3.3 do not modify the operation and hence the accuracy of the protocol in any manner.

4.2   Security

As a consequence of the procedures introduced in Section 3.3 the row spaces and null spaces of the parties are hidden from each another. In the multiparty scenario, the protocol is also robust to collusion between parties with data, although not to collusion between Trent and any of the other parties. If two parties out of N collude, they will find information about each other, but will not learn anything about the data of the remaining $N - 2$ parties.

What remains is the information which can be obtained from the sequence of u_i vectors. Alice receives the following two sets of matrices:

$$U = \{u_1, u_2, u_3, \ldots\}, \quad U' = \{u_1', u_2', \ldots\}$$

representing the outcomes of valid iterations and the random vectors respectively. In the absence of the random data U', Alice only receives U. As mentioned in Section 3.3, $u_i = (MM^T)^i u_0$ which is a sequence of vectors from the Krylov space of the matrix $AA^T + BB^T$ sufficient to determine all eigenvectors of MM^T. For k-dimensional data, it is sufficient to have any sequence of k vectors in U to determine MM^T. Hence, if the vectors in U were not interspersed with the vectors in U', the algorithm essentially reveals information about all eigenvectors to all parties. Furthermore, given a sequence $u_i, u_{i+1}, u_{i+2}, \ldots, u_{i+k-1}$ vectors from U, Alice can *verify* that they are indeed from the Krylov space.[1] Introducing random scaling $r_i u_i$ makes it harder still to verify Krylov space. While solving for k vectors, Alice and Bob need to solve for another k parameters $r_1, \ldots, r_k$.

Security is obtained from the following observation: although Alice can *verify* that a given set of vectors forms a sequence in the Krylov space, she cannot *select* them from a larger set without exhaustive evaluation of all k sets of vectors. If the shortest sequence of k vectors from the Krylov space is embedded in a longer sequence of N vectors, Alice needs $\binom{N}{k}$ checks to find the Krylov space, which is a combinatorial problem.

4.3   Efficiency

First we analyze the computational time complexity of the protocol. As the total the number of iterations is data dependent and proportional to $\left| \frac{\lambda_1}{\lambda_2} \right|$, we analyze the cost per iteration. The computation is performed by the individual parties in parallel, though synchronized and the parties also spend time waiting for intermediate results from other parties. The oblivious transfer introduces extra iterations with random data, on average the number of iterations needed for convergence increase by a factor of $\frac{1}{p}$, where p is the probability of Trent sending a non-random vector. As the same operations are performed in an iteration with a random vector, its the time complexity would be the same as an iteration with a non-random vector.

In the ith iteration, Alice and Bob individually need to perform two matrix multiplications: $A\alpha_i$ and $A^T(A\alpha_i + B\beta_i)$, $B\beta_i$ and $B^T(A\alpha_i + B\beta_i)$ respectively. The first part involves multiplication of a $k \times m$ matrix by a m dimensional vector which is $O(km)$ operations for Alice and $O(kn)$ for Bob. The second part involves multiplication of a $m \times k$ matrix by a k dimensional vector which is $O(km)$ operations for Alice and $O(kn)$ for Bob. Calculating $\|A^T(A\alpha_i + B\beta_i)\|^2$ involves $O(m)$ operations for Alice and analogously $O(n)$ operations for Bob. The final step involves only a normalization by a scalar and can be again done in linear time, $O(m)$ for Alice and $O(n)$ for Bob. Therefore, total time complexity of computations performed by Alice and Bob is $O(km) + O(m) = O(km)$ and $O(kn) + O(n) = O(kn)$ operations respectively. Trent computes an element-wise product of two k dimensional vectors $A\alpha_i$ and $B\beta_i$ which is $O(k)$ operations. The multiplication of two encrypted scalar requires only one operation, making Trent's total time complexity $O(k)$.

In each iteration, Alice and Bob encrypt and decrypt two vectors and two scalar normalization terms which is equivalent to performing $k + 1$ encryptions and $k + 1$ decryptions individually, which is $O(k)$ encryptions and decryptions.

---

[1] If the spectral radius of MM^T is 1.

In the ith iteration, Alice and Bob each need to transmit k dimensional vectors to Trent who computes $E(A\alpha_i + B\beta_i)$ and transmits it back: involving the transfer of $4k$ elements. Similarly, Alice and Bob each transmit one scalar norm value to Trent who sends back another scalar value involving in all the transfer of 4 elements. In total, each iteration requires the transmission of $4k + 4 = O(k)$ data elements.

To summarize, the time complexity of the protocol per iteration is $O(km)$ or $O(kn)$ operations whichever is larger, $O(k)$ encryptions and decryptions, and $O(k)$ transmissions. In practice, each individual encryption/decryption and data transmission take much longer than performing computation operation.

5 Conclusion

In this paper, we proposed a protocol for computing the principal eigenvector of the combined data shared by multiple parties coordinated by a semi-honest arbitrator Trent. The data matrices belonging to individual parties and correlation matrix of the combined data is protected and cannot be reconstructed. We used randomization, data padding, and oblivious transfer to hide the information which the parties can learn from the intermediate results. The computational cost for each party is $O(km)$ where k is the number of features and m data instances along with $O(k)$ encryption/decryption operations and $O(k)$ data transfer operations.

Potential future work include extending the protocol to finding the complete singular value decomposition, particularly with efficient algorithms like thin-SVD. Some of the techniques like data padding, oblivious transfer we applied to increase the security of the protocol can be used in other problems as well. We are working towards a unified theoretical model for applying and analyzing these techniques in general.

References

1. Canny, J.: Collaborative filtering with privacy. In: IEEE Symposium on Security and Privacy (2002)
2. Evfimievski, A.V.: Randomization in privacy-preserving data mining. SIGKDD Explorations 4(2), 43–48 (2002)
3. Goldberg, K., Roeder, T., Gupta, D., Perkins, C.: Eigentaste: A constant time collaborative filtering algorithm. Information Retrieval 4(2), 133–151 (2001)
4. Golub, G.H., Van Loan, C.F.: Matrix Computations, 2nd edn. The Johns Hopkins University Press, Baltimore (1989)
5. Han, S., Ng, W.K., Yu, P.S.: Privacy-preserving singular value decomposition. In: IEEE International Conference on Data Mining, pp. 1267–1270. IEEE, Los Alamitos (2009)
6. Massy, W.F.: Principal component analysis in exploratory data research. Journal of the American Statistical Association 60, 234–256 (1965)
7. Page, L., Brin, S., Motwani, R., Winograd, T.: The pagerank citation ranking: Bringing order to the web. Technical report, Stanford University, Stanford, CA (1998)

8. Paillier, P.: Public-key cryptosystems based on composite degree residuosity classes. In: Stern, J. (ed.) EUROCRYPT 1999. LNCS, vol. 1592, p. 223. Springer, Heidelberg (1999)
9. Papoulis, A.: Probability, Random Variables, and Stochastic Processes, 2nd edn. McGraw-Hill, New York (1984)
10. Rabin, M.: How to exchange secrets by oblivious transfer. Technical Report TR-81, Harvard University (1981)
11. Sewell, G.: Computational Methods of Linear Algebra, 2nd edn. Wiley-Interscience, Hoboken (2005)

Appendix

Proof (Lemma 1). We have,

$$\bar{M}^T \bar{M} = \begin{bmatrix} M^T M & M^T P \\ P^T M & I \end{bmatrix}.$$

Multiplying by the eigenvector $\bar{v} = \begin{bmatrix} v_{t \times 1} \\ v'_{s \times 1} \end{bmatrix}$ gives us

$$\bar{M}^T \bar{M} \begin{bmatrix} v \\ v' \end{bmatrix} = \begin{bmatrix} M^T M v + M^T P v' \\ P^T M v + v' \end{bmatrix} = \lambda \begin{bmatrix} v \\ v' \end{bmatrix}.$$

Therefore,

$$M^T M v + M^T P v' = \lambda v, \tag{6}$$

$$P^T M v + v' = \lambda v'. \tag{7}$$

Since $\lambda \neq 1$, Equation (7) implies $v' = \frac{1}{\lambda - 1} P^T M v$. Substituting this into Equation (6) and the orthogonality of P gives us

$$M^T M v + \frac{1}{\lambda - 1} M^T P P^T M v = \frac{\lambda}{\lambda - 1} M^T M v = \lambda v.$$

Hence, $M^T M v = (\lambda - 1) v$. □

Content-Based Filtering in On-Line Social Networks

Marco Vanetti, Elisabetta Binaghi, Barbara Carminati,
Moreno Carullo, and Elena Ferrari

Department of Computer Science and Communication
University of Insubria
21100 Varese, Italy
{marco.vanetti,elisabetta.binaghi,barbara.carminati,
moreno.carullo,elena.ferrari}@uninsubria.it

Abstract. This paper proposes a system enforcing content-based message filtering for On-line Social Networks (OSNs). The system allows OSN users to have a direct control on the messages posted on their walls. This is achieved through a flexible rule-based system, that allows a user to customize the filtering criteria to be applied to their walls, and a Machine Learning based soft classifier automatically labelling messages in support of content-based filtering.

Keywords: On-line Social Networks, Short Text Classification, Text Filtering, Filtering Policies.

1 Introduction

In the last years, On-line Social Networks (*OSNs*) have become a popular interactive medium to communicate, share and disseminate a considerable amount of human life information. Daily and continuous communication implies the exchange of several types of content, including free text, image, audio and video data. The huge and dynamic character of these data creates the premise for the employment of web content mining strategies aimed to automatically discover useful information dormant within the data and then provide an active support in complex and sophisticated tasks involved in social networking analysis and management. A main part of social network content is constituted by short text, a notable example are the messages permanently written by OSN users on particular public/private areas, called in general *walls*.

The aim of the present work is to propose and experimentally evaluate an automated system, called *Filtered Wall* (FW), able to filter out unwanted messages from social network user walls. The key idea of the proposed system is the support for content-based user preferences. This is possible thank to the use of a Machine Learning (ML) text categorization procedure [21] able to automatically assign with each message a set of categories based on its content. We believe that the proposed strategy is a key service for social networks in that in today social networks users have little control on the messages displayed on their walls. For example, Facebook allows users to state who is allowed to insert messages in their walls (i.e., friends, friends of friends, or defined groups of friends). However, no content-based preferences are supported. For instance, it is not possible to prevent political or vulgar messages. In contrast, by means of the proposed mechanism, a user can specify what contents should not be displayed

C. Dimitrakakis et al. (Eds.): PSDML 2010, LNAI 6549, pp. 127–140, 2011.
© Springer-Verlag Berlin Heidelberg 2011

on his/her wall, by specifying a set of *filtering rules*. Filtering rules are very flexible in terms of the filtering requirements they can support, in that they allow to specify filtering conditions based on user profiles, user relationships as well as the output of the ML categorization process. In addition, the system provides the support for user-defined blacklists, that is, list of users that are temporarily prevented to post messages on a user wall.

The remainder of this paper is organized as follows: in Sect. 2 we describe work closely related to this paper, Sect. 3 introduces the conceptual architecture of the proposed system. Sect. 4 describes the ML-based text classification method used to categorize text contents, whereas Sect. 5 provides details on the content-based filtering system. Sect. 6 describes and evaluates the overall proposed system with a case study prototype application. Finally, Sect. 7 concludes the paper.

2   Related Work

In the OSN domain, interest in access control and privacy protection is quite recent. As far as privacy is concerned, current work is mainly focusing on privacy-preserving data mining techniques, that is, protecting information related to the network, i.e., relationships/nodes, while performing social network analysis [4]. Work more related to our proposals are those in the field of access control. In this field, many different access control models and related mechanisms have been proposed so far (e.g., [5,23,1,9]), which mainly differ on the expressivity of the access control policy language and on the way access control is enforced (e.g., centralized vs. decentralized). Most of these models express access control requirements in terms of relationships that the requestor should have with the resource owner. We use a similar idea to identify the users to which a filtering rule applies. However, the overall goal of our proposal is completely different, since we mainly deal with filtering of unwanted contents rather than with access control. As such, one of the key ingredients of our system is the availability of a description for the message contents to be exploited by the filtering mechanism as well as by the language to express filtering rules. In contrast, no one of the access control models previously cited exploits the content of the resources to enforce access control. We believe that this is a fundamental difference. Moreover, the notion of blacklists and their management are not considered by any of these access control models.

Content-based filtering has been widely investigated by exploiting ML techniques [2,13,19] as well as other strategies [12,7]. However, the problem of applying content-based filtering on the varied contents exchanged by users of social networks has received up to now few attention in the scientific community. One of the few examples in this direction is the work by Boykin and Roychowdhury [3] that proposes an automated anti-spam tool that, exploiting the properties of social networks, can recognize unsolicited commercial e-mail, spam and messages associated with people the user knows. However, it is important to note that the strategy just mentioned does not exploit ML content-based techniques.

The advantages of using ML filtering strategies over ad-hoc knowledge engineering approaches are a very good effectiveness, flexibility to changes in the domain and portability in different applications. However difficulties arise in finding an appropriate set of features by which to represent short, grammatically ill formed sentences and in providing a consistent training set of manually classified texts.

3 Filtered Wall Conceptual Architecture

The aim of this paper is to develop a method that allows OSN users to easily filter undesired messages, according to content based criteria. In particular, we are interested in defining an automated language-independent system providing a flexible and customizable way to filter and then control incoming messages.

Before illustrating the architecture of the proposed system, we briefly introduce the basic model underlying OSNs. In general, the standard way to model a social network is as directed graph, where each node corresponds to a network user and edges denote relationships between two different users. In particular each edge is labeled by the *type* of the established relationship (e.g., friend of, colleague of, parent of) and, possibly, the corresponding *trust* level, which represents how much a given user considers trustworthy with respect to that specific kind of relationship the user with whom he/she is establishing it. Therefore, there exists a direct relationship of a given type RT and trust value X between two users, if there is an edge connecting them having the labels RT and X. Moreover, two users are in an indirect relationship of a given type RT if there is a path of more than one edge connecting them, such that all the edges in the path have label RT [11].

In general, the architecture in support of OSN services is a three-tier structure. The first layer commonly aims to provide the basic OSN functionalities (i.e., profile and relationship management). Additionally, some OSNs provide an additional layer allowing the support of external Social Network Applications (SNA).[1] Finally, the supported SNA may require an additional layer for their needed graphical user interfaces (GUIs). According to this reference layered architecture, the proposed system has to be placed in the second and third layers (Fig. 1), as it can be considered as a SNA. In particular, users interact with the system by means of a GUI setting up their filtering rules, according to which messages have to be filtered out (see Sect. 5 for more details). Moreover, the GUI provides users with a FW, that is, a wall where only messages that are authorized according to their filtering rules are published.

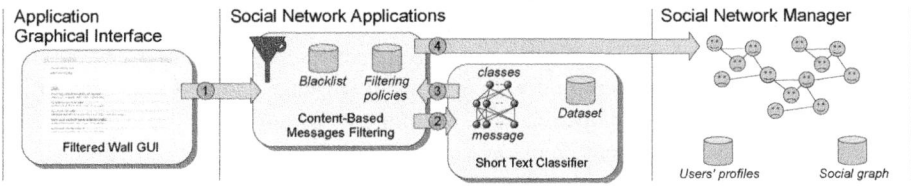

Fig. 1. Filtered Wall Conceptual Architecture

---

[1] See for example the Facebook Developers documentation, available on-line at
`http://developers.facebook.com/docs/`

The core components of the proposed system are the *Content-Based Messages Filtering* (CBMF) and the *Short Text Classifier* (STC) modules. The latter component aims to classify messages according to a set of categories. The strategy underlying this module is described in Sect. 4. In contrast, the first component exploits the message categorization provided by the STC module to enforce the filtering rules specified by the user. Note that, in order to improve the filtering actions, the system makes use of a *blacklist* (BL) mechanism. By exploiting BLs, the system can prevent messages from undesired users. More precisely, as discussed in Sect. 5, the system is able to detect who are the users to be inserted in the BL according to the specified user preferences, so to block all their messages and for how long they should be kept in the BL.

4   Short Text Classifier

Established techniques used for text classifications work well on datasets with large documents such as newswires corpora [16] but suffer when the documents in the corpus are short. In this context critical aspects are the definition of a set of characterizing and discriminant features allowing the representation of underlying concepts and the collection of a complete and consistent set of supervised examples.

The task of semantically categorizing short texts is conceived in our approach as a multi-class soft classification process composed of two main phases: text representation and ML-based classification.

4.1   Text Representation

The extraction of an appropriate set of features by which representing the text of a given document is a crucial task strongly affecting the performance of the overall classification strategy. Different sets of features for text categorization have been proposed in the literature [21], however the most appropriate feature types and feature representation for short text messages have not been sufficiently investigated. Proceeding from these considerations and basing on our experience documented in previous work [6], we consider two types of features, *Bag of Words* (BoW) and *Document properties* (Dp), that are used in the experimental evaluation to determine the combination that is most appropriate for short message classification (see Sect. 6).

The underlying model for text representation is the Vector Space Model [17] for which a text document d_j is represented as a vector of binary or real weights $d_j = w_{1j}, \ldots, w_{|\mathcal{T}|j}$, where $\mathcal{T}$ is the set of terms (sometimes also called features) that occur at least once in at least one document of the collection of document $\mathcal{T}r$, and $w_{kj} \in [0; 1]$ represents how much term t_k contributes to the semantics of document d_j. In the BoW representation, terms are identified with words. In the case of non-binary weighting, the weight w_{kj} of term t_k in document d_j is computed according to the standard Term Frequency - Inverse Document Frequency (tf-idf) weighting function [20], defined as

$$tf - idf(t_k, d_j) = \#(t_k, d_j) \cdot \log \frac{|\mathcal{T}_r|}{\#\mathcal{T}_r(t_k)} \tag{1}$$

where $\#(t_k, d_j)$ denotes the number of times t_k occurs in d_j, and $\#\mathcal{T}_r(t_k)$ denotes the document frequency of term t_k, i.e., the number of documents in $\mathcal{T}r$ in which t_k

occurs. Domain specific criteria are adopted in choosing an additional set of features concerning orthography, known words and statistical properties of messages. In more details:

- *Correct words:* express the amount of terms $t_k \in \mathcal{T} \cap \mathcal{K}$, where t_k is a term of the considered document d_j and $\mathcal{K}$ is a set of known words for the domain language. This value is normalized by $\sum_{k=1}^{|\mathcal{T}|} \#(t_k, d_j)$.
- *Bad words:* are computed similarly to the *Correct words* feature, whereas the set $\mathcal{K}$ is a collection of "dirty words" for the domain language.
- *Capital words:* express the amount of words mostly written with capital letters, calculated as the percentage of words within the message, having more than half of the characters in capital case. For example, the value of the feature for the document "To be OR NOt to BE" is 0.5 since the words "OR" "NOt" and "BE" are considered as capitalized ("To" is not uppercase since the number of capital characters should be strictly greater than the characters count).
- *Punctuations characters:* calculated as the percentage of the punctuation characters over the total number of characters in the message. For example, the value of the feature for the document "Hello!!! How're u doing?" is $5/24$.
- *Exclamation marks:* calculated as the percentage of exclamation marks over the total number of punctuation characters in the message. Referring to the aforementioned document the feature value is $3/5$.
- *Question marks:* calculated as the percentage of question marks over the total number of punctuations characters in the message. Referring to the aforementioned document the feature value is $1/5$.

4.2   Machine Learning-Based Classification

We address the short text categorization as a hierarchical two-level classification process. The first-level classifier performs a binary hard categorization that labels messages as *Neutral* and *Non-Neutral*. The first-level filtering task facilitates the subsequent second-level task in which a finer-grained classification is performed. The second-level classifier performs a soft-partition of *Non-neutral* messages assigning with a given message a gradual membership to each of the non neutral classes. Among the variety of multi-class ML models well-suited for the text classification, we choose the *Radial Basis Function Network* (RBFN) model [18] for its proven robustness in dealing with inherent vagueness in class assignments and for the experimented competitive behavior with respect to other state-of the-art classifiers. The first and second-level classifiers are then structured as regular RBFNs, conceived as hard and soft classifier respectively. Its non-linear function maps the feature space to the categories space as a result of the learning phase on the given training set constituted by manually classified messages. As will be described in Sect. 6, our strategy includes the availability of a team of experts, previously tuned on the way with which to intend the interpretation of messages and their categorization, provide manually classified examples.

We now formally describe the overall classification strategy. Let Ω be the set of classes to which each message can belong to. Each element of the supervised collected set of messages $D = \{(m_i, \boldsymbol{y}_i), \ldots, (m_{|D|}, \boldsymbol{y}_{|D|})\}$ is composed of the text m_i and the supervised label $\boldsymbol{y}_i \in \{0, 1\}^{|\Omega|}$ describing the belongingness to each of the defined classes. The set D is then split into two partitions, namely the training set TrS_D and the test set TeS_D.

Let M_1 and M_2 be the first and second level classifier respectively and $\boldsymbol{y}_1$ be the belongingness to the *Neutral* class. The learning and generalization phase works as follows:

1. each message m_i is processed such that the vector $\boldsymbol{x}_i$ of features is extracted. The two sets TrS_D and TeS_D are then transformed into $TrS = \{(\boldsymbol{x}_i, \boldsymbol{y}_i), \ldots, (\boldsymbol{x}_{|TrS_D|}, \boldsymbol{y}_{|TrS_D|})\}$ and $TeS = \{(\boldsymbol{x}_i, \boldsymbol{y}_i), \ldots, (\boldsymbol{x}_{|TeS_D|}, \boldsymbol{y}_{|TeS_D|})\}$ respectively.
2. a binary training set $TrS_1 = \{(\boldsymbol{x}_j, \boldsymbol{y}_j) \in TrS \mid (\boldsymbol{x}_j, y_j), y_j = \boldsymbol{y}_{j_1}\}$ is created for M_1.
3. a multi-class training set $TrS_2 = \{(\boldsymbol{x}_j, \boldsymbol{y}_j) \in TrS \mid (\boldsymbol{x}_j, \boldsymbol{y}'_j), \boldsymbol{y}'_{j_k} = \boldsymbol{y}_{j_{k+1}}, k = 2, \ldots, |\Omega|\}$ is created for M_2.
4. M_1 is trained with TrS_1 with the aim to recognize whether or not a message is *Non-Neutral*. The performance of the model M_1 is then evaluated using the test set TeS_1.
5. M_2 is trained with the *Non-Neutral* TrS_2 messages with the aim of computing gradual membership to the *Non-Neutral* classes. The performance of the model M_2 is then evaluated using the test set TeS_2.

To summarize the hierarchical system is then composed of M_1 and M_2, where the overall computed function $f : R^n \to R^{|\Omega|}$ is able to map the feature space to the class space, that is to recognize the belongingness of a message to each of the $|\Omega|$ classes. The membership values for each class of a given message computed by f are then exploited by the CBMF module described in the following section.

5   Content-Based Filtering with Blacklist

In this section, we introduce the rules adopted for filtering unwanted messages. In defining the language for filtering rules specification, we consider three main issues that, in our opinion, should affect the filtering decision. The first aspect is related to the fact that, in OSNs like in everyday life, the same message may have different meanings and relevances based on who writes it. As a consequence, filtering rules should allow users to state *constraints on message creators*. Thus, creators on which a filtering rule applies should be selected on the basis of several different criteria, one of the most relevant is by imposing conditions on user profile's attributes. In such a way it is, for instance, possible to define rules applying only to young creators, to creators with a given religious/political view, or to creators that we believe are not expert in a given field (e.g., by posing constraints on the work attribute of user profile).

Given the social network scenario, we see a further way according to which creators may be identified, that is, by exploiting information on their social graph. This implies to state conditions on type, depth and trust values of the relationship(s) creators should be involved in order to apply them the specified rules.

Another relevant issue to be taken into account in defining a language for filtering rules specification is the support for *content-based rules*. This means filtering rules identifying messages according to constraints on their contents. In order to specify and enforce these constraints, we make use of the two-level text classification introduced in Sect. 4. More precisely, the idea is to exploit classes of the first and second level as well as their corresponding membership levels to make users able to state content-based constraints. For example, it would be possible to identify messages that, with high probability, are neutral or non-neutral, (i.e., messages with which the *Neutral/Non-Neutral* first level class is associated with membership level greater than a given threshold); as well as, in a similar way, messages dealing with a particular second level class.

Another issue we believe it is worth being considered is related to the difficulties an average OSN user may have in defining the correct threshold for the membership level. To make the user more comfortable in specifying the membership level threshold, we believe it would be useful allowing the specification of a *tolerance value* that, associated with each basic constraint, specifies how much the membership level can be lower than the membership threshold given in the constraint. Introducing the tolerance would help the system to handle, in some way, those messages that are very close to satisfy the rule and thus they might deserve a special treatment. In particular, these messages are those with a membership level less than the membership level threshold indicated in the rule but greater or equal to the specified tolerance value. As an example, we might have a rule requiring to block messages with violence class with a membership level greater than 0.8. As such messages with violence class with membership level of 0.79 will be published, as they are not filtered by the rule. However, introducing a tolerance value of 0.05 in the previous content-based constraint allows the system to automatically handle these messages. How the system has to behave with messages caught just for the tolerance value is a complex issue to be dealt with that may entail several different strategies. Due to its complexity and, more importantly, the need of an exhaustive experimental evaluation, in this paper we adopt a naïve solution according to which the system simply notifies the user about the message asking for him/her decision. We postpone the investigation of these strategies as future work.

The last component of a filtering rule is the *action* that the system has to perform on the messages that satisfy the rule. The possible actions we are considering are "block", "publish" and "notify", with the obvious semantics of blocking/publishing the message, or notify the user about the message so to wait him/her decision.

A filtering rule is therefore formally defined as follows.

Definition 1. *A filtering rule fr is a tuple $(creatorSpec, contentSpec, action)$, where:*

- *creatorSpec denotes the set of OSN users to which the rule applies. It can have one of the following forms, possibly combined: (1) a set of attribute constraints of the form an OP av, where an is a profile attribute name, av is a profile attribute value, whereas OP is a comparison operator compatible with an's domain; (2) a set of relationship constraints of the form $(m, rt, maxDepth, minTrust)$, denoting all the OSN users participating with user m in a relationship of type rt, having a depth less or equal to maxDepth, and a trust value greater than or equal to minTrust.*
- *contentSpec is a Boolean expression defined on content constraints. In particular, each content constraint is defined as a triple (C, ml, T), where C is a class of the first or second level, ml is the minimum membership level required to class C to make the constraint satisfied, and T is the tolerance for the constraint.*

- $action \in \{block,\ publish,\ notify\}$ denotes the action to be performed by the system on the messages matching $contentSpec$ and created by users identified by $creatorSpec$.

Example 1. The filtering rule $((Bob,\ friendOf,\ 10,\ 0.10),\ (Sex,\ 0.80,\ 0.05),\ block)$ blocks all the messages created by those users having a direct or indirect friendship relationship with Bob at maximum distance 10 and minimum trust level 0.10. In particular, it blocks only those messages with which the *Sex* second level class has been associated with a membership level greater than 0.80; whereas those with membership level greater than 0.75 and less than 0.80 are notified to the wall's owner.

As introduced in Sect. 3, we make use of a BL mechanism to avoid messages from undesired creators. BL is managed directly by the system, which according to our strategy is able to: *(1)* detect who are the users to be inserted in the BL, *(2)* block all their messages, and *(3)* decide when users retention in the BL is finished. To make the system able to automatically perform these tasks, the BL mechanism has to be instructed with some rules, hereafter BL rules. In particular, these rules aim to specify *(a)* how the BL mechanism has to identify users to be banned and *(b)* for how long the banned users have to be retained in the BL, i.e., the retention time. Before going into the details of BL rules specification, it is important to note that according to our system design, these rules are not defined by the Social Network manager, which implies that these rules are not meant as general high level directives to be applied to the whole community. Rather, we decide to let the users themselves, i.e., the wall's owners to specify BL rules regulating who has to be banned from their walls. As such, the wall owner is able to clearly state how the system has to detect users to be banned and for how long the banned users have to be retained in the BL. Note that, according to this strategy, a user might be banned from a wall, by, at the same time, being able to post in other walls.

In defining the language of BL rule specification we have mainly considered the issue of how to identify users to be banned. We are aware that several strategies would be possible, which might deserve to be considered in our scenario. Among these, in this paper we have considered two main directions, postponing as future work a more exhaustive analysis of other possible strategies. In particular, our BL rules make the wall owner able to identify users to be blocked according to their profiles as well as their relationships. By means of this specification, wall owners are able to ban from their walls, for example, users they do not know directly (i.e., with which they have only indirect relationships), or users that are friend of a given person as they may have a bad opinion of this person. This banning can be adopted for an undetermined time period or for a specific time window. Moreover, banning criteria take in consideration also users' behavior in the OSN. More precisely, among possible information denoting users' bad behavior we have focused on two main measures. The first is related to the principle that if within a given time interval a user has been inserted into the BL for several times, say greater than a given threshold, he/she might deserve to stay in the BL for another while, as his/her behavior is not improved. This principle works for those users that have been already inserted in the BL at least one time. To catch new bad behaviors, we use the *Relative Frequency* (RF), defined later in this section. RF let the system be able to detect those users whose messages continue to fail the filtering rules. A BL rule is therefore formally defined as follows.

Definition 2. *A BL rule is a tuple* $(author, creatorSpec, creatorBehavior, T)$, *where:*

- *author is the OSN user who specifies the rule, i.e., the wall owner;*
- *creatorSpec denotes the set of OSN users to which the rule applies. It can have one of the following forms, possibly combined: (1) a set of attribute constraints of the form an OP av, where an is a profile attribute name, av is a profile attribute value, whereas OP is a comparison operator compatible with an's domain; (2) a set of relationship constraints of the form $(m, rt, maxDepth, minTrust)$, denoting all the OSN users participating with user m in a relationship of type rt, having a depth less or equal to maxDepth, and a trust value greater or equal to minTrust.*
- *creatorBehavior = $RFBlocked \lor minBanned$. In particular, $RFBlocked = (RF, mode, window)$ is defined such that:*
  - $RF = \frac{\#bMessages}{\#tMessages}$, *where $\#tMessages$ is the total number of messages that each OSN user identified by creatorSpec has tried to publish in the author wall (mode = $myWall$) or in all the OSN walls (mode = SN); whereas $\#bMessages$ is the number of messages among those in $\#tMessages$ that have been blocked.*
  - *mode $\in \{myWall, SN\}$ specifies if the messages to be considered for the RF computation have to be gathered from the author's wall only (mode = $myWall$) or from the whole community walls (mode = SN).*
  - *window is the time interval of creation of those messages that have to be considered for RF computation;*

  $minBanned = (min, mode, window)$ *is defined such that min is the minimum number of times in the time interval specified in window that OSN users identified by creatorSpec have to be inserted into the BL due to BL rules specified by author wall (mode = me) or other OSN users (mode = SN) in order to satisfy the constraint.*
- *T denotes the time period the users identified by creatorSpec or creatorBehavior have to be banned from author wall.*

Example 2. **The BL rule** $(Alice, (Age < 16), (0.5, myWall, 1\ week), 3\ days)$ inserts into the BL associated with Alice's wall those young users (i.e., with age less than 16) that in the last week have a relative frequency of blocked messages greater than or equal to 0.5. Moreover, the rule specifies that these banned users have to stay in the BL for three days.

6   A Case Study: DicomFW

In this section we illustrate how our system can be applied in a real OSN, that is, Facebook. In the following we describe the prototype implementation details, we then provide some preliminary experiments in order to evaluate the performance of our system.

6.1   Problem and Dataset Description

We have built a dataset[2] D of messages taken from Facebook. We have selected an heterogeneous set of publicly visible user groups in italian language. The set of classes

---

[2] http://www.dicom.uninsubria.it/~marco.vanetti/wmsnsec/

$\Omega = \{Neutral, Violence, Vulgar, Offensive, Hate, Sex\}$ is considered, where $\Omega - \{Neutral\}$ belongs to the second level classes. The set D has 1266 elements, where the percentage of elements in D that belongs to the *Neutral* class is 31%. In order to deal with intrinsic ambiguity in assigning messages to classes, we conceive that a given message belongs to more than one classes. In particular, on the average, a message belongs to two classes (*Vulgar* and *Offensive* are the most related classes). Each message has been labeled by a group of five experts and the class membership values $y_j \in \{0,1\}^{|\Omega|}$ for a given message m_j were computed by majority voting. Within *Non-Neutral* classes, the resulting final distribution of the sub-classes is uniform.

6.2   Demo Application

Throughout the development of the prototype[3] we have focused our attention on filtering rules, leaving BL implementation as a future improvement. The filtering rules functionality is critical since permits the STC and CBMF components to interact.

To summarize, our application (Fig. 2) permits to: (1) view the list of users' FWs (see Fig. 2(a)), (2) view messages on a FW, (3) post a message on other FWs, (4) define filtering rules for the FWs. When a user tries to post a message on a FW, if it is blocked by a filtering rule, he/she receives an alerting message (see Fig. 2(b)).

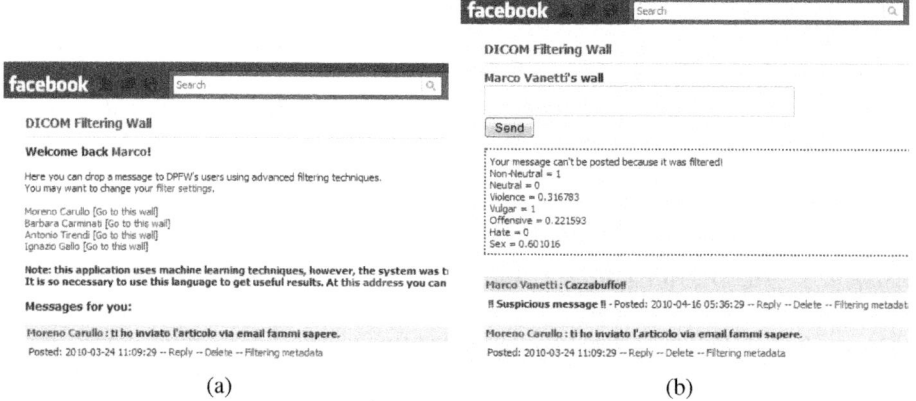

(a)   (b)

Fig. 2. Two relevant use cases of the DicomFW application: (a) start page proposes the list of walls the OSN user can see, (b) a message filtered by the wall's owner filtering rules

6.3   Short Text Classifier Evaluation

Evaluation Metrics. Two different types of measures will be used to evaluate the effectiveness of first level and second level classifications. In the first level, the short text classification procedure is evaluated on the basis of the contingency table approach. In particular the derived well known Overall Accuracy (OA) index capturing the simple

---

[3] http://apps.facebook.com/dicompostfw/

percent agreement between truth and classification results, is complemented with the Cohen's KAPPA (K) coefficient thought to be a more robust measure that takes into account the agreement occurring by chance [14].

At second level, we adopt measures widely accepted in the Information Retrieval and Document Analysis field, that is, Precision (P), that permits to evaluate the number of false positives, Recall (R), that permits to evaluate the number of false negatives, and the overall metric F-Measure (F_β), defined as the harmonic mean between the above two indexes [10]. Precision and Recall are computed by first calculating P and R for each class and then taking the average of these, according to the macro-averaging method [21], in order to compensate unbalanced class cardinalities. The F-Measure is commonly defined in terms of a coefficient β that defines how much to favor Recall over Precision. We chose to set $\beta = 1$.

Numerical Results. By trial and error we have found a quite good parameters configuration for the RBFN learning model. The best value for the M parameter, that determines the number of Basis Function, seems to be $N/2$, where N is the number of input patterns from the dataset. The value used for the spread σ, which usually depends on the data, is $\sigma = 32$ for both networks M_1 and M_2. As mentioned in Sect. 4.1, the text has been represented with the BoW feature model together with a set of additional features Dp based on document local properties. To calculate the first two features we used two specific italian word-lists, one of these is the CoLFIS corpus [15]. The cardinalities of TrS_D and TeS_D, subsets of D with $TrS_D \cap TeS_D = \emptyset$, were chosen so that TrS_D is twice larger than TeS_D. Table 1 exposes the main results varying used features and term weighting for BoW.

Table 1. Results for the two stages of the proposed hierarchical classifier

Configuration		First level		Second Level		
Features	BoW TW	OA	K	P	R	F_1
BoW	binary	72.9%	28.8%	69%	36%	48%
BoW	tf-idf	73.8%	30.0%	75%	38%	50%
BoW+Dp	binary	73.8%	30.0%	73%	38%	50%
BoW+Dp	tf-idf	75.7%	35.0%	74%	37%	49%
Dp	-	69.9%	21.6%	37%	29%	33%

Network M_1 has been evaluated using the OA and the K value. Precision, Recall and F-Measure were used for the M_2 network because, in this particular case, each pattern can be assigned to one or more classes.

Table 1 shows how different features configuration and term weighting (for the BoW features) impact on the results. The numbers prove that, for the first classification stage, Dp features are important in order to distinguish neutral messages from others. BoW features better support the classification task if used with the term weighting as seen in Table 1. The last consideration that we can do on the results is that the network M_2 works better using only the BoW features. This happens because Dp features are too

Table 2. Results of the proposed model in term of Precision, Recall and F-Measure values for each class

	First level		Second Level				
Metric	Neutral	Non-Neutral	Violence	Vulgar	Offensive	Hate	Sex
P	77%	69%	92%	69%	86%	58%	75%
R	92%	38%	32%	53%	27%	26%	52%
F_1	84%	49%	47%	60%	41%	36%	62%

general in order to contribute significantly in the second stage classification, where there are more than two classes, all of non-neutral type, and it is required a greater effort in order to understand the semantics of the message.

Table 2 exposes detailed results for the best classifier (BoW+Dp with tf-idf term weighting for the first stage and BoW with tf-idf term weighting for the second stage). Precision, Recall and F-Measure values, related to each class, show that the most problematic cases are the *Hate* and *Offensive* classes. Messages with hate and offensive contents often hold quite complex concepts that hardly may be understood using a term based approach. The behavior of the system on the *Non-Neutral* classes is to be interpreted in light of the intrinsic difficulty of short message semantics.

6.4   Overall Performance and Discussion

In order to provide an overall assessment of how effectively the system will apply a filtering rule, we look again at Table 2. This table allows us to estimate the Precision and Recall of our filtering rules, since values reported in Table 2 have been computed for filtering rules with content specification component set to $(C, 0.5, 0.0)$, where $C \in \{Neutral, Non-Neutral, Violence, Vulgar, Offensive, Hate, Sex\}$. Let us suppose that the system applies a given rule on a certain message. As such, Precision reported in Table 2 is the probability that the decision taken on the considered message (that is blocking it or not) is actually the correct one. In contrast, Recall has to be interpreted as the probability that, given a rule that must be applied over a certain message, the rule is finally enforced. Let us now discuss, with some examples, the results presented in Table 2, which reports Precision and Recall values. The second column of Table 2 represents the Precision and the Recall value computed for the filtering rule with $(Neutral, 0.5, 0.0)$ content constraint. In contrast, the fifth column stores the Precision and the Recall value computed for the filtering rule with $(Vulgar, 0.5, 0.0)$ constraint.

Results obtained for the content-based specification component, on the first level classification, can be considered good enough and aligned with those obtained by well-known information filtering techniques [12]. Results obtained for the content-based specification component on the second level must be interpreted in view of the intrinsic difficulties in assigning to a messages a semantically most specific category (see the discussion in Sect. 6.3). As such we are optimistic that after having improved the text classifier strategies such to overcome these difficulties, results on second level will be aligned with those on the first level. More precisely, improvements we are planning and carrying on focus on reducing the inconsistency in the collection of manually classified examples and improving the message representation with the inclusion of contextual information.

7 Conclusions

In this paper, we have presented a system to filter out undesired messages from OSN walls. The system exploits a ML soft classifier to enforce customizable content dependent filtering rules. Moreover, the flexibility of the system in terms of filtering options is enhanced through the management of BLs.

This work is the first step of a wider project. The early encouraging results we have obtained on the classification procedure prompt us to continue with other work that will aim to improve the quality of classification. Additionally, we plan to enhance our filtering rule system, with a more sophisticated approach to manage those messages caught just for the tolerance and to decide when a user should be inserted into a BL. For instance, the system can automatically take a decision about the messages blocked because of the tolerance, on the basis of some statistical data (e.g., number of blocked messages from the same author, number of times the creator has been inserted in the BL) as well as data on creator profile (e.g., relationships with the wall owner, age, sex). Further, we plan to test the robustness of our system against different adversary models. The development of a GUI to make easier BL and filtering rule specification is also a direction we plan to investigate.

However, we aware that a new GUI could not be enough, representing only the first step. Indeed, the proposed system may suffer of problems similar to those in the specification of privacy settings in OSN. In this context, many empirical studies [22] show that average OSN users have difficulties in understanding also the simple privacy settings provided by today OSNs. To overcome this problem, a promising trend is to exploit data mining techniques to infer the best privacy preferences to suggest to OSN users, on the basis of the available social network data [8]. As future work, we intend to exploit similar techniques to infer BL and filtering rules.

References

1. Ali, B., Villegas, W., Maheswaran, M.: A trust based approach for protecting user data in social networks. In: Proceedings of the 2007 Conference of the Center for Advanced Studies on Collaborative Research, pp. 288–293. ACM, New York (2007)
2. Amati, G., Crestani, F.: Probabilistic learning for selective dissemination of information. Information Processing and Management 35(5), 633–654 (1999)
3. Boykin, P.O., Roychowdhury, V.P.: Leveraging social networks to fight spam. IEEE Computer Magazine 38, 61–67 (2005)
4. Carminati, B., Ferrari, E.: Access control and privacy in web-based social networks. International Journal of Web Information Systems 4, 395–415 (2008)
5. Carminati, B., Ferrari, E., Perego, A.: Enforcing access control in web-based social networks. ACM Trans. Inf. Syst. Secur. 13(1), 1–38 (2009)
6. Carullo, M., Binaghi, E., Gallo, I.: An online document clustering technique for short web contents. Pattern Recognition Letters 30, 870–876 (2009)

7. Churcharoenkrung, N., Kim, Y.S., Kang, B.H.: Dynamic web content filtering based on user's knowledge. In: International Conference on Information Technology: Coding and Computing, vol. 1, pp. 184–188 (2005)
8. Fang, L., LeFevre, K.: Privacy wizards for social networking sites. In: WWW 2010: Proceedings of the 19th International Conference on World Wide Web, pp. 351–360. ACM, New York (2010)
9. Fong, P.W.L., Anwar, M.M., Zhao, Z.: A privacy preservation model for facebook-style social network systems. In: Backes, M., Ning, P. (eds.) ESORICS 2009. LNCS, vol. 5789, pp. 303–320. Springer, Heidelberg (2009)
10. Frakes, W., Baeza-Yates, R. (eds.): Information Retrieval: Data Structures & Algorithms. Prentice-Hall, Englewood Cliffs (1992)
11. Golbeck, J.A.: Computing and Applying Trust in Web-based Social Networks. Ph.D. thesis, Graduate School of the University of Maryland, College Park (2005)
12. Hanani, U., Shapira, B., Shoval, P.: Information filtering: Overview of issues, research and systems. User Modeling and User-Adapted Interaction 11, 203–259 (2001)
13. Kim, Y.H., Hahn, S.Y., Zhang, B.T.: Text filtering by boosting naive bayes classifiers. In: SIGIR 2000: Proceedings of the 23rd Annual International ACM SIGIR Conference on Research and Development in Information Retrieval, pp. 168–175. ACM, New York (2000)
14. Landis, J.R., Koch, G.: The measurement of observer agreement for categorical data. Biometrics 33(1), 159–174 (1977)
15. Laudanna, A., Thornton, A., Brown, G., Burani, C., Marconi, L.: Un corpus dell'italiano scritto contemporaneo dalla parte del ricevente. III Giornate Internazionali di Analisi Statistica dei Dati Testuali 1, 103–109 (1995)
16. Lewis, D.D., Yang, Y., Rose, T.G., Li, F.: RCV1: A new benchmark collection for text categorization research. Journal of Machine Learning Research (2004)
17. Manning, C., Raghavan, P., Schütze, H.: Introduction to Information Retrieval. Cambridge University Press, Cambridge (2008)
18. Moody, J., Darken, C.: Fast learning in networks of locally-tuned processing units. Neural Computation 1, 281–294 (1989)
19. Pérez-Alcázar, J.d.J., Calderón-Benavides, M.L., González-Caro, C.N.: Towards an information filtering system in the web integrating collaborative and content based techniques. In: LA-WEB 2003: Proceedings of the First Conference on Latin American Web Congress, p. 222. IEEE Computer Society, Washington (2003)
20. Salton, G., Buckley, C.: Term-weighting approaches in automatic text retrieval. Information Processing and Management 24(5), 513–523 (1988)
21. Sebastiani, F.: Machine learning in automated text categorization. ACM Computing Surveys 34(1), 1–47 (2002)
22. Strater, K., Richter, H.: Examining privacy and disclosure in a social networking community. In: SOUPS 2007: Proceedings of the 3rd Symposium on Usable Privacy and Security, pp. 157–158. ACM, New York (2007)
23. Tootoonchian, A., Gollu, K.K., Saroiu, S., Ganjali, Y., Wolman, A.: Lockr: social access control for web 2.0. In: WOSP 2008: Proceedings of the First Workshop on Online Social Networks, pp. 43–48. ACM, New York (2008)

Author Index